Managing Innovation and Cultural Management in the Digital Era

The world-class National Palace Museum (NPM) in Taiwan possesses a repository of the largest collection of Chinese cultural treasures of outstanding quality. Through implementing a two-organizational restructuring, and shifting its operational focus from being object-oriented to public-centered, it aims to capture the attention of people and promote awareness of the culture and traditions of China. In this vein, the NPM combines its expertise in museum service with the possibilities afforded by information technology (IT). This book analyzes the research results of a team sponsored by the National Science Council in Taiwan to observe the development processes and accomplishments, and to conduct scientific researches covering not only the technology and management disciplines, but also the humanities and social science disciplines.

The development process of new digital content and IT-enabled services of NPM would be a useful benchmark for museums, cultural and creative organizations, and traditional organizations in Taiwan and around the world.

Rua-Huan Tsaih is Professor at the Department of Management Information Systems, National Chengchi University, Taiwan.

Tzu-Shian Han is Professor at the Department of Business Administration, National Chengchi University, Taiwan.

T0371829

Routledge Frontiers of Business Management

Managing Innovation and Cultural Management in the Digital Era

The case of the National Palace Museum

**Edited by
Rua-Huan Tsaih and
Tzu-Shian Han**

Routledge
Taylor & Francis Group

LONDON AND NEW YORK

First published 2016
by Routledge
2 Park Square, Milton Park, Abingdon, Oxon OX14 4RN

and by Routledge
605 Third Avenue, New York, NY 10017

First issued in paperback 2020

*Routledge is an imprint of the Taylor & Francis Group,
an informa business*

British Library Cataloguing in Publication Data
A catalogue record for this book is available from the British Library

Library of Congress Cataloging-in-Publication Data
Names: Tsaih, Rua-Huan. | Han, Tzu-Shian.
Title: Managing innovation and cultural management in the digital
    era : the case of the National Palace Museum / edited by
    Rua-Huan Tsaih and Tzu-Shian Han.
Description: Milton Park, Abingdon, Oxon : Routledge, 2016.
Identifiers: LCCN 2015034191 | ISBN 9781138885141 (hardback) |
    ISBN 9781315715643 (ebook)
Subjects: LCSH: Guo li gu gong bo wu yuan—Management. |
    Guo li gu gong bo wu yuan—Data processing. |
    Museums—Collection management—Taiwan—Taipei. |
    Museums—Taiwan—Taipei—Data processing. | Technological
    innovations—Taiwan—Taipei. | Digital media—Taiwan—Taipei. |
    Cultural property—Protection—Taiwan—Taipei. | Cultural
    property—Taiwan—Taipei—Management.
Classification: LCC AM101.T23 M36 2016 | DDC 069/.068—dc23
LC record available at http://lccn.loc.gov/2015034191

ISBN 13: 978-0-367-85960-2 (pbk)
ISBN 13: 978-1-138-88514-1 (hbk)

Typeset in Galliard
by Apex CoVantage, LLC

Contents

Figures

Tables

Contributors

Chen-Wo Kuo is a Section Chief in the Department of Education, Exhibition, and Information Service at the National Palace Museum, Taiwan.

Chih-Lin Hu is Associate Professor at the Department of Communication Engineering, National Central University, Taoyuan, Taiwan. He is also a member of the ACM and the IEEE.

Chun-Ko Hsieh is a Senior Specialist and is in charge of digital museum projects in the Department of Education, Exhibition, and Information Service at the National Palace Museum, Taiwan. He received his doctoral degree in computer science from National Taiwan University.

Eldon Y. Li is University Chair Professor and Chairperson of Department of Management Information Systems at National Chengchi University in Taiwan. He is also editor of several international journals, and he was the president of International Consortium for Electronic Business and Asia Pacific Decision Sciences Institute during 2007–08.

Fang Yu is Associate Professor in the Department of Management Information Systems at National Chengchi University. He is the current executive editor of *International Journal of Information and Computer Security*.

Hsin-Lu Chang is Associate Professor at the Department of Management Information Systems, National Chengchi University.

Hsu-Hsin Chiang is Associate Professor at the Graduate Institute of Human Resource and e-Learning Technology, National Hsinchu University of Education, Taiwan.

Hung-Chin Jang is Associate Professor in computer science, the Chief Executive Officer of Mater Program in Computer Science for Professional Education, and Director of the Mobile Computing and Communication Lab, National Chengchi University.

Jerry G. Fong is Professor of law at National Chengchi University. His research focuses on intellectual property related subjects, including patent law, copyright law, trademark law, and related management issues. He has published more than 100 academic articles, over 200 non-academic articles, and a dozen books.

Kai Wang is Associate Professor and Chairman of Department of Information Management at National University of Kaohsiung, Taiwan.

Laurence F. K. Chang is a Ph.D. candidate at the department of Management Information Systems at National Chengchi University. He has over 10 years of experience in software development, system implementation, and administration, especially in the e-government sector.

Ming-Chu Fung is Director of the National Palace Museum. She has played an integral role in the development of the culture and creative industries of the NPM, including launching and implementing the NPM Digital Archives Project. She was also the Chairperson of the Chinese Association of Museums for two consecutive terms from 2010–14.

Pei-Jeng Kuo is Assistant Professor at National Chengchi University.

Quo-Ping Lin is a senior researcher and chief of the education, exhibition, and information service division, National Palace Museum (NPM), Taipei, Taiwan.

Rua-Huan Tsaih is Vice Dean of Office of Research and Development and a professor in the Department of Management Information Systems, College of Commerce at National Chengchi University at Taipei, Taiwan.

Shoou-Shyan Yen is a research assistant of the Department of Education, Exhibition and Information Services, National Palace Museum. She received her master's degree in Art Management and Culture Policy from National Taiwan University of Arts in 2014.

Tzu-Chieh Tsai was the Chair of Department of Computer Science, and Director of the Master's Program in Digital Content & Technologies at National Cheng-Chi University, Taipei, Taiwan. He is currently Associate Professor at the Computer Science Department, National Cheng-Chi University, Taipei, Taiwan. He has served as the technical committee for several international conferences, and as one of editorial board for *International Journal on Advances in Networks and Services*.

Tzu-Shian Han is Professor at National Chengchi University where he teaches human resource management, cultural and creativity entrepreneurship, design thinking, and innovation. His research focuses on strategic talent management, strategic innovation, and corporate governance.

Yao-Nan Lien is Professor at the Department of Computer Science at National Chengchi University in Taiwan. He was the Deputy Director of the Computer Software Technology Division at ITRI/CCL.

Yi-An Chen has a master's degree in museum education and was formerly a research assistant to Professor Tzu-Shian Han in conducting research on the innovation management in museum settings. She currently works at Xue Xue Foundation in Taipei.

Preface

The National Palace Museum (NPM) in Taiwan possesses a repository of a great number of Chinese cultural treasures of outstanding quality. Like other prestigious museums around the world, the NPM is not exposed to competition from other local museums. Nevertheless, one of its aims is to capture the attention of young people and promote awareness of ancient Chinese cultures and traditions among them. To do this, as stated by Hume (2011) and Hume and Mills (2011), the content and services provided by the museum are in a sense competing with other counterparts for the attraction of young people, such as games, television programs, and video offerings available on the market. Therefore, the NPM incorporates popular elements and digital technologies to add creativity to its content and services.

To this end, the NPM implemented two organizational restructuring efforts (Yeh, 2008), issuing an advertisement image titled "Old Is New" based on "A Letter on Floral Fragrances" by Song Dynasty calligrapher Tingjian Huang in 2006 and announcing its new vision of "Reviving the Charm of an Ancient Collection and Creating New Values for Generations to Come" in 2010. Furthermore, the NPM has shifted its operational focus from being object-oriented to being public-centered in recent years. For instance, it began participating in the National Digital Archives Program sponsored by the National Science Council (which became the Ministry of Science and Technology on February 3, 2014) in Taiwan in 2002; the Cultural and Creative Project in 2010; and the Museum Information Application Project of Mobile e-Government sponsored by the Research, Development and Evaluation Commission in Taiwan in 2011. Via these projects, the NPM has begun to develop digital archives and offer new types of services enabled by information technology.

In sum, digital archives and innovations in IT-enabled services are the key endeavors for infusing life into ancient artifacts and texts, sustaining the public's curiosity about Chinese culture and history, and invoking its desire to visit the NPM in person. Adopting digital technologies and innovative services can have a positive effect on the museum. These technologies and services have changed the NPM's image from one of a traditional antique silo into one of an active participant in social education. The museum's archived collections have taken on a refreshingly new image. People can engage with them interactively and online and connect them to their daily lives.

Although the digital archives and new IT-enabled services have created new demand and interest among the public, their development processes and accomplishments have faced many challenges, such as contrary opinions from the public, government, and academia. From the academic perspective, the process of developing digital archives and new IT-enabled services is a benchmark for the museum, cultural and creative industries, and brick-and-mortar industries both in Taiwan and around the world. The development of the NPM's digital archives and new IT-enabled services can provide a broad and interdisciplinary experimental context to the (academic) observer. The observer can examine the aforementioned challenges that the senior managers of the NPM tackle currently and will tackle in the foreseeable future, and can take further steps to conduct the scientific research necessary to derive advice about the development of the NPM's digital archives and new IT-enabled services.

Therefore, during 2012–14, the National Science Council sponsored a research team to observe the developments of these archives and services and to conduct scientific research that covered not only the technology and management disciplines, but also the humanities and social science disciplines.

This book, *Managing Innovation and Cultural Knowledge Successfully: the case of the National Palace Museum,* summarizes the results of this research in several chapters outlined as follows.

The chapter titled "Transforming traditional organizations: a model and challenges" depicts the challenges facing the use of IT in transforming a traditional organization such as a museum and a model for addressing these challenges. The NPM wants to extend beyond its traditional functions and become closer to the public. To do so, it announced its new vision, implemented two organizational restructuring efforts, and spent more than a decade conducting a sequence of IT applications to develop new IT-generated content and IT-enabled services. This chapter addresses several of the challenges facing the NPM in terms of policies, strategies, management, and technology.

The chapter titled "Application and interdisciplinary integration of digital technology and humanities: using the history of the development of digital assets in the National Palace Museum as an example" discusses the recent endeavors of the NPM to enrich the display of its collections of ancient Chinese artifacts via new digital technologies, including the building of Internet resources, the development of multimedia videos and the use of interactive devices and new media. By using these new forms of technology in its exhibitions, the NPM can enhance its service quality and finally fulfill its mission of becoming a cultural missionary.

The chapter titled "Measurement development of service quality for museum websites displaying artifacts" investigates the effects of a newly launched video-based website platform known as iPalace on users' satisfaction and reuse intention. A survey of online users of the NPM's iPalace and text-based website platforms found that iPalace outperformed the text-based counterpart in many aspects related to service quality, which led to higher satisfaction and reuse intention in users. These findings have implications for museum management and practices given the advancement of new IT.

In the chapter titled "Organizational issues in implementing ICT technology in museums: the case of the National Palace Museum," the authors discuss some of the organizational issues that may deter the diffusion of ICT-enabled services in the NPM, including its organizational culture and management practices. To facilitate the pace of ICT-enabled service innovation, the authors suggest adopting a constructive model of strategic implementation that is conducive to the building of an innovative culture for the acceleration of this service innovation in the NPM and considers effective leadership, communication, and social aspects. This chapter examines how such a strategic plan can assist the NPM in fulfilling its mission and becoming a museum that embraces innovation.

Protection of intellectual property (IP) rights is a major issue encountered by many cultural and creative organizations. In the chapter titled "Legal issues regarding innovative museum services in a mobile and cloud computing environment: examples of copyright and licensing issues for the National Palace Museum," the author discusses the legal issues associated with using mobile and cloud computing technologies in the NPM. This chapter provides insightful suggestions for protecting IP rights using the NPM's digital content and services. If the NPM decides to promote innovative services within a mobile/cloud computing structure to make the best use of its digital content, then the key factors to be considered are the legal and IP issues related to the protection and use of the NPM's digital content and services, as such issues have definitive effects on the ultimate success of such innovative services.

In the chapter titled "Developing the cloud services adoption strategy for the National Palace Museum," the authors mention that cloud services could offer the NPM a different way of organizing and presenting information on multiple levels and from multiple perspectives and dimensions, transforming the museum from a "collection-driven" museum into an "audience-driven" museum. However, how the NPM can successfully implement cloud services remains unclear. The study aims to develop a cloud adoption framework that identifies cloud readiness factors that permit the better adoption of cloud services and evaluates the effects on performance so that the NPM is able to choose adoption priorities, design diffusion paths and predict value outcomes.

In the chapter titled "Mobilizing digital museums," the authors use the NPM as a reference museum for the application of cloud computing and mobile communication technologies to mobilize digital museums. A set of design guidelines specific to the NPM's services is formulated and a few prototype systems are implemented based on these guidelines, including (1) Qingming Painting and Mao Gong Ding Inscription graphical exhibition systems, (2) Mobile Digital Museum Explorer, (3) a live voice interactive museum guiding system, and (4) an edutainment system. Via mobilization, the NPM and other museums should be able to lift their world-class services to another level for the benefit of all.

In the chapter titled "Design factors of a mobile museum navigation system: the case of the National Palace Museum in Taiwan," the authors mention that integrating a mobile museum navigation system into smartphones to improve the learning experience of tourists is becoming increasingly important to museum tourism. The study focuses on visitors of the NPM as research participants and derives seven design guidelines with 38 influencing factors based on an extensive literature review and detailed analysis of personal digital navigation systems. Using an analytic hierarchy process, the study identifies that the information quality in navigation systems and convenience of communication between users and the system are the two most critical design factors in a successful navigation system.

In the chapter titled "Investigating security mechanisms for the ICT-enabled services of the National Palace Museum," the authors direct their attention to service security and investigate mechanisms that provide system, application, and content protection. They focus on an elastic cloud platform with virtual intro-spection, which provides a reliable cloud environment for deploying distributed ICT-enabled services. The authors develop static program analysis techniques to detect and patch Web application vulnerabilities and use static binary analysis to reveal the behavior of mobile applications, providing systematic approaches to analyzing mobile and Web applications. The authors also discuss the data-hiding techniques used to authenticate digital content.

The chapters in this book present the results of some other scientific research related to the development of the NPM's new IT-generated content and IT-enabled services. The advice derived from these results can be transformed into concrete recommendations for improving the policies, strategies, management, and technical issues related to the IT-generated content and IT-enabled services of the NPM (in addition to museums, cultural and creative organizations, and traditional organizations in Taiwan and around the world). The derived advice can also serve as a reference model for the humanities and social sciences disciplines.

References

Hume, M. (2011). How do we keep them coming? Examining museum experiences using a services marketing paradigm, *Journal of Nonprofit and Public Sector Marketing, 23*(1), 71–94.

Hume, M., and Mills, M. (2011). Building the sustainable iMuseum: Is the virtual museum leaving our museums virtually empty? *Journal of Nonprofit and Public Sector Marketing, 16*(3), 275–289.

Yeh, K. (2008). Evaluating the museum organization, *Museology Quarterly, 22*(1), 5–20. (Chinese version).

Part I
NPM-related issues

Part I

NPM-related Issues

1 Challenges and adaptations

The transformation of the National Palace Museum over the past 30 years

Ming-Chu Fung

Introduction

In 2013, the International Committee of Museums (ICOM) proposed the theme of "Museums (Memory + Creativity) = Social Change" for International Museum Day. The INTERCOM and FIHRM 2014 were held in Taipei covering the theme of the social impact of museums, which explored how the museums of the era had responded to the continuous changes in politics, economy, and social environments and whether they had reacted appropriately in their management and operations. The INTERCOM and FIHRM invited me to present the keynote speech, giving me the opportunity to carefully consider how the National Palace Museum (NPM) had responded to the pressures brought on by social changes.

On October 10, 1925, the Palace Museum was erected within the compounds of the Forbidden Palace. This national museum inherited the cultural treasures of the Qing imperial family, offering a collection of premium artifacts from the many previous dynasties in Chinese civilization. When the Sino-Japanese War broke out in 1933, the Palace Museum selected the best artifacts of the collection for crating. These 19,557 crates escaped the Forbidden Palace and were moved southwest in five separate groups. In the same year, the Palace Museum changed its name to the National Palace Museum of Beiping, establishing the Preparatory Office of the National Central Museum. After the end of the Sino-Japanese War in 1945, the artifacts were transferred back to Nanjing, the capital of the Republic of China at the time. When civil war broke out between the Nationalists and Communists in 1948, the National Palace Museum of Beiping again selected artifacts to be sent to Taiwan. In total, 3,824 crates of artifacts from the National Palace Museum of Beiping and the Preparatory Office of the National Central Museum were moved in three separate shipments, a mere quarter of the artifacts moved from the Forbidden Palace to Nanjing. In 1949, the National Palace Museum of Beiping constructed a storeroom in Beikou, Wufeng Village in Taichung County, thus beginning the museum's Beikou period. In 1965, for the centennial celebration of Dr. Sun Yat-sen, the National Palace Museum of Beiping and the Preparatory Office of the Central Museum combined to form the NPM and reopened at Waishuangxi in Taipei. The NPM has been operating for 90 years, or 50 years if one counts from the museum's reopening in Taipei.

Looking back at certain events and milestones over the past 90 years, the history of the NPM can be divided into five periods.

Founding period (1925–33): This period covered the founding of the Palace Museum to the time of the Sino-Japanese War. Artifacts were moved out of the Palace Museum to ensure their safety.

Moving period (1933–38): The artifacts of the Palace Museum were separated into three groups and moved out of the museum to Southwest China. After the Sino-Japanese War, the artifacts were moved back to Nanjing.

Beikou period (1948–64): The artifacts of the museum were shipped to Taiwan. They arrived at Beikou Village, Wufeng Town in Taichung, where they remained for more than a decade.

Growth period (1965–83): The National Palace Museum of Beiping and Preparatory Office of the National Central Museum combined to form the NPM in Waishuangxi, Taipei. The various operations of the museum developed quickly. Its number of visitors rose continuously along with its popularity and fame.

Reinvention period (1983–present): Taiwanese society, politics, and economy have undergone rapid changes since the time of former museum director Chin Hsiao-yi. The NPM has transformed itself in the face of these challenges and reinvented itself to become the museum it is today.

This chapter focuses on the NPM's reinvention period.

Challenges facing the NPM over the past 30 years

The NPM has undergone rapid change over the past 30 years in response to the changes in Taiwan's social and economic development. For example, changes in the era and environment resulted in changes to the museum's facilities in addition to its relocation and expansion. To discuss the NPM's transformation over the past 30 years, we must identify the challenges it faces and which social changes have affected the NPM enough to make the necessary changes. Analysis reveals that the following six social challenges influenced the NPM to take action and transform its policies.

- Challenges presented by the arrival of the digital technology era.
- Challenges presented by the regional Taiwanese culture.
- Challenges presented by the Taiwanese public's demand for equity in cultural resources for both Northern and Southern Taiwan.
- Challenges presented by the needs of disadvantaged communities.
- Challenges presented by the rise of the cultural creativity industry.
- Challenges presented by the NPM's expanding operations and the consequent lack of space on the museum grounds.

I discuss the NPM's responses to the aforementioned challenges as follows.

Challenges presented by the arrival of the digital technology era

Digital technology has undeniably brought about revolutionary change to human civilization. In response to the challenges presented by the advent of digital technology, the NPM quickly addressed its archives management, education, services, and new media applications in ways that changed the museum's original operation model, reinvented its image, and transformed it from a traditional museum into a "museum without walls." The NPM's digital development can be divided into the following stages.

- **Transformation from the Information Services Center into the Department of Education, Exhibition and Information Services**

  In 1987, the NPM established the Information Technology Center for IT affairs and began to research the application of digital technology to artifact archiving and preservation. The Information Technology Center gradually expanded its scope due to the heavy demands of projects and tasks. Finally, in 2011, it was combined with the Department of Exhibition to form the Department of Education, Exhibition and Information Services, under which the Information Technology Education and Information Services sections spearhead museum projects such as the research, planning, management, and maintenance of IT software and facilities and network services. This transformation marked an innovation made by the NPM in response to the advent of the digital technology era.

- **Digital archiving**

  It is widely known that computer technology can systematically integrate, transport, and propagate complex information. Of course, digitally archiving the NPM's 70,000-piece collection required a great amount of labor, material, and finance. In 2002, the government launched a preliminary version of the Digital Archives Program to provide necessary resources for the NPM to completely digitize its archives. At the beginning of the program, the NPM participated in six projects. After a decade of effort, the museum had established 21 databases, cementing the foundation of its digitization efforts. All digital archiving databases are helpful, whether in terms of artifact management, preventative restoration, exhibition planning and design, education programming, research and publication, new media and digital art creation or innovations in cultural creativity and visitor services. With the use of IT, they enhance the functionality and quality of the NPM's service, making the museum's rich and fine collection more valuable and effective.

- **Museum without walls**

  In 1997, the NPM launched a global website in both English and Chinese, adding nine languages later on (Japanese, Korean, French, German,

Spanish, Russian, and Arabic). In conjunction with the opening of the NPM Southern Branch Museum of Asian Art and Culture on December 28, 2015, versions in Southeast Asian languages such as Thai, Cambodian, Indonesian, Vietnamese, and others are currently being added and are due to appear online in August. In December 2002, the NPM began circulating its e-newsletter in both Chinese and English. It has since launched various learning resources for the artifacts, made the archives database public and produced and released 33 thematic websites and 3D virtual displays, truly becoming a "museum without walls."

- **New media art creation**

  In 2006, based on the digital archives, the NPM began to cooperate with various educational institutions and industries, combining technology with art and stepping into the field of new media art creation. Its efforts in this area have fallen under the following categories.

  - **Painting animation**

    In 2006, the NPM worked with Professor Chiu Chia-hua from the Chungyuan Christian University to interpret the painting *One Hundred Horses* by Giuseppe Castiglione of the Qing Dynasty. Using new media technology, they created and imagined day–night, time and weather transitions and movement in the painting, bringing Castiglione's quiet world to life. In 3 short minutes, the environment within the painting undergoes a series of weather changes as its 100 horses charge ahead, creating a grand scene that has captivated audiences. The NPM has developed six additional painting animations since 2010, including *Imitating Zhao Bosu's Latter Ode on Red Cliff, Spring Morning in the Han Palace, Return Clearing, Up the River During Qingming, Activities of the Twelve Months,* and *Syzygy of the Sun and Moon and the Five Planets.* These paintings are currently on view on a rotational schedule in the Painting Animation corridor.

  - **3D animated films**

    In 2006, the NPM began working with Digimax Inc. and Director Tom Sito from Hollywood, USA, to produce a 3D animated film titled *Adventures in the NPM.* Four films in the *Adventures in the NPM* series have been produced since, bringing audiences closer to the ancient artifacts and serving as a great educational tool for children and school students.

  - **New media arts exhibition**

    In 2011, the NPM worked with new media artists for the first time to simultaneously produce new media art for an exhibition at the NPM titled "Landscape Reunited: Huang Gongwang and Dwelling in the

Table 1.1 List of accolades for the *Adventures in the NPM* series by the NPM

Product Time	Product Awarded	Competition Name	Category	Prize Awarded
2007	*Adventures in the NPM*	The 2007 Festival International de l'Audiovisuel et du Multimédia sur le Patrimoine	Audiovisuals	Prize "Coup de Coeur"
		Tokyo International Animation Fair 2008	Grand Prize	Animation of the Year
2008	*Adventures in the NPM: Meet the Painting and Calligraphy Masterpieces*	The 46th Annual WorldFest-Houston International Film Festival	Film and Video Productions	Gold Award
		2012 International Audiovisual Festival on Museums and Heritage (FIAMP) Awards	Shot Film	Sliver Prize
2011	*Adventures in the NPM: Lost in the Art of Landscape Painting*	The 46th Annual WorldFest-Houston International Film Festival	TV Commercials and Public Service PSAs	Platinum Award
2013	*Adventures in the NPM: The Formosa Odyssey*	The 47th Annual WorldFest-Houston International Film Festival	Film and Video Productions	Platinum Remi

Fuchun Mountains." The two curatorial teams partnered together to organize "Beyond Landscape: Meeting Huang Gongwang and New Deductions of the Landscape." Inspired by the tradition of Chinese scholarly ink-wash painting found in *Dwelling in the Fuchun Mountains* and the legends surrounding the painting, the new media art curatorial team developed five new media artworks that combined techniques from digital technology, art, literature, music, and theatre to present a new interpretation of East Asian aesthetics as envisioned by contemporary artists using modern technology. On April 29, 2012, the installation was awarded the Gold Prize in the Interpretive Interactive Installation category at the MUSE awards held by the American Association of Museums.

In 2013, in conjunction with the exhibitions entitled "Voyage with the Tailwind: Qing Archival and Cartographical Materials on Maritime History in the National Palace Museum" and "The All Complete Qianlong: A Special Exhibition on the Aesthetic Tastes of the Qing Emperor Gaozong," the NPM organized the accompanying big-scale new media arts exhibition, once again blurring the boundaries of technology, historical studies, and art.

- **Mobile museum**

  In an effort to amass diverse and rich new media art creations, the NPM began to plan for new media arts exhibitions and became closer to the people. In addition to participating in the various digital technology expos organized by the Ministry of Science and Technology, the NPM stepped onto campuses and exhibited at various school levels. In 2008, the NPM was invited to permanently display digital creations at the Customer Service Area of Terminal 2 of the Taoyuan International Airport. In 2012, the NPM installed the "Future Museum" exhibition, which changes every 6 months and will serve visitors of the airport until 2016. Also in 2012, the NPM was invited by the Huashan Creative Park to create digital art shows and cultural creativity products for visitors to the park for 3 years. The outcomes from this collaboration have been fruitful and will benefit the management of the park. From 2013 to 2014, under the auspices of the Taiwanese government's i-Taiwan 12 Projects, the NPM combined digital shows and its cultural creative merchandise to organize the CHAO Exhibition, which was based on the concept of a mobile museum and traveled around Taiwan.

  In 2012, the NPM launched the first smartphone and tablet app to provide artifact information and offer a gallery guided tour function and interactive features. In December 2014, the NPM and National Center for High-Performance Computing officially launched iPalace Channel, providing educational services on the cloud platform. In response to the challenges posed by the digital technology era, the NPM made organizational and structural changes, and its staff ceaselessly pursued learning, applications, research, and innovations to achieve excellence and enable the museum's successful application of digital technology.

Challenges presented by regional Taiwanese culture

The NPM is a national museum that inherited the cultural treasures of the Qing imperial palace. It serves as an institution for the imperial art collection. For a long time, it has been questioned whether the NPM's lofty position as a cultural guardian separates it too greatly from audiences. In response to the Taiwanese public's interest in local history and culture, the NPM has arranged and published Taiwanese historical materials from the Qing Dynasty in its collection since the 1980s. In the 1990s, the NPM began organizing exhibitions of Taiwanese historical documents, model books, and related paintings in an attempt to improve the connection between its collection and local Taiwanese culture. In 1994, the NPM organized the "Taiwanese Historical Material in the Collection of the NPM" and has since launched similar exhibitions of Taiwanese historical material every 2–3 years. To meet the needs of these exhibitions, the NPM has included Taiwanese historical files and documents as parts of its acquisition interest. The NPM organized the "Beginnings of Modernization in Taiwan" in 1999, "The Land and Her People: Active Figures in the History of Taiwan During the Ch'ing Dynasty" in 2001 (July 5 to October 4) and "Ilha Formosa: the Emergence of Taiwan on the World Scene in the 17th Century" in 2003 (January 24 to May 14). With its experience organizing the Taiwanese history exhibition series, the NPM's Department of Rare Books and Historical Documents learned how to converse with regional audiences and respond to their interest in local Taiwanese history.

Apart from regional history, the aboriginal community has been a topic of interest. In 2005, the Member of Parliament Aboriginal Representative rebuked the NPM for being haughty and not allowing aboriginal art in its exhibition halls. In response to this issue, the NPM explained that each museum had its own missions, and that the NPM was indeed not fit to compete with museums that focused on aboriginal interests and organized exhibitions with aboriginal themes. In 2006, the NPM organized its first exhibition with an aboriginal theme. Titled "Early Dwellers of Taiwan: Illustrated Historical Documents in the Collections of the National Palace Museum" (June 11 to December 19), the exhibition lasted for half a year and received high praise from the aboriginal community. It also led the National Museum of Prehistory to invite the NPM to collaborate on organizing the "Hundred Years of Historical Views about Taiwan: Historical Materials about Taiwan, Taitung and Taiwanese Aborigines" in 2007 (July 21 to October 21). The NPM's aboriginal historical documents and image files were sent to Taitung to allow audiences on the east coast of Taiwan to engage with them. Since then, documents related to the Taiwanese aborigines have always been exhibited in the Rare Books and Historical Documents galleries. The NPM has also started employing curators who specialize in Taiwanese historical research to strengthen the museum's capacity for meaningful engagement in the field. In 2013, NPM staff used the hunters of the Plains aboriginal tribe and hunting dogs in *Illustrations of the Tribute Missions* as inspirations to produce the 3D animation film *Adventures in the NPM*. The film received high praise and continues to screen in various schools and on NPM channels. In 2014, in an effort to use different methods to engage with the local indigenous culture, the curators at the Department of Rare Books and Historical Documents organized "In Their Footsteps: A Special Exhibition of Images and Documents on Indigenous Peoples in Taiwan," in which sand painting was used to trace history, and filmed *An Imperial Audience: Legend of Taiwanese Aborigines Entering the Imperial Palace*.

Challenges presented by the Taiwanese public's demand for equity in cultural resources for both Northern and Southern Taiwan

Located at Waishuangxi in Taipei, the NPM is hard to reach for visitors from Central, Southern, and Eastern Taiwan and the islands. Students often only get to visit the NPM on graduation trips. With this in mind, since 1979, the NPM has taken necessary actions to plan replica artifact exhibitions that are sent to different regions around Taiwan in different years. In 1997, in response to the call for "cultural equity," the NPM organized the "Best Hundred Objects in the National Palace Museum" touring exhibition, which was shown at various cultural centers and museums around Taiwan. During the 2000 presidential elections, presidential candidate Mr. Chen Shui-pian proposed a cultural policy for ensuring cultural equity between Northern and Southern Taiwan and promised to supervise the building of a branch of the NPM in Central or Southern Taiwan. In 2003, the Executive Yuan passed the "National Palace Museum Southern Branch Construction Project." After more than a decade of effort, the NPM Southern Branch Museum of Asian Art and Culture is scheduled to open on December 28, 2015, in Taibao City, Chiayi County, Tainan.

Challenges presented by the needs of disadvantaged communities

In addition to taking care of the needs of indigenous communities, the NPM attempts to respond to disadvantaged communities by providing the following services.

- **Guided tour services for mentally and physically disadvantaged groups**

  The NPM exhibits social responsibility toward disadvantaged communities via expressions of humanity and kindness. It provides several services to disadvantaged groups, including barrier-free environments and websites, guided tours delivered with sign language, tours for the visually impaired, and the barrier-free program known as "Beyond Barriers, Appreciating Beauty." The construction of the NPM Southern Branch Museum of Asian Art and Culture also accounts for the needs of disadvantaged communities.

- **Services for senior citizens**

  To meet the needs of a society with an increasing number of senior citizens, the NPM offers free admission to retirees and organizes service trips to nursing homes.

- **Services for immigrants**

  Apart from those who hail from mainland China, the immigrants in Taiwan hail mostly from Southeast Asia, Japan, and Korea. The NPM Southern Branch Museum was built to serve as an Asian art and culture museum. Its website will include various regional languages to service these immigrant communities. In 2004, the NPM organized the "Cultures of Asia" exhibition (January 18 to April 18) at Chiayi Performing Arts Center. In March 2008, the NPM organized "Exploring Asia: Episode One of the NPM Southern Branch" in Taipei. In October 2008, the exhibition travelled to Chiayi Performing Arts Center. In 2009, the NPM collaborated again with the Cultural Affairs Bureau in Chiayi City to organize "Rising Lotus: Exquisite Vietnamese Blue and White Wares from the Sea" (October 31, 2009, to March 14, 2010) at the Chiayi Municipal Museum. It has also hosted activities for the Vietnamese Culture Festival.

- **Services for remote villages and the training of new recruits**

    To service a diverse range of audience and promote the sharing of artistic and cultural resources, the NPM Artifact Replica Exhibition has traveled around Taiwan since 1979. In recent years, in collaboration with the new media arts exhibitions, the Replica Exhibition has visited remote schools to provide artistic and cultural education to students in remote areas. In 2010, the program began its expansion into correctional institutions such as Taipei Prison, Taoyuan Women's Prison, Taoyuan Reform School, Ming Yang High School, and Chengjheng High School, providing communities that could not visit the NPM with an opportunity to receive an aesthetic education.

    Through the public's calls for "Interests in Local Culture," "Equity in Resources," and "Care for Disadvantaged Communities," the NPM has taken appropriate actions at its policy-making, management, and operational levels, allowing itself to become closer to the public and contribute more significantly to society. Today, the NPM is no longer a cultural ivory tower beyond the reach of the public. Indeed, it is a true national museum.

Challenges presented by the rise of the cultural creativity industry

The NPM exhibits artifacts in its collection and promotes creativity. Producing souvenir items is almost a staple for museums. In 1965, when the NPM first reopened in Taipei, it focused on publishing catalogues and printing postcards and replica paintings/images of the artifacts. In 1968, the Publications Department was established, specializing in the publishing affairs of the NPM. In 1970, the Technology Section was established and started producing replica artifacts and gradually accumulating material resources. In 1983, Director Chin Hsiao-yi (1921–2007) was appointed, and he proposed a vision for "Innovating Tradition, Uniting Art and Lifestyle" and initiated the development of the NPM's cultural creativity. The NPM staff began to find inspiration in the ancient artifacts, designing scarves, ties, umbrellas, table cloths, dining mats, tie clips, cufflinks, brooches, lipstick containers, mirrors, textiles, lifestyle tools, and stationery among other items to define the NPM brand. Through its brand licensing, image authorization, cooperative development, and commissioned selling efforts, the NPM collaborated with a diverse range of merchandisers, using the NPM collection as the main inspiration for a vibrant development of its cultural creativity.

Director Tu Cheng-sheng was appointed in 2000 and called for a new design of the NPM logo. At that time, the NPM brand had been established and led to the development of many offshoot industries. Until the first half of 2015, 20 merchandisers had the NPM Brand License, 126 had the NPM Cooperative Development License and 24 had the Commissioned Selling License. The museum became a mid-size business operation with an annual income of over NTD $8 billion.

Since 2009, the development of the NPM's cultural creativity has faced a new upturn. Other than producing its own merchandizing, brand licensing, and collaborative development projects, the NPM launched the Workshop on Cultural Creativity Industries Development in collaboration with NPM curators, artists from outside of the NPM and renowned designers. Through this workshop, which is based on the artifacts at the NPM, participants interested in cultural creativity and working with the NPM familiarize themselves with the artifacts at a deeper level and use them as bases for designs. The goal is to provide NPM resources and an educational platform to increase the significance and quality of museum-related industries and establish collaborative and commercial relationships between the NPM and various industries. The previous five workshops had 72 participating merchandizing groups. The NPM is currently organizing the sixth session, which will feature famous Taiwanese jewelry brands and *falan* porcelain brands. Some of the workshop outcomes were included in the March 2014 edition of *Album of the NPM Workshop on Cultural Creativity Industries Development*.

Since 2010, the NPM has organized the design competition for the *Derivative Merchandize of the National Treasures* to encourage more youth to join the field of cultural creativity design. Participants are required to attend aesthetics lectures organized by the NPM to familiarize themselves with the museum's artifacts before entering the competition and engaging in creative designs. The NPM announces the outcome of the competition and organizes the touring exhibition titled "New Waves of NPM: The Union of National Treasures and Creative Design." In addition, it collaborates with merchandisers and competition winners to mass-produce the winning designs. Over the past 6 years, the competition has indeed brought a new degree of creativity and culturally creative trendiness to NPM's value-added merchandizing practices.

Challenges presented by the NPM's expanding museum operations and the consequent lack of space on the museum grounds

Other than meeting and adapting to the challenges presented by digital technology, cultural creativity, north–south equity, and calls from the local community, the NPM has continuously expanded its operations over the past 30 years by acquiring new artifacts, adding scientific analytical laboratories, expanding its organizational structure, diversifying its offered services, hiring more curators, and increasing its number of visitors. This has resulted in a serious shortage of space at the NPM. The NPM has expanded five times since its 1965 reopening. However, a major challenge arose in 2009, when the Taiwanese government adopted the new immigration rule allowing mainland

Chinese visitors to visit across the straits to Taiwan. Visitor numbers at the NPM have risen rapidly ever since, from 2.24 million in 2008 to 5.4 million in 2014. The NPM has proposed short-term solutions and strategies for adapting to the lack of reception space, such as controlling the number of visitors to the NPM by establishing a limit of 2,800 persons per time. The opening hours for Monday–Thursday were also extended by 2 hours (8:30 a.m. to 6:30 p.m.). On Fridays and Saturdays, the museum stays open until 9 p.m. However, more significantly, the NPM proposed a plan to expand in Taipei. On January 1, 2010, President of the Republic of China Ma Ying-jeou announced that the Grand NPM Plan would be an important cultural project for Taiwan. The plan was officially launched on October 7, 2011, and after 4 years of effort, it has matured significantly. The plan should include both the construction of the Southern Branch Museum and the expansion of the Taipei museum grounds. The construction of the Southern Branch will be completed on December 28, 2015. The expansion of the Taipei museum grounds is currently in its second phase of environmental evaluation, and all involved hope it will advance smoothly.

The contents of the Grand NPM Plan to expand the museum grounds in Taipei include the renovation of the main exhibition building; the expansion and construction of various landscaping projects; a makeover of the old buildings constructed since 1965; and the expansion of services, exhibition and storage spaces and research capacity. Furthermore, the first national Research Center for Scientific Preservation, a world-class Research and Development Center for Digital Art Performance and the NPM Creative Base, which is the first cultural creativity research institution attached to a museum, will be built on the 4.8 hectares of the Art and Culture Park. The makeover aims to provide sufficient space for the NPM's development and adaptation to social changes.

Concluding remarks

On the Double Tenth day of 2015, the NPM will enter into its 90th year since its establishment, or 50th year if one counts from its reopening at Waishuangxi, Taipei in 1965. Together with the political changes occurring in the Republic of China, the NPM has continued through its founding, moving, Beikou, growth, and reinvention periods. Over the past 30 years, it has stayed abreast with the times and transformed itself according to social demand. The NPM is currently stepping into the age of digital technology. In addition to digitizing its collection, the NPM is using digital technology applications to enhance its exhibitions and launch e-learning practices, allowing it to develop into a "museum without walls." It is also organizing new media art exhibitions, stepping outside of the museum to become closer to the people. The "Qian Long C.H.A.O – New Media Art Exhibition" has already toured to various locations in Taiwan, allowing the NPM to transform from a virtual museum into a mobile museum. In recent years, the NPM has also achieved great outcomes in the development of its cultural creativity based on its digitized artifact collection, not only promoting cultural creativity education but also causing a chain reaction in the cultural creativity landscape of Taiwan. In response to the call for north–south equity and the needs of disadvantaged audiences, the NPM has taken appropriate actions, providing services for remote areas, disadvantaged groups, and new immigrants. Since the launch of the iPalace Channel in December 2014, the coverage of NPM's educational efforts has widened. The museum hopes to achieve more in this area and influence society more proactively.

2 Transforming traditional organizations

A model and challenges

Rua-Huan Tsaih

Effect of information technology on traditional organizations

There has been a widespread and dramatic growth in information technology (IT) applications, due to the convergence of information and communication technologies that include the Internet, the communications standard TCP/IP (Transfer Control Protocol/Internet Protocol), the URL address system, personal computers (PCs), customer databases, free and user-friendly browsers, portable devices (tablet PCs and smartphones), multi-media, cloud computing,[1] smart TV, global telephone systems, and third- and fourth-generation mobile telecommunications technologies,[2] among others. These advances in IT provide a cheaper infrastructure that effectively and efficiently links people, content (as information, knowledge, or entertainment), organizations, information systems, and heterogeneous devices (e.g., portable equipment, smart TVs, and the Internet of Things[3]) together, facilitating the development of new IT-generated content and IT-enabled services for individual customers in general, and for members of the younger generation in particular. Hereafter, content in digital form (or resulting from digital practice) is referred to as IT-generated content. IT-enabled services denote instantaneous and interactive services supported by IT. For instance, a number of IT-enabled services are provided via mobile applications.[4] Individual customers pay less now than ever before to acquire new IT-generated content or IT-enabled services. A pressing need for new IT-generated content and IT-enabled services has recently emerged. It should also be noted that to create a competitive advantage, such content and services should by nature be customer-oriented and radically innovative.

However, the deployment of complex IT in a traditional (bricks-and-mortar) organization with less advanced IT expertise entails many challenges, arising from the interdisciplinary nature of content and services, which requires integration of IT, processes, customer demands, and social aspects. A deeper understanding of the potential challenges may lead to a more systematic approach to preparing adequately for the effective and efficient development, deployment, and diffusion of new IT-generated content or IT-enabled services.

In the literature on the deployment of complex IT in traditional organizations, the most relevant studies are in the discipline of service science. However, although this discipline aims to explain and improve the interactions through which multiple entities can work together to achieve mutual benefit, the relevant studies have been summarized as "too much, too little, too soon" (Spohrer and Maglio, 2009: 5). First, service science represents a quest for a holistic, integrative discipline and there is therefore too much content for a single, coherent discipline. Second, the concept of service science seeks to add value to many existing disciplines through focusing on value co-creation and on the dynamic configuration of all associated service ecosystem entities. However, this concept is not sufficiently different to warrant a separate discipline; in many existing disciplines, service science is viewed as merely a conceptual shift in focus or a condensing of case examples. Third, the emerging profession associated with service science depends, critically, on a tool that will probably not be built for at least another decade, and both the emerging discipline and the profession are held by many to be simply premature, it being too soon for them to become established.

The case of the National Palace Museum (NPM) in Taiwan is an excellent example of the deployment of complex IT in a traditional organization. The NPM has received ongoing funding from the Taiwanese government for digitizing the cultural assets of its collection to create new IT-generated content and IT-enabled services. For instance, as shown in Figure 2.1, programs funded by the Taiwanese government include the National Digital Archives Program[5] sponsored by the National Science Council (NSC, which became the Ministry of Science and Technology on February 3, 2014) in 2002, the Cultural and Creative Projects sponsored by the Executive Yuan in 2010, the Museum Information Application Projects of Mobile e-Government sponsored by the Research, Development and

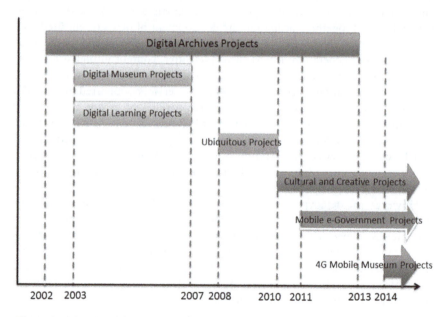

Figure 2.1 Timeline of projects implemented by the NPM

Evaluation Commission in 2011, and the 4G Mobile Museum Projects sponsored by the Executive Yuan in 2014. In short, the NPM has implemented a series of IT applications to develop new IT-generated content and IT-enabled services over more than a decade.

The NPM development process may serve as a model for traditional organizations around Taiwan and the world that wish to transform themselves through frequent application of up-to-date IT for developing new IT-generated content or IT-enabled services, and may also provide a set of broad and interdisciplinary experimental scenarios. A research team sponsored by the NSC is therefore observing the NPM's process for developing its new IT-generated content and IT-enabled services. This research team has received subsidies for two integrated projects, comprising five 3-year sub-projects running from January 1, 2012, to December 31, 2014, and three 2-year sub-projects running from January 1, 2013, to December 31, 2014.[6] Table 2.1 lists these NSC projects.

Table 2.1 The list of NSC projects that are referred to in this book

Integrated Project	Sub-project	NSC No.
Innovations in IT-enabled Services of the National Palace Museum	Designing IT-enabled Services for the National Palace Museum	101–2420-H-004–005-MY3
	The Innovation of IT-enabled Services of the National Palace Museum: Research into Mobile and Cloud Technologies for the National Palace Museum Digital Library	101–2420-H-004–006-MY3
	A Study of the New Internet Platform of the National Palace Museum and Its Effects on Users' Satisfaction and Brand Equity	101–2420-H-004–007-MY3
	Personalized Mobile Navigation Cloud Service System for the Palace Museum: Model Development, System Implementation, and Performance Evaluation	101–2420-H-004–008-MY3
	Exploring the Legal and Intellectual Property Issues of the IT-enabled Services of the National Palace Museum	101–2420-H-004–009-MY3
The Innovations of ICT-Enabled Services of the National Palace Museum and their Effects	The iPalace Video Channel Service and Its Project Management	102–2420-H-004–006-MY2
	The Adoption Strategy for Cloud Services in the National Palace Museum: IT Roadmap, Readiness, and Valuation	102–2420-H-004–004-MY2
	The Applications of Images of Cultural Artifacts in the National Palace Museum for Interactive Media Design, New Communication Technology, and Learning Effect Evaluation	102–2420-H-004–005-MY2

We (the academic observers) have investigated the challenges that the senior NPM managers have dealt with in the past and will face within the foreseeable future. We have also conducted relevant scientific research that covers not only the disciplines of technology and management, but also the humanities and social science.

Part II of this chapter covers the aforementioned development process of the NPM in detail. Some of the related challenges and associated scientific research are then discussed in Part III.

The NPM and its new IT-generated content and IT-enabled services

Like other prestigious museums around the world, the NPM is not exposed to competition from other nearby museums. The NPM is famous for its extensive and intricate collection of artifacts from the Chinese civilization,[7] making it one of the most popular destinations in Taiwan for international tourists.

Unlike many Western museums, the NPM is government operated; in terms of administrative ranking, the NPM is the most prestigious museum in Taiwan. As shown in Figure 2.2, the museum's administration is led by a director who is also a cabinet member of the Executive Yuan in Taiwan. The director, two deputy directors, and a secretary general are required to report to the Legislative Yuan in Taiwan on a regular basis. There are seven departments (Department of Antiquities, Department of Painting and Calligraphy, Department of Rare Books and Historical Documents, Department of Registration and Conservation, Department of Education, Exhibition and Information Service, Department of Cultural Creativity and Marketing, and Department of the Southern Branch Museum Affairs) and five offices (Secretariat and General Affairs Office, Personnel Office, Accounting and Statistics Office, Security Management Office, and Civil Service Ethics Office). Funding for the museum is derived mainly from allowances provided by the central government.

Transition actions of the NPM

The NPM has decided to move beyond its traditional functions to interact more closely with the public (who represent potential visitors to the NPM). For instance, the NPM wishes to capture the attention of members of the younger generation to promote awareness of the culture and traditions of China. As Hume (2011) and Hume and Mills (2011) stated, the content and services provided by the museum are thus, in a sense, competing for the attention of young people with other diversions available in the market, such as games, TV programs, and videos. To capture the attention of these young people, the NPM needs to find out how to incorporate popular elements, digital technology, and creativity into its new content and services.

To achieve its aims, the NPM implemented two rounds of organizational restructuring (Yeh, 2008), issued an image-based advertising campaign "Old Is New," based on "A Letter on Floral Fragrances" by the Song Dynasty calligrapher

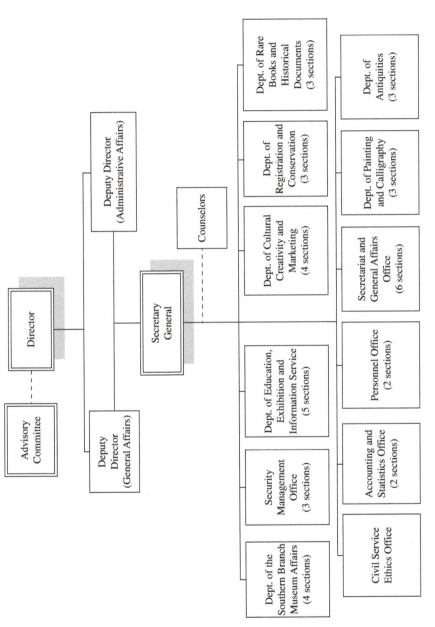

Figure 2.2 The organizational chart of the NPM from 1/1/2012 to the present

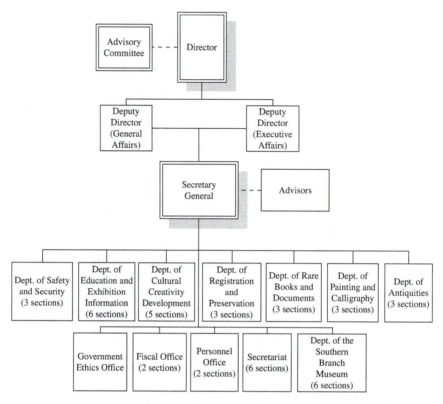

Figure 2.3 The organizational chart of the NPM from 11/2/2009 to 12/31/2011

Tingjian Huang, in 2006, and announced its new vision "Reviving the Charm of an Ancient Collection and Creating New Values for Generations to Come" in 2010. In contrast to its previous organizational structures, shown in Figures 2.3 and 2.4, the NPM's Department of Education, Exhibition, and Information Service now integrates the three major functions of educational and awareness programs, exhibition services, and IT. In addition, the Department of Cultural Creativity and Marketing has been established to strengthen the NPM's marketing capabilities.

In recent years, the NPM has also shifted its operational focus from being object-oriented to being public-centered. For instance, since 2002, the NPM has carried out the projects shown in Figure 2.1, which aim to provide content or services that, from a museum perspective, are not traditional. We briefly discuss some of these projects below.

Projects related to new content and services

From 2002 onward, the NPM carried out numerous digital archiving projects, as shown in Table 2.2, to form a basis for digital archives and new IT-generated

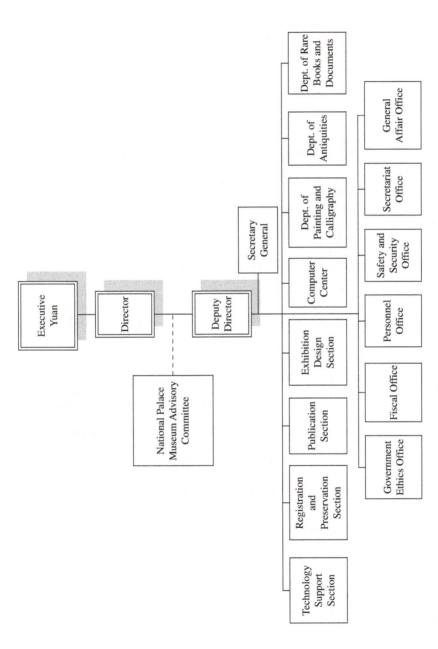

Figure 2.4 The organizational chart of the NPM from 1986 to 2008

Table 2.2 National Digital Archives Program implemented by the NPM

Year	Project Contents
2002	Sub-project 1: Project Integration Sub-project 2: NPM Antiques Digital Archives Sub-project 3: NPM Painting and Calligraphy Digital Archives Sub-project 4: NPM Ch'ing Files Digital Archive Sub-project 5: NPM Artifact Database Creation and Management Sub-project 6: NPM Digital Archives Computer Application System Sub-project 7: NPM Digital Archives Computer Network System
2003–04	Sub-project 1: Project Integration Sub-project 2: NPM Antiques Digital Archives Sub-project 3: NPM Painting and Calligraphy Digital Archives Sub-project 4: NPM Ch'ing Files Digital Archive Sub-project 5: NPM Rare Books Digital Archives Sub-project 6: NPM Artifact Database Creation and Management Sub-project 7: NPM Digital Archives Computer Application System Sub-project 8: NPM Digital Archives Computer Network System
2005–06	Sub-project 1: Project Integration Sub-project 2: NPM Antiques Digital Archives Sub-project 3: NPM Painting and Calligraphy Digital Archives Sub-project 4: NPM Ch'ing Files Digital Archive Sub-project 5: NPM Rare Books Digital Archives Sub-project 6: NPM Artifact Database Creation and Management Sub-project 7: NPM Digital Archives Computer Application System Sub-project 8: NPM Digital Archives Computer Network System Sub-project 9: Establishing the System for the Conservation Records of NPM Artifacts
2007	Sub-project 1: Project Integration Sub-project 2: NPM Antiques Digital Archives Sub-project 3: NPM Painting and Calligraphy Digital Archives Sub-project 4: NPM Books and Historical Documents Digital Archives Sub-project 5: Establishing the System for the Conservation Records of NPM Artifacts Sub-project 6: Establishing and Application of NPM Artifacts and Knowledge Database
2008–10	Sub-project 1: Project Integration Sub-project 2: NPM Antiques Digital Archives Sub-project 3: NPM Painting and Calligraphy Digital Archives Sub-project 4: NPM Books and Historical Documents Digital Archives Sub-project 5: Establishing the System for the Conservation Records of NPM Artifacts Sub-project 6: Establishing and Application of NPM Artifacts and Knowledge Database Sub-project 7: NPM Digital Archives of Ming and Ch'ing Cartographic Materials in the National Palace Museum

2011–12   Sub-project 1: Project Integration
                 Sub-project 2: NPM Antiques Digital Archives
                 Sub-project 3: NPM Painting and Calligraphy Digital Archives
                 Sub-project 4: NPM Books and Historical Documents Digital
                               Archives
                 Sub-project 5: Digital Archiving of 3D Computed Tomography
                               Images
                 Sub-project 6: Establishing and Application of NPM Artifacts and
                               Knowledge Database
                 Sub-project 7: NPM Digital Archives of Ming and Ch'ing
                               Cartographic Materials in the National Palace
                               Museum

content. In these projects, the NPM used up-to-date high-tech methods such
as digital photography and 3D modeling to digitize its collection, allowing the
museum to retain the appearance and value of its collection indefinitely in the
digital era.

Further value was then added to the NPM's digital archives, with the resulting value-added elements being grouped into the following seven categories
(National Palace Museum, 2010b).

1 **Website and various theme-based webpages:** Images and metadata created
   for the National Digital Archives Program provide the best source of materials needed to create the website and other theme-based webpages.
2 **Multimedia interactive CD-ROM:** CDs such as *Era of the Khans*, *The
   Grand Collection of Books*, and *Buddhist Sutras with Picture Annotations*
   provide the general public with an interactive means of understanding the
   national treasure.
3 **NPM e-newsletter:** The e-newsletter provides pro-active and instantaneous information about ongoing exhibits and the latest events held at the
   NPM.
4 **NPM movies:** Movies are used as a novel means of introducing historical
   treasures and reviving interest in ancient artifacts.
5 **Image-based advertisements:** Different methods of presentation exploit
   imaginative opportunities to help people living in the modern era to become
   connected with historical artifacts.
6 **Commercial value-adding:** Resources generated for the National Digital
   Archives Program are used to create marketable items such as picture albums,
   hanging ornaments, and souvenirs.
7 **Digital learning:** Tools such as the learning equipment, online learning,
   and interactive games provided in the exhibits help to people gain a more
   comprehensive understanding of the artifacts.

People in Taiwan have recently begun to think highly of cultural consumption.
Within this phenomenon and in the service economy of today, content plays a

vital role. The Taiwanese government has acknowledged this trend and formed a plan for helping the cultural and creative industries in Taiwan to thrive. The NPM has been asked to act as the flagship of this plan. In response to government policy, the NPM has considered how to transform the historical spirit, cultural meaning, and formal aesthetics of its Chinese cultural relics into contemporary cultural and creative products. Two strategies adopted by the NPM are dedicated commitment to digitizing the museum's collection and the use of the digital outcome. As shown in Figure 2.5, Cultural and Creative Projects are thus initiated to encourage interdisciplinary cultural creativity that combines cultural and technological elements.

These projects rely on using the cultural wealth and international fame of the NPM to construct a platform for the cultural and creative industries that will simultaneously trigger interdisciplinary integration of culture and technology, promote the adoption of cultural and creative elements by technological industries, lead to online events and training programs to promote culture and creativity, and enhance the aesthetic tastes and cultural creativity of the public by providing new inspiration from the integration of technology and culture (National Palace Museum, 2010a).

The Museum Information Application Project of Mobile e-Government carried out by the NPM focuses on delivering its services to the PCs or mobile equipment (e.g., tablet PCs or smartphones) of museum visitors to improve the quality of the museum's services. These services will increase visitor interaction

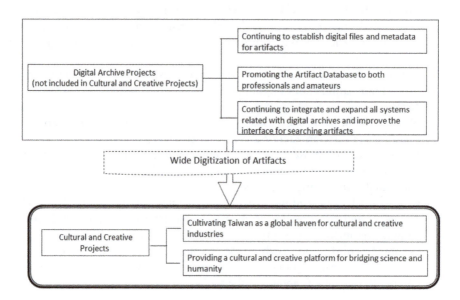

Figure 2.5 The vision blueprint of the NPM's Cultural and Creative Projects
Source: National Palace Museum, 2010a

with and participation in the museum and will further the museum's mission of promoting culture and education. In the next step, through new services enabled by up-to-date information and communication technologies such as social media platforms, the iOS platform, and cloud-computing technology, the NPM wishes to attract a wider range of younger people who are much more familiar with the digital world, and so create a modern, vibrant image both in Taiwan and abroad and concurrently enhance its global exposure (National Palace Museum, 2011).

In summary, the achievements that the aforementioned projects aim to deliver can be grouped into two conceptual levels, a fundamental level involving the creation of digital materials and digital databases of artifacts and knowledge relating to the museum's extensive collection; and an application level involving transformation of this digital material into IT-generated content for the purposes of digital learning, marketing, cultural product creation, or art exhibition via new media.

The activities and results of the aforementioned projects are summarized in Figure 2.6. Using digital creativity and digital practices, the NPM is transforming historical treasures into new IT-generated content by producing either "old wine in new bottles" or "new wine in new bottles." The NPM is using this new content to provide services (exhibition, marketing, or digital learning) via either a traditional platform or a new digital platform. Regardless of the platform, the

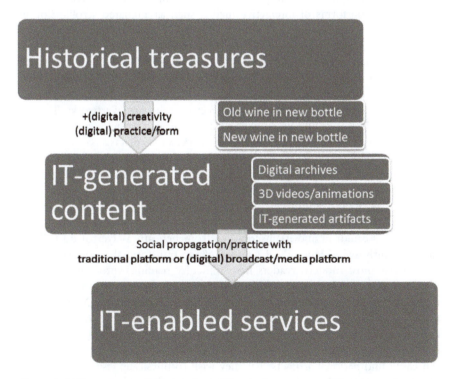

Figure 2.6 The process of moving from historical treasures to IT-generated content and IT-enabled services

services enabled by the IT-generated content are IT-enabled services. Viewers are able to familiarize themselves with the limitless degree of innovation and convenience made possible by IT as they experience, engage with, admire, and interact with the exhibits. Via interactive technologies, the public is able to engage with the essence of the historical artifacts, while digital multimedia such as animations and videos can be used to admire artifacts in greater detail.

Theoretically, IT-enabled services provide IT empowerment for viewers, giving them a novel and independent role as active participants within a self-directed service system. IT-enabled services can improve customization, accuracy, ease-of-use, control, and service-related satisfaction ratings. In general, IT-enabled services are characterized by a rich source of information and by being intelligent, automated, and self-directed.

Below, we describe several IT-enabled services that are provided by the NPM.

The IT-enabled services of the NPM

The *Royal Garden of Emperor Huizong of Song* exhibit makes extensive use of interactive multimedia to present historical artifacts. No physical artifacts are actually shown. Visitors are able to examine the intricate details of artworks and other items through digital images shown on a computer display. They can use new and unique forms of interactive media, such as animated scrolling of an artwork at the same scale as the original. Detailed contextual background information is provided as visitors wave a fan to browse through *Children Playing*, *Literary Gathering*, and *Cat and Peonies*. They can also unfurl a scroll to admire the calligraphy of Emperor Huizong's *Couplet*, Su Tung-po's *Cold Food Observance*, and Liu Sung-nien's *Elegant Gathering at the Western Garden*. Interactive devices allow visitors to answer questions posted directly on the virtual artworks. The use of interactive learning and gaming within a digital art exhibit helps visitors to gain a deeper understanding of Song Dynasty artworks and artifacts.

To achieve better interaction with members of the younger generation and to generate interest among them, the NPM's audio tours include Virtual Artifact Interaction Exhibits to support existing audio recordings. Two apps, titled *NPM on the Go* and *Standing Exhibits of the NPM*, have been developed to create a dynamic cultural exhibit. Users can blow across their iPad[8] to expose Duke Mao's cauldron and its inscriptions from beneath a layer of dust. They can also softly swipe Huaisu's *Autobiography* to transform the original cursive script (that most modern readers have difficulty reading) into regular script. The most popular element of *NPM on the Go* is the interactive exhibition of 100 national treasures and 20 virtual artifacts. *Standing Exhibits of the NPM* features a selection of nearly 400 artifacts. It allows readers to browse the collection with commentary in Chinese, English, or Japanese. Quick response (QR) codes[9] with tour guide functions are also provided for each displayed artifact, so that visitors can easily find national artifacts that they wish to physically visit. Visitors have only to activate the QR code application to broaden the scope and depth of their museum experience.

In 2011, the NPM hosted the much anticipated exhibit *Landscape Reunited – Huang Gongwang and Dwelling in the Fuchun Mountains* in both China and Taiwan. The historically significant reunion of the two sections, *The Remaining Mountain* and *The Wuyong Version*, was achieved for the first time in 360 years. To expose members of the younger generation to the paintings and calligraphic works of ancient Chinese literati, the NPM also implemented *Landscape Reunited – A New Multimedia Gallery of Huang Gongwang's Dwelling in the Fuchun Mountains* and created the 3D animated *Dwelling in the Fuchun Mountains*. Fifty projectors were used to display the entire work, which measures 180 cm long. Overlapping digital projections were used to generate animated and lifelike motions within the landscape painting. Visitors were able to interact with the exhibit through different movements and behavior. For example, clapping and shouting made the characters within *Dwelling in the Fuchun Mountains* turn their heads, wave their fans, or cast lines to begin fishing. Visitors could make the water in the painting ripple or shimmer by waving their hands.

In 2012, the NPM joined the Google *Art Project* to promote worldwide the exquisite beauty of Chinese treasures. The webpage section on collections from the NPM allowed the NPM to publicly display its collections and exhibits via an online platform, allowing it to overcome temporal and spatial boundaries between the museum and the rest of the world. For this collaborative project, the NPM selected 18 popular artifacts that the general public was most familiar with: famous calligraphic works and paintings such as Guo Xi's *Early Spring* of the Song Dynasty and artifacts such as the *Ding Cauldron of Duke Mao* of the Western Zhou Dynasty and the *Jadeite Cabbage* of the Qing Dynasty. One particular work of note was Zhao Chang's *Picture of the New Year*, which was depicted using gigapixel technology so that online viewers could study the revitalized colors in detail.

In 2013, the NPM published its first 3D epic movie, titled *Rebuilding the Tongan Ships*, to re-imagine the historical grandeur of these vessels from the 19th century. The NPM invited experts, pioneering directors, and 3D animators to jointly create a 50-minute-long 3D documentary. *Rebuilding the Tongan Ships* had a budget of over 3 million NT dollars and took 2 years to complete. The NPM also produced the *Rebuilding the Tongan Ships – New Media Art Exhibit*, in which auto-stereoscope and augmented-reality technologies were used as special exhibit features. Visitors can acquire augmented reality (AR)[10] cards for a co-playing experience, becoming either a Qing Dynasty official or the pirate lord Cai Qian. Their photos can also be uploaded to social media such as Facebook.

The examples described above show that IT can be used to revive ancient artworks by allowing interactive and/or dreamlike experiences of journeying through the worlds depicted within them. For instance, the *New Media Art Exhibit* created a new aesthetic experience of appreciation of and interaction with art. Novel means of art appreciation and modern digital visual experiences can help to generate new connections with an artwork and create inspiring memories of cultural experiences and classical works. These examples clearly show that the adoption of digital technologies and innovative services can have positive effects for the museum.

Summary

The abovementioned content and services have changed the NPM's image from that of a traditional antiques silo to that of an active participant in social education. Archived collections of the NPM that have been given a refreshing new image are promoted to people who can view them interactively and online, and in this way become connected with people's daily lives. Among these endeavors for infusing life into ancient artifacts and texts, sustaining the interest of the public in Chinese culture and history and invoking their desire to visit the NPM in person, the keys to success are IT-generated content and IT-enabled services.

Hsu and Tsaih (2014) stated that the NPM has worked out how to use a community of practice (CoA&A) to develop IT-generated content. For each area of IT-generated content, the NPM sets up a CoA&A, comprising the project manager, experts on relics from the NPM, and ICT experts from (external) IT firms. Within the CoA&A, as shown in Figure 2.7, community members interact frequently to work, learn, and innovate. To develop a new type of IT-generated content, members of the CoA&A learn from practicing and innovate on the basis of their learning.

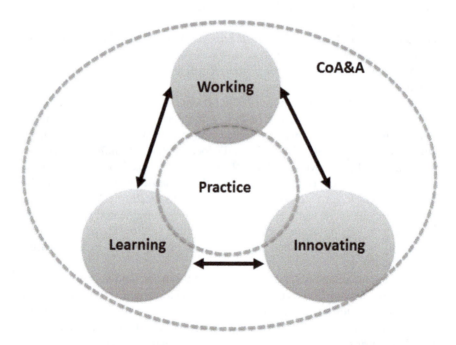

Figure 2.7 The operations of a community of practice
Source: adapted from Hsu and Tsaih, 2014

Scientific research on the development of new IT-generated content and IT-enabled services by the NPM

In this section, we first take the case of the iPalace Video Channel service (iPalace), an exploratory and experimental IT-enabled service created within the subproject "Designing IT-enabled Services of the National Palace Museum," to illustrate the type of scientific research being conducted on IT-enabled services. We then return to the macro perspective of the NPM experience to explore the vital issues that affect all of the relevant NPM projects.

Research issues relating to the iPalace video channel service

Based on its joint collaboration experience with Google and its extensive ownership of high-quality videos, the NPM aspires to create a video-streaming website that will allow members of the younger generation to gain access to its collections of Chinese relics. This aspiration has led to the iPalace initiative.

The strategic service vision of iPalace is shown in Table 2.3. The target audience is young people who use Web browsers, are interested in Chinese heritage, and enjoy watching videos. The service concept involves curating well-organized video exhibitions to deliver fresh and attractive video content smoothly, providing viewers with a TV program that offers a wonderful viewing experience of

Table 2.3 Strategic service vision of iPalace (adapted from Tsaih et al., 2012, and Huang et al., 2013)

Service Delivery System	Operating Strategy	Service Concept	Target Market Segments
1. Fresh and attractive video content 2. Well-defined NPM experiences • NPM images • Easy to use • Profound sense of Chinese culture and aesthetic pleasure 3. Smooth video delivery	1. Continual provision of new video exhibitions 2. Periodically changing interface appearance 3. Effective load balancing • Task-oriented process design • Elastic Web service infrastructure • Peer-to-peer networking • Multitasking and distributed system architecture	1. A video service that smoothly displays NPM relics • Well-arranged exhibition • Available any time and anywhere • Uninterrupted multicasting 2. A user interface that is easy to use and offers a profound sense of Chinese culture and aesthetic pleasure	Young people who use Web browsers • are interested in Chinese heritage • enjoy watching videos

NPM artifacts. Delivery is achieved through the operating strategies of (1) a video production process that produces new videos/animations that are fresh and attractive, (2) periodically updating the appearance of the interface to facilitate delivery, and (3) effective load balancing through such features as a task-oriented process design, an elastic Web service infrastructure, and a peer-to-peer networking capability. As an online medium of the NPM, the service delivery system of iPalace must not only meet its high-quality brand image, but must also be able to cope with potentially large peaks in demand.

From the museum's perspective, iPalace is a radical innovation in IT-enabled services. Although primarily a video-streaming service based on Web technology, it requires expertise in sophisticated cloud-computing technology that the NPM does not possess itself. From the viewers' perspective, iPalace is radically different from the NPM's current text-based webpages. Typical museum video channels, such as that of the British Museum, offer a variety of video clips accessed by individual clicks. In contrast, iPalace operates in a similar way to a television program, broadcasting continuously until the viewer turns the channel off.

We can classify the research conducted on iPalace into the following two categories.

Technical issues

As iPalace is a radically new service, there are design issues for the IT-enabled service and its associated information system, and for the cloud-based system in terms of coping with potentially large peaks in demand.

Huang, Chao, and Tsaih (2013) integrated approaches from the disciplines of service and system engineering to derive a communication tool for designing such new IT-enabled services. The derived communication tool helps the designer to comprehensively describe the strategic vision for the service, the blueprint for the IT-enabled service, the interface table for encounters with the IT-enabled service, and the pseudo code for the middle-office and back-office activities that cross intra-organizational business processes and inter-organizational workflows. Yu, Wan, and Tsaih (2014) constructed a general service framework for cloud-based streaming services and formalized its queuing models. They then discussed the queuing and quantitative analysis of the service framework, along with the theoretical deduction of stationary closed-form expressions for the number of customers, waiting times, the number of employed virtual machines, and their lifecycle.

Strategic and managerial issues

Each new IT-enabled service entails a complementary IT system involving customer devices, industry-wide IT development, and nation-wide IT infrastructure, each of which is difficult for any individual organization to control. The IT predicament refers to the complementary IT system not being adequate to deliver the promised quality of the new IT-enabled service. Given the IT predicament, an organization faces the dilemma of whether to launch or postpone the new service. In addition, to adopt up-to-date IT and new media tools to give their patrons access to the services provided, traditional museums need to form a value-chain-wide solution due to the interdisciplinary nature of the desired services. Furthermore, they need to implement the new value chain even if they lack advanced IT expertise and other required non-domain expertise.

In the case of iPalace, Chang, Tsaih, Yen, and Han (2013) proposed the following process for resolving the dilemma posed by the IT predicament. (1) Identify the counterpart, which is an existing service providing a similar purpose to the new service. (2) Establish a causal model for measuring the new service and its counterpart. (3) Develop an instrument for measuring users' perceived service quality regarding the new service and its counterpart. (4) Set up a survey environment to collect data. (5) Compare the performances of the new service and the counterpart by analyzing the collected survey data. (6) Support the finding that the advantages of the new service outweigh its disadvantages when the performance of the new service surpasses that of its counterpart.

Through exploring the iPalace case, Tsaih, Yen, and Chang (2014) highlighted the challenges associated with the deployment of complex technology in a traditional organization such as a museum. Specifically, through explaining the relationship between the deployment of technology in museums and the value-chain concept, their study broadened the scope of research on technological innovation by demonstrating that it was embedded within a larger network of relationships. To explicate this broader network, the authors used the concept of the value chain from business studies to help provide understanding of the challenges and opportunities of service innovation in traditional organizations. Tsaih, Yen, and Chang (2014) stated that managers must have an in-depth understanding of all of the business partners/stakeholders involved in the embedded value chain. Additionally, carrier-rights agreements and creative-rights agreements must be carefully developed and examined. The managers of an organization must also develop an effective business model (e.g., income sharing) to ensure success. As in the case of iPalace, trust is also an issue.

Research issues relating to the NPM experience

We can classify the vital issues that affect all of the relevant NPM projects into the following categories.

The innovation management issue

A traditional organization such as a museum needs to know how to develop new IT-generated content and IT-enabled services into innovations that are viable in the market. As shown in Figure 2.8, there is a "Valley of Death" between invention and innovation (Auerswald and Branscomb, 2003). A traditional organization must obtain funding and experience to enable the development of viable IT-generated content and IT-enabled services. Furthermore, as shown in

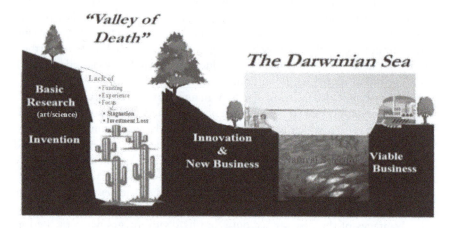

Figure 2.8 The "Valley of Death" and the Darwinian Sea between invention, innovation, and viable business

Source: adapted from Auerswald and Branscomb, 2003

Figure 2.8, there is a Darwinian Sea between innovation and viable business. A traditional organization is faced with the tough scenario of natural selection – its customers decide which content/services are viable and have a competitive advantage in the market.

In the case of the NPM, the museum has received ongoing funding for many projects, shown in Figure 2.1, for which the objective is to digitize the cultural asset represented by its collection into new IT-generated content and IT-enabled services. The NPM has therefore gained much experience in the development of such content and services.

Various factors may drive the funding of new content and new services for the NPM over such a long period. It is, however, clear that the Taiwanese government wishes to (1) shift the weight of economic development toward the appreciation of cultural assets and (2) ensure that the cultural and creative industries become important elements of the national competitive advantage. In other words, funding for the aforementioned projects of the NPM represents a government tactic for enhancing the human and social effects of new IT-generated content and IT-enabled services.

From this perspective, even though the NPM has achieved excellent results from participating in international competitions relating to the use of digital technologies to share collections, it still needs to make its new content and services viable in terms of their human and social effects. The NPM needs to ensure that its IT-generated content and IT-enabled services truly compete for the attention of young people with other diversions available in the market, such as games, TV programs, and videos. Another important issue is measurement of the social value of the NPM's IT-generated content and IT-enabled services.

The knowledge management (KM) issue

Museums are organizations for preserving, creating, and sharing knowledge. In a museum, ancient wisdom is preserved in objects and rediscovered through research. In terms of their intellectual contribution, museums traditionally create knowledge by recruiting researchers and providing them with the required incentives and resources. As a result, museums create abundant knowledge. In the past, professional researchers worked independently to enhance expertise in their own academic fields, rather than for the benefit of the general public. Meanwhile, although museums staged exhibitions to display certain objects, viewers were rarely afforded an intimate view of these objects, which needed to be protected and preserved.

However, the International Council of Museums (2007) redefined the museum as:

> A non-profit, permanent institution in the service of society and its development, open to the public, which acquires, conserves, researches, communicates, and exhibits the tangible and intangible heritage of humanity and its environment for the purposes of education, study, and enjoyment.

Additionally, in line with social development, the function of museums has gradually changed in recent years from object-oriented (before the 1980s), to education focused (the 1980s to the 2000s) and finally to public-centered (after the 2000s) (Chang, 2011).

It should be noted that different museum functions lead to different types of knowledge. Different types of knowledge should thus have different KM mechanisms for creating and sharing knowledge.

In the case of the NPM, the museum needs to have KM mechanisms that regularly create and share new knowledge through IT-generated content and IT-enabled services even when its expertise in up-to-date IT is lacking. Hsu and Tsaih (2014) stated that the NPM has worked out a CoA&A mechanism for creating new knowledge related to IT-generated content and IT-enabled services through collaboration between internal (domain) professionals and external (IT application) experts. Hsu and Tsaih (2014) adapted the SECI mode (Nonaka, 1994) to summarize the knowledge creation process of the CoA&A mechanism, as shown in Figure 2.9.

However, as shown in Table 2.4, the external IT partner associated with each NPM project varies. Therefore, despite already using the CoA&A mechanism, the NPM needs to develop an effective CoA&A capability that regularly creates and shares knowledge related to IT-generated content and IT-enabled services.

The NPM also needs to know what conflicts will arise from the new IT-generated content and IT-enabled services, and decide whether the museum really wants to have both traditional and IT-generated knowledge available. If yes, the museum needs to implement effective KM mechanisms for both traditional and

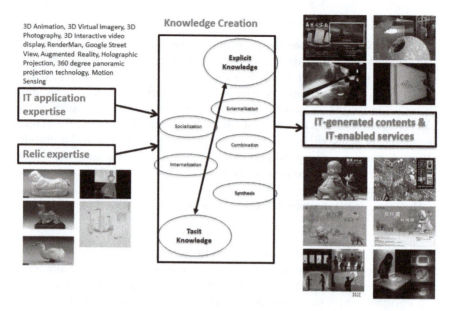

Figure 2.9 The knowledge creation process, from knowledge of historical relics to knowledge related to IT-generated content

Source: adapted from Hsu and Tsaih, 2014

Table 2.4 Some NPM projects and their external IT partners

Year	NPM Project	Partners
2005	Peach Blossoms and Two Swallows	• Techart Group Co. • Bright Ideas Design Co. • Acer Group
2006	A Letter on Floral Fragrances	• Aegus Co.
2007	The Adventures in the NPM	• Digimax, Inc.
2010	The 2011 National Treasure Exhibit	• Blue Phoenix New Media Arts • ASUS Design
2011	Landscape Reunited – Huang Gongwang's Dwelling in the Fuchun Mountains	• Blue Phoenix New Media Arts • Delta Group
2012	Google Art Project	• Google
2013	Rebuilding the Tongan Ships	• Bronze Visual Art

Source: adapted from Hsu and Tsaih, 2014

IT-generated knowledge, and solve any conflicts at strategic, managerial, and operational levels.

The inheritance and evolution of cultural relics

The NPM ensures that its digital creativity and new digital practice/forms lead to the sound inheritance and evolution of historical treasures. In a sense, the NPM places a frame around its digital creativity and new digital practice/forms. Exploration of the appropriate framing of the NPM's digital creativity and new digital practice/forms is of interest. Another issue relates to measuring the inheritance and evolution of historical treasures under the influence of new IT-generated content and IT-enabled services.

Conclusion and summary

The NPM's development process may serve as a model for traditional organizations around Taiwan and the world that wish to transform themselves through frequent application of up-to-date IT to develop new IT-generated content or IT-enabled services. For instance, the transition actions adopted by the NPM in its transformation may serve as a reference for traditional organizations.

This chapter has also discussed several challenges and the scientific research associated with these. Although its IT-generated content and IT-enabled services are creating new demand and interest from the public, the NPM has faced numerous challenges in terms of policy, strategy, management, and technology. For instance, the effective application of complex IT to the development of new IT-generated content and IT-enabled services is a challenge for the NPM. As discussed above, meeting this challenge involves both technical and non-technical issues. Furthermore, the NPM intends its new IT-generated content and IT-enabled services to infuse new life into ancient artifacts and texts, sustaining the interest of the public in Chinese culture and history, and invoking the public's desire to visit the NPM in person. The NPM is also concerned about the effects that new IT-generated content and IT-enabled services will have on the historical treasures. As discussed above, these issues are still under study.

In summary, the challenges involved with developing new IT-generated content and IT-enabled services, and the associated scientific research, are grouped into the following categories.

1   Technical issues

Issues related to the design of the content/services in terms of up-to-date IT.

2   Innovation management

Issues related to the setting up of new IT-enabled service systems, the management of IT-enabled services, business models, interdisciplinary integration, culture and arts innovation, social capital, knowledge management, intellectual capital, and others.

3   The human and social effects of IT applications

Issues related to the effects of IT-generated content and IT-enabled services on the humanities, arts, life, law, psychology, social, and other aspects.

4   The inheritance and evolution of cultural relics

Issues related to the metamorphosis of the universal values and historical heritage of the NPM's historical treasures under the influence of new IT-generated content and IT-enabled services.

Notes

1 The U.S. Government's National Institute of Standards and Technology (NIST) states that cloud computing is a model for enabling ubiquitous, convenient, on-demand network access to a shared pool of configurable computing resources (e.g., networks, servers, storage, applications, and services) that can be rapidly provisioned and released with minimal management effort or service provider interaction (Liu et al., 2011).
2 4G, short for fourth generation, is the fourth generation of mobile telecommunications technology, succeeding 3G and preceding 5G. A 4G system, in addition to the usual voice and other services of 3G, provides mobile ultra-broadband Internet access, for example to laptops with USB wireless modems, to smartphones, and to other mobile devices. Possible applications include amended mobile web access, IP telephony, gaming services, high-definition mobile TV, video conferencing, 3D television, and cloud computing. Source: Wikipedia 2014/8/27, accessed on 2014/9/11 via http://en.wikipedia.org/wiki/4G.
3 The Internet of Things (IoT) refers to the interconnection of uniquely identifiable embedded computing-like devices within the existing Internet infrastructure. Typically, IoT is expected to offer advanced connectivity of devices, systems, and services that goes beyond machine-to-machine communications (M2M) and covers a variety of protocols, domains, and applications. Source: Wikipedia 2014/9/16, accessed on 2014/9/18 via http://en.wikipedia.org/wiki/Internet_of_Things.
4 Mobile applications (usually abbreviated to mobile apps or simply apps) refer to computer software applications designed for smartphones, tablets, or other mobile devices. Source: Wikipedia 2013/11/22, accessed on 2013/11/27 via http://en.wikipedia.org/wiki/Mobile_app.
5 The National Digital Archives Program, the only national program in the field of humanities and culture sponsored by the NSC, places equal emphasis on culture and technology. The National Digital Archives Program also aims to accelerate improvements in the cultural and information industries and help to establish a competitive advantage for academic developments. This program has the objectives of showcasing the diversity of Taiwanese culture and nature, improving the integration of museum collection and technology with educational, research, industrial and social developments, promoting globalization of the museum collection, establishing and implementing a global collaboration network, and bridging the technological gap (National Digital Archives Program, 2008).
6 The research team has also obtained sponsorship for these studies from other organizations. For instance, in 2010, the Networked Communications Program Office in Taiwan authorized the project "The Server Architecture of Video-Based

Marketing Platform for National Palace Museum." For this project, the research team was able to use 50 virtual machines in Hicloud CaaS provided by the Chunghwa Telecom Co. up until the end of July 2012. We have also received 100 virtual machines fully sponsored by Quanta Co. in Taiwan since July 2012.

7 The collections comprise more than 690,000 ancient cultural artifacts, including bronzes, jade carvings, ceramics, lacquer-ware, curios, calligraphy, paintings, rare books, and documents.

8 iPad is a line of tablet computers designed and marketed by Apple Inc. and running the iOS operating system developed by the same company. Source: Wikipedia 2013/11/26, accessed on 2013/11/27 via http://en.wikipedia.org/wiki/iPad.

9 A quick response (QR) is a type of dimensional code developed by the Japanese company DENSO WAVE in 1994. The contents encoded within a QR code are designed to be deciphered quickly. QR codes are most commonly seen in Japan, where they are currently the most popular two-dimensional barcode system. QR codes can store more information than traditional codes. Unlike traditional barcodes that must be scanned as a straight line, QR codes are not restricted by orientation. Source: Wikipedia, accessed on 2013/11/27 via http://en.wikipedia.org/wiki/QR_code.

10 Augmented reality (AR) is a technology, first proposed in 1990, in which the position and angle of a camera are calculated in real time and supplemented using corresponding images. The aim of AR is to add interactive virtual elements to the real world. As the processing capabilities of mobile devices increase, the use of AR is expected to become increasingly widespread. Source: Wikipedia 2013/11/17, accessed on 2013/11/18 via http://en.wikipedia.org/wiki/Augmented_reality.

References

Auerswald, P. E., and Branscomb, L. M. (2003). Valleys of Death and Darwinian Seas: Financing the invention to innovation transition in the United States, *The Journal of Technology Transfer, 28*(3–4), 227–239.

Chang, W., Tsaih, R. H., Yen, D. C., and Han, T. S. (2013). *The ICT predicament of New ICT-enabled service*, Working paper.

Chang, Y. (2011). *The constitution and understanding of marketing functions in the museum sector.* Unpublished Ph.D. Thesis. King's College London, London.

Hsu, C.-C., and Tsaih, R. H. (2014). *The adapted SECI model for innovative it applications in B&M organizations*, presented at the 2014 International Conference on Information and Social Science (ISS 2014), International Business Academics Consortium (iBAC), Nagoya, Japan.

Huang, S. Y., Chao, Y. T., and Tsaih, R. H. (2013). ICT-enabled service design suitable for museums – The case of the iPalace channel of the national palace museum in Taipei, *Journal of Library and Information Science, 39*(1), 84–97. (Chinese version).

Hume, M. (2011). How do we keep them coming? Examining museum experiences using a services marketing paradigm, *Journal of Nonprofit and Public Sector Marketing, 23*(1), 71–94.

Hume, M., and Mills, M. (2011). Building the sustainable iMuseum: Is the virtual museum leaving our museums virtually empty? *Journal of Nonprofit and Public Sector Marketing, 16*(3), 275–289.

International Council of Museums. (2007). *ICOM definition of a museum.* Retrieved on 20/08/2012 from http://icom.museum/definition.html

Liu, F., Tong, J., Mao, J., Bohn, R., Messina, J., Badger, L., and Leaf, D. (2011). *NIST cloud computing reference architecture*. National Institute of Standards and Technology Special Publication 500-292, Gaithersburg, MD. http://www.nist.gov/customcf/get_pdf.cfm?pub_id=909505

National Digital Archives Program. (2008). *National digital archives program phase 2 program summary*. Retrieved on 27/11/2013 from http://www.ndap.org.tw/1_intro/intro.php. (Chinese version).

National Palace Museum. (2010a). *The National Palace Museum cultural and creative resources website*. Retrieved on 27/11/2013 from http://ccp.npm.gov.tw/content/plans/plans_01.aspx. (Chinese version).

National Palace Museum. (2010b). *What is the digital archive?* The NPM Program for Establishing a Digital Knowledge and Intricate Collection Database. Retrieved on 27/11/2013 from http://www.npm.gov.tw/da/ch-htm/about03-1.html

National Palace Museum. (2011). Museum information application project of mobile e-government, *Internal document*. (Chinese version).

Nonaka, I. (1994). A dynamic theory of organizational knowledge creation, *Organization Science, 5*(1), 14–37.

Spohrer, J., and Maglio, P. P. (Eds.). (2009). *Service science: Toward a smarter planet*. New York, NY: John Wiley & Sons.

Tsaih, R. H., Lin, Q. P., Han, T. S., Chao, Y. T., and Chan, H. C. (2012). *New ICT-enabled services of national palace museum and their designs*. The 17th International Conference on Cultural Economics, Kyoto, Japan.

Tsaih, R. H., Yen, D. C., and Chang, Y. C. (2014). Challenges of deploying complex technologies in a traditional organization – The case of national palace museum, *Communications of the ACM, 58*(8), 70–75.

Yeh, K. (2008). Evaluating the museum organization, *Museology Quarterly, 22*(1), 5–20. (Chinese version).

Yu, F., Wan, Y.-W., and Tsaih, R. H. (2014). *On simulating cloud-based streaming services*, Working paper.

3 Application and interdisciplinary integration of digital technology and the humanities

Using the history of the development of digital assets in the National Palace Museum as an example

Quo-Ping Lin, Chen-Wo Kuo, Shoou-Shyan Yen, and Chun-Ko Hsieh

Program history

Rapid developments in science and technology have promoted digitization worldwide. The traditional working methods used by museums for the registration of artifacts, research and publication, and the curating of exhibitions are also undergoing significant change. The National Palace Museum (NPM) houses a rich and diverse collection of artifacts. Since joining the Taiwan e-Learning and Digital Archives Program in 2002, the NPM has combined the humanities with technology to convert substantial amounts of precious artifact data into digital data. These digital data have become the foundation of much digital development by the NPM and facilitate the building of databases, the development of multimedia videos and display devices, and the curating of exhibitions using new media.

The NPM has continued to cooperate with the Taiwanese government to promote various digital programs: for example, the Digital Museum Project, which aims to take advantage of the convenience of the Internet to allow viewers from Taiwan and abroad to browse through the NPM's digital data regardless of time zone and physical location; the National e-Learning Program, which involves the development of e-learning websites and interactive learning tools to allow the public to gain access to the NPM's artifacts and art collections in a faster and more convenient manner; the National Palace Museum Ubiquitous Project, which uses wireless sensors and emerging technologies to combine digital databases with a wireless network to provide information services; and the Cultural and Creative Environment Project, which focuses on the application and interdisciplinary integration of the humanities and technology, aimed at developing online marketing and digital content for cultural and creative videos. Each of these programs/projects has made great use of the achievements in the digital archiving area, extending the digitization of museums into various dimensions.

In anticipation of the advent of a 4G smart living environment, the NPM has vigorously promoted the concept of the NPM 4G Mobile Museum since 2014, developing innovative 4G applications, content, and experiences to expedite the availability of mobile broadband services, enrich digital content, and take advantage of technology from various domains.

Although the names and objectives of these programs may change at various stages, the goal of using emerging technologies to digitize the NPM's artifact collection to meet international trends and give artifacts a brand-new look remains the same.

Achievements in the application of digital assets

With the NPM being involved in various digital programs over the years and working toward the interdisciplinary integration of technology and creative thinking, the museum has had the freedom to use and promote its collection. The NPM's efforts have allowed the public to overcome restrictions of time and location and to gain access to the NPM's collection in a variety of ways, strengthening the museum's educational role and facilitating interdisciplinary cooperation between technology and the humanities to create a synergistic effect. In this chapter, the current state of development and application of the NPM's digital assets will be outlined by examining the NPM's achievements in various areas: Internet resources, multimedia discs, videos, interactive installations, animations of paintings, and art exhibitions using new media.

Internet resources and multimedia discs

Website

The NPM website is the gateway for the public to learn more about the museum. More importantly, it is a treasure chest full of rich cultural resources. The NPM's website can currently be viewed in nine languages and has an internationalized structure designed to attract viewers from all over the world. Statistics have shown that the NPM website receives more than 2 million visits per year. The website offers a selection of themes, such as paintings and calligraphy, antiquities, rare books, and historical documents, and a variety of technologies; its rich content and elegant styling (Figure 3.1) have captured the interest of the public and won the NPM numerous awards both at home and abroad (Table 3.1).

For e-learning, online learning channels such as *NPM e-Learning*, *NPM's M-learning Portal Site*, and *e-Learning at the NPM* have been established. Of these online learning channels, *NPM e-Learning* has achieved the most: it groups information about the various artifacts into different categories and introduces it to the public through an online platform (Figure 3.2). *NPM e-Learning* features exciting ceramics, calligraphy, painting, and artifact restoration lessons for viewers to browse through online.

Figure 3.1 Screenshots of *Tracing the Che School in Chinese Painting* and the website's interactive timeline

Table 3.1 Awards won for website

Awards	Entries	Category	Result	Organizer	Year
The 17th Annual Communicator Awards	World Wide Website of the NPM	Interactive Media – Educational	Silver	International Academy of the Visual Arts	2011
International Audiovisual Festival on Museums and Heritage (FIAMP) Awards	Tracing the Che School in Chinese Painting	Website	Silver	ICOM International Committee for Audiovisual and New Technologies of Image and Sound (AVICOM)	2008
MUSE Awards	Tracing the Che School in Chinese Painting	Online Presence	Bronze	American Alliance of Museums (AAM)	2008
MUSE Awards	The Calligraphic World of Mi Fu's Art	Online Presence	Gold	American Alliance of Museums (AAM)	2007
Golden Learning Award	e-Learning Course on Bronzes at the National Palace Museum	Website	Golden Learning Award	Ministry of Education, Overseas Chinese Affairs Commission, National Science Council, and Institute for Information Industry, R.O.C.	2004

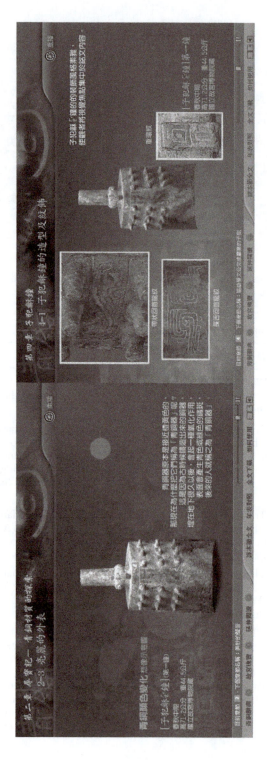

Figure 3.2 The National Palace Museum artifact e-learning project *A Marvelous Journey Through Bronzes!*

Multimedia discs

Much of the NPM's themed website and e-learning material is available on discs, including a tour of the NPM and some of its antiquities, paintings, calligraphy, rare books, and historical documents. Most of the material has been translated into different languages. The general public is able to use these discs to gain full access to the artifacts, enriching their experience both before and after a visit to the museum, and allowing artifact education by the NPM to become a part of their lives.

The multimedia discs are beautifully made and feature a wealth of content, making them ideal supportive tools for promoting arts education. They have received affirmation from government units such as the Research, Development and Evaluation Commission of the Executive Yuan, the Ministry of Education, and the Institute for Information Industry. In addition, they have received a number of awards from various organizations (Table 3.2).

Databases

Under the impetus of the Taiwan e-Learning and Digital Archives Program, the NPM has carried out artifact digitization and developed a database archival system comprised of 21 databases: the Digital Archives System of Antiquities, the Painting and Calligraphy Collections Management System, Digital Images of Qing Palace Memorials and Archives of the Grand Council, Digital Images of Rare Books, and the Ming and Qing Cartographical Materials Database.

Some of these databases are open to the public (Figure 3.3), either free of charge or at a cost, whereas others are storeroom management databases used exclusively by the museum. All of the databases, which contain a wealth of

Table 3.2 Awards won for multimedia discs

Awards	Entries	Category	Result	Organizer	Year
13th Annual Interactive Competition	*Precious Ju Ware – The Infinity of Aestheticism*	Digital Disc	Award of Excellence (Info Design)	Communication Arts Magazine	2007
2006 Innovation Awards for Digital Publishing	*Precious Ju Ware – The Infinity of Aestheticism*	Digital Disc	Bronze	Government Information Office, Executive Yuan	2006
MUSE Awards	*Convergence of Radiance: Tibeto-Chinese Buddhist Scripture Illustrations*	Collection Database or Reference	Silver	American Alliance of Museums (AAM)	2004

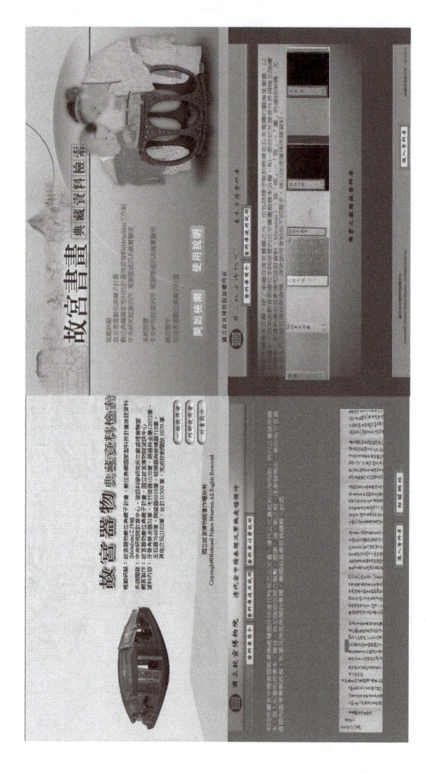

Figure 3.3 Examples of the National Palace Museum's artifact collection databases which are open to the public

content, provide users with the necessary information for studying or browsing. To render the databases more complete and convenient, functions such as input, saving, and retrieval are constantly updated to enable the resources stored in the databases to gain further value and influence.

Mobile applications

The development of smart mobile devices has changed the way in which modern-day people obtain real-time information. To keep pace with the mobile era, the NPM has launched a number of mobile device apps since 2012. The first of these, *Discover NPM*, was the first app in Taiwan to contain interactive features for artifacts. Users of this app are able to browse through and interact with the NPM's virtual artifacts, during which process they gain knowledge of the artifacts. The next app launched was *NPM InSight*, which features eight types of artifact (ceramics, jades, bronzes, curios, paintings, calligraphy, rare books, and historical documents) selected from the NPM's permanent exhibitions. It also offers visitors two tour routes, the "fine artifact collection" route and the "Chinese treasures" route. Both of these apps provide visitor information and artifact-learning functions in an entertaining and interactive manner. The content is also rich and practical.

Videos

Images facilitate a more vivid presentation of artifacts. In recent years, the NPM has planned and shot various creative short films, animated films, micro-movies, dramas, and documentaries. Using diverse technologies, such as multimedia and 3D animation, and containing fascinating plots, characters, and scenes, these films tell stories through captivating images, naturally drawing the audience closer to the artifacts.

Advertisement-type creative short films

Since developing the 3D Virtual Collection Exhibition System in 2003, the NPM has digitized five of its treasured artifacts, *Boat Carved from an Olive Pit*, *Ivory Ball*, *Revolving Vase*, *Jadeite Cabbage*, and *Mao-Kung Ting* (bronze vessel). Using X-ray, microscope and 3D-interactive images, structural analyses, and simulations, intricate details of the artifacts are displayed in videos. For example, the video for *Boat Carved from an Olive Pit* features the "Odes to the Red Cliff" and contains images of various components of the boat obtained by a simulated dismantling of it; that for *Ivory Ball* contains revolving simulations and endoscopic videos (Figure 3.4); *Revolving Vase* provides structural analyses and a revolving simulation; *Jadeite Cabbage* presents a simulation of the process of its construction; and *Mao-Kung Ting* shows the original colors of the vessel and compares ancient and modern versions of its inscriptions. All of the functions exemplify the NPM's use of digital technology to enhance the online navigation experience. In

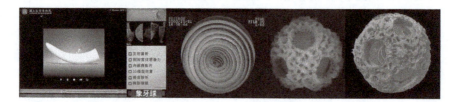

Figure 3.4 The 3D Virtual Collection Exhibition System playing the *Imagination in NPM: Ivory Ball* creative short film, which uses endoscopic videos, 3D models, and structural analyses to dissect and present the many "faces" of the ivory ball

addition, animated 3D short films about the unique features of each of the five artifacts have been made, with interesting plots and innovative 3D images added to present the virtual artifacts, creating new images for viewers to enjoy.

Adventures in the NPM-animated series

In 2007, the NPM collaborated with international teams from France and the United States, using the latest computer animation technology to produce the breathtaking 3D animated film *Adventures in the NPM*. Adopting an anthropomorphic approach, the film features three protagonists, a white Ding ware pillow in the shape of a child, a Song Dynasty jade duck, and a Han Dynasty jade pi-hsieh (evil-averting beast), based on the original artifacts. Humorous plots are used to raise people's awareness of NPM artifacts and the history of their relocation. In 2012, the NPM produced two sequels, *Adventures in the NPM: Meet the Painting and Calligraphy Masterpieces* and *Adventures in the NPM 2: Lost in the Art of Landscape Painting*, in which the three protagonists again lead the audience into various scenes created using 3D stereoscopic technology, allowing them to learn about classical masterpieces and enjoy the beauty of Chinese landscape paintings. In 2013, the NPM introduced *Adventures in the NPM: The Formosa Odyssey*, in which the three protagonists embark on a Ji-type Tongan ship on a trip to Taiwan, beginning a journey into the unknown and experiencing the beautiful scenery and culture of Taiwan. The *Adventures in the NPM* 3D animated series uses realistic animation techniques that fully retain the styles of the original paintings, clearly demonstrating the charm of the NPM artifacts, and are both entertaining and educational. In addition to Chinese and English language options, *Adventures in the NPM* is also voiced in Japanese with Japanese subtitles; *Adventures in the NPM: The Formosa Odyssey* is even voiced in Taiwanese to add authenticity for the audience. The different languages allow audiences from a variety of backgrounds to enjoy the animated films.

The *Adventures in the NPM* animated series has received numerous international awards (Table 3.3). These achievements highlight the unique, groundbreaking technology and presentation of the animated films, which allow them

Table 3.3 Awards won for the *Adventures in the NPM* animated series

Awards	Entries	Category	Result	Organizer	Year
The 47th Annual WorldFest – Houston International Film and Video Festival	*Adventures in the NPM: The Formosa Odyssey*	Film and Video Productions	Platinum Remi	WorldFest – Houston International Film and Video Festival	2014
The 46th Annual WorldFest – Houston International Film and Video Festival	*Adventures in NPM: Lost in the Art of Landscape Painting*	TV Commercials and Public Service Announcements	Platinum Remi	WorldFest – Houston International Film and Video Festival	2013
The 46th Annual WorldFest – Houston International Film and Video Festival	*Adventures of NPM: Meet the Painting and Calligraphy Masterpieces*	Film and Video Productions	Gold Remi	WorldFest – Houston International Film and Video Festival	2013
International Audiovisual Festival on Museums and Heritage (FIAMP) Awards	*Adventures of NPM: Meet the Painting and Calligraphy Masterpieces*	Audiovisuals	Silver Short Film Award	ICOM International Committee for Audiovisual and New Technologies of Image and Sound (AVICOM)	2012
Tokyo International Animation Fair 2008	*Adventures in the NPM*	Grand Prize	Animation of the Year	Tokyo International Animation Fair	2008
International Audiovisual Festival on Museums and Heritage (FIAMP) Awards	*Adventures in the NPM*	Audiovisuals	"Coup de Coeur" Award	ICOM International Committee for Audiovisual and New Technologies of Image and Sound (AVICOM)	2007

to mesmerize audiences on the international stage and have resulted in their acknowledgment as masterpieces among the NPM's animated films.

Micro-movies

In 2012, the NPM introduced the app micro-movie *A Trip to the Present (Lost in Time)*. This was the first micro-movie made by the NPM, made to complement the *Discover NPM* app. In the micro-movie, actor Chin Shih-Chieh assumes the role of Han Dynasty court painter Mao Yan-Shou; he and a number of other historical figures can be summoned to modern-day Taipei City using the virtual interactive features of the app, with which they can roam the city's streets, shopping malls, and MRT stations. *A Trip to the Present* is highly ingenious and witty; it is guaranteed to put a smile on viewers' faces.

Figure 3.5 The *Adventures in the NPM* 3D animated series

Table 3.4 Award won for micro-movie

Awards	Entries	Category	Result	Organizer	Year
The 46th Annual WorldFest-Houston International Film and Video Festival	*A Trip to the Present (Lost in Time)*: App Micro-movie	TV Commercials and Public Service Announcement category	Platinum Remi	WorldFest – Houston International Film and Video Festival	2013

Figure 3.6 Images from the micro-movie *A Trip to the Present*

Dramas

Th*e Passage*, directed by Cheng Wen-Tang, was the first drama film produced by the NPM. The historical background of the NPM and its artifacts are presented using an enchanting, movie-like atmosphere that resonates with viewers. *Cold Food Observance*, Su Shi's calligraphy masterpiece, was the inspiration for the touching story featured in the drama: three protagonists living in three worlds are brought together by the masterpiece and a wonderful and moving story ensues. Director Cheng has said that the film has a quiet and reserved atmosphere to correspond to the essence of Chinese artifacts, revealing the spirit of oriental aesthetics.

Documentaries

The documentary *In the Golden Age of Chinese Craftsmanship*, directed by Hou Hsiao-hsien in 2005, uses a unique narrative technique to describe the style, beauty, and texture of arts and crafts created during the progress of human civilization. In addition, it reveals the consummate craftsmanship of the artisans and

Table 3.5 Awards won for dramas

Awards	Entries	Category	Result	Organizer	Year
The 17th Tokyo International Film Festival Awards	*The Passage*	Film	Nominated for Competition	Tokyo International Foundation for Promotion of Screen Image Culture	2004
The 41st Golden Horse Awards	*The Passage*	Film	Nominated for Best Original Screenplay	Taipei Golden Horse Film Festival Executive Committee	2004
The 41st Golden Horse Awards	*The Passage*	Film	Best Sound Effects	Taipei Golden Horse Film Festival Executive Committee	2004

Figure 3.7 Images from the National Palace Museum drama *The Passage*

Figure 3.8 The beauty of craftsmanship as shown in the documentary *In the Golden Age of Chinese Craftsmanship*

Figure 3.9 Images from the documentary *Rebuilding the Tongan Ships*

Table 3.6 Awards won for documentaries

Awards	Entries	Category	Result	Organizer	Year
The 47th Annual WorldFest – Houston International Film and Video Festival	*Rebuilding the Tongan Ships*	Film and Video Productions	Gold Remi	WorldFest – Houston International Film and Video Festival	2014
2006 Digital Archives Commercial Application Contest	*In The Golden Age of Chinese Craftsmanship*	Film	Digital Archives / Award of Excellence	Digital Archives e-Park	2006

the detailed, complicated process of their production. The documentary can be viewed in a variety of languages (Chinese, English, Japanese, and French).

Rebuilding the Tongan Ships, a documentary produced by the NPM in 2012, primarily introduces the *Tongan ship "Ji" Diagram* and the *Tongan ship "No. 1" Diagram*. After conducting in-depth investigations and research, the NPM used post-production technologies that include model-making and 3D technology to reproduce the ancient sailing ships in detail. The origins of the diagrams and their significance are also explored, and the historical ties between Tongan natives Li Changgeng and Cai Qian are analyzed. The documentary presents the results of the NPM's rich and rigorous research to the modern-day public, bringing them closer to the elegant oceanic times of the Qing Dynasty.

Interactive installations

Continuous technological innovation has led museums to use new technologies such as human–machine interface technology, virtual reality technology, and biological sensing technology. These technologies transcend the previous static method of exhibition by using lively and creative interactions to spark the interest of visitors. A range of options for manipulating these interactive installations is available to visitors, creating a museum in which the exhibition pieces are able to "communicate" with their audience. Such "communication" allows the audience to be moved by and to resonate with the artifacts and motivates them to delve into the history behind the mysterious relics. A selection of representative interactive devices produced by the NPM and details of the NPM's achievements with interactive devices are listed below.

Interactive tables

The NPM has developed interactive tables using high-technology projection and touchscreens to display classic artifacts in an interactive manner. The *Must See Paintings and Calligraphies* interactive table contains 15 of the NPM's paintings and calligraphy masterpieces, such as *Clearing After Snowfall*, *Autobiography*, *Travelers Among Mountains and Streams*, *Dwelling in the Fuchun Mountains*, and *Along the River During the Qingming Festival* (painted by five Qing imperial court painters). New technology has overcome the problem of ancient paintings and calligraphy masterpieces being too fragile to withstand regular exhibition. Visitors are able to operate the touchscreens freely and examine the classic pieces in detail. The *Chinese Characters on Mao-Kung Ting* interactive installation uses digital content to reveal the evolution of the Chinese characters inscribed inside the *Mao-Kung Ting*. The ancient-to-modern character-conversion function provides viewers with a better understanding of the inscriptions and their cultural connotations. The interactive tables combine technology and the humanities and

Figure 3.10 Users operating the *Must See Paintings and Calligraphies* interactive tabletop and the *Chinese Characters on Mao-Kung Ting* interactive installation

bring audiences closer to the NPM's collection of masterpieces, delivering profound cultural education via exciting human-artifact interactions.

Magic Crystal Ball

The *Magic Crystal Ball* interactive device features images of *Jadeite Cabbage, Boat Carved from an Olive Pit, Mao-Kung Ting, Ivory Ball,* and *Revolving Vase,* taken by 3D panoramic photography. Users press buttons to make 3D virtual images appear inside the crystal ball, allowing them to touch and play with these artifacts as ancient emperors might have done. The colors of the lights on the outside of the ball also change as the artifacts shown inside change. This spherical device displays novel technology, while the artifacts reveal aesthetic craftsmanship.

A Tang Palace Rhapsody

In 2009, the NPM drew on *A Tang Palace Concert* as the inspiration for developing the interactive installation *A Tang Palace Rhapsody,* which incorporates interactive devices such as pressure-sensitive floors and distance sensors. An animated film shows the palace ladies traveling through time and space to enjoy enriching experiences in Taiwan, New York, and Paris. When visitors activate the sensors, the palace ladies hurry back to the original painting, where they once again play their Tang Dynasty musical instruments.

Figure 3.11 Visitors operating the interactive device the *Magic Crystal Ball*

Table 3.7 Award won for the interactive installation *A Tang Palace Rhapsody*

Awards	Entries	Category	Result	Organizer	Year
The 17th Annual Communicator Awards	A Tang Palace Rhapsody	Interactive Media	Educational- Silver Awards	International Academy of the Visual Arts	2011

Figure 3.12 Images from the interactive installation *A Tang Palace Rhapsody*

Table 3.8 Award won for the interactive installation *It's a Big World: Globetrotting*

Awards	Entries	Category	Result	Organizer	Year
MUSE Awards	*It's a Big World: Globetrotting*	Games and Augmented Reality	Silver	American Alliance of Museums (AAM)	2013

Figure 3.13 Images from the *It's a Big World: Globetrotting* exhibition hall

It's a Big World: Globetrotting

The interactive installation *It's a Big World: Globetrotting* is based on the *Kunyu Quantu* (*World Map*) by Ferdinand Verbiest, Qing dynasty. Kinect somatosensory interactive devices and large projection floors are used to allow visitors to move freely around hemispheric map images, view stars on a panoramic screen, and experience the conditions in which ancient people studied astronomy and geography. The animated odd beast theater that is part of the installation is suitable for families. This lively and dynamic interactive theater, which features a game-type animation design, won silver in the 2013 MUSE Awards.

Four Seasons of the NPM

The *Four Seasons of the NPM* exhibit, opened in 2011, features four famous paintings from the NPM's collection. Novel technology was adopted to provide visitors with a new way of viewing paintings rather than the conventional static way; visitors are able to "feel" the beauty of the four seasons with various senses. The interactive paintings displayed in the exhibit are *Spring Birth*, *Summer Lotus*, *Autumn Colors*, and *Winter Snow*. *Spring Birth*, based on *Immortal Blossoms in an Everlasting Spring* by Giuseppe Castiglione, Qing Dynasty, uses movement-activated sensors and voice-activated technology to make the flowers and birds in the painting sway and dance according to movements and sounds made by visitors, recreating a garden full of life in the spring. *Summer Lotus*, based on *Lotuses in the Wind at Taiye* by Feng Dayou, Song Dynasty, integrates image-sensing technology with devices such as fans to interact with visitors. The visitors' steps and the wind generated move the fish and lotuses in the projections. *Autumn Colors*, based on *Autumn Colors on the Qiao and Hua Mountains* by Zhao Mengfu, Yuan Dynasty, uses dynamic infrared cameras to capture visitors' hand movements and enlarge the original painting, producing magnificent and detailed images. *Winter Snow*, based on *Deep Snow in Mountain Passes* by Wen Zhengming, Ming Dynasty, uses an electronically controlled dimming glass and vision-detection technology to induce color changes to portray the cycle of a day. The positions of viewers are also detected and used to adjust the clarity of the display glass. The application of a myriad novel technology renders this exhibition remarkably captivating and highly interactive, and it won an award from I.T. Month in 2012.

Table 3.9 Award won for *Four Seasons of the NPM*

Awards	Entries	Category	Result	Organizer	Year
Outstanding I.T. Application and Products Award	New Multimedia Art Exhibition, *Four Seasons of the NPM*	Digital Multimedia	Outstanding I.T. Application and Products Award	I.T. Month	2012

Figure 3.14 Visitors operating interactive installations at *Four Seasons of the NPM*

Painting animations

The NPM carefully selected six famous paintings from its collection to produce full-sized, high-resolution painting animations: *Return Clearing* by an anonymous artist, Ming Dynasty; *Spring Morning in the Han Palace* by Qiu Ying, Ming Dynasty; *Imitating Zhao Bosu's Latter Ode on Red Cliff* by Wen Zhengming, Ming Dynasty; *Syzygy of the Sun, Moon, and the Five Planets* by Xu Yang, Qing Dynasty; *Along the River During the Qingming Festival* by the Qing Court artists; and *Activities of the Twelve Months* by anonymous Qing court artists. Four high-resolution projectors in conjunction with seamless fusion technology are used to build an 8-meter-wide elongated screen. The painting animation series are true to the original paintings to facilitate interpretations of these classic masterpieces.

To celebrate the advent of the Year of the Horse, in 2013 the NPM outdid itself by curating a higher-caliber exhibition, *Painting Animation: One Hundred Horses*. For this exhibition, the number of projectors was increased to six and a plot created around the caring of horses by horse officers. The beauty of day-to-night and sunshine-to-rain cycles are displayed elegantly and various activities engaged in by the horses, such as crossing the river, galloping, resting, and playing, are vividly portrayed. The high-resolution presentation brings the magnificent horses created by Giuseppe Castiglione back to life, giving the illusion that the audience has moved into the painting and is experiencing the essence of Chinese scroll painting.

Table 3.10 Awards won for painting animations

Awards	Entries	Category	Result	Organizer	Year
The 47th Annual WorldFest – Houston International Film and Video Festival	*Painting Animation: One Hundred Horses*	Film and Video Productions	Gold Remi	WorldFest – Houston International Film and Video Festival	2014
The 47th Annual WorldFest – Houston International Film and Video Festival	*Painting Animation: Imitating Zhao Bosu's Latter Ode on Red Cliff*	Film and Video Productions	Silver Remi	WorldFest – Houston International Film and Video Festival	2014
The 46th Annual WorldFest – Houston International Film and Video Festival	*Painting Animation: Along the River During the Qingming Festival*	Film and Video Productions	Gold Remi	WorldFest – Houston International Film and Video Festival	2013
MUSE Awards	*Painting Animation: Along the River During the Qingming Festival*	Multimedia Installations	Gold	American Alliance of Museums (AAM)	2012

Figure 3.15 The painting animation *One Hundred Horses* displayed in Gallery 102 at the National Palace Museum

The painting animations series, which uses delicate animation and projects a simulation of a painting scroll on a wall, provide visitors with a stunning visual experience that is highly praised. Such achievements show just how much effort is being made by the NPM to combine new media with traditional paintings and positive feedback received from international communities.

New media art exhibitions

The NPM has been committed to developing digital technology for many years. Since 2013, the NPM has combined its digital achievements, such as multimedia movies and interactive devices, to organize its New media art exhibitions, producing exhibitions that feature strong and memorable themes, powerful interactive functions, and appealing content.

Rebuilding the Tongan Ships – New Media Art Exhibition

In 2013, the NPM introduced *Rebuilding the Tongan Ships – New Media Art Exhibition*. Floating projections, autostereoscopic displays, augmented reality, and somatosensory interactive technologies, allow visitors to re-examine the glorious days of the Tongan ships and experience China's power and strength in oceanic affairs in East Asia during the 19th century. The exhibition features

Figure 3.16 Visitors operating the interactive installations *Breaking Waves* (left) and
The Augmented Reality Clothes Changing System (right) at the *Rebuilding the Tongan Ships* exhibition

devices such as the kinect somatosensory interactive installation *Breaking Waves*, which uses three-sided surround projection to enable audiences to experience the setting of the sails, the operation of cannons, and the pursuit of pirates, reproducing the experience aboard a real Tongan ship. *Deconstruct the Tongan Ships* uses a laser detection interactive device to allow visitors to disassemble and reassemble the 3D Tongan ship models via intuitive movements such as touching and dragging. *Crossover Dialogues: Holographic Projection* uses advanced floating projection technology to facilitate meetings between the Jiaqing Emperor, Viceroy Li Changgeng, and pirate leader Cai Qian via a process that overlaps virtual and real life. Through operating these devices, visitors gain a deeper understanding of the structure, equipment, and functions of the Tongan ships and the historical events associated with these vessels.

Qianlong C.H.A.O. – New Media Art Exhibition

Opened in 2013, the *Qianlong C.H.A.O. – New Media Art Exhibition* includes situation-oriented interactive installations, films, and displays of actual artifacts. Qianlong Emperor's artistic life is interpreted from a modern perspective using modern art techniques. The exhibition is divided into various themes. *Tree of Colors* is based on an artifact from Qianlong Emperor's collection. *Vase with Decoration of Floral Pattern and Landscape in Yangcai Painted Enamels* uses color-sensing devices to detect visitors' apparel for instant color analysis, after which the colors of the visitors' clothing are regrouped and projected onto the vase, allowing visitors to produce artwork featuring their unique personal style. *Stamps of Landscape*, which is based on the *Activities of the Twelve Months*, allows visitors to move various stamps (elements) of the painting, such as the mountains, stones, trees, and people, to put together their own landscape painting, in imitation of the hobby of the Qianlong Emperor, who enjoyed stamping and commenting on paintings. The painting animation installation *City's Spring Festival* combines projectors and large display devices to redraw the *Court Version of "Spring Dawn in the Han Palace."* The facial expressions of visitors are captured

Table 3.11 Awards won for *The Qianlong C.H.A.O. – New Media Art Exhibition*

Awards	Entries	Category	Result	Organizer	Year
MUSE Awards	*Qianlong C.H.A.O. – New Media Art Exhibition*	Interpretive Interactive Installations	Silver	American Alliance of Museums (AAM)	2014
The 47th Annual WorldFest – Houston International Film and Video Festival	*Qianlong C.H.A.O. – New Media Art Exhibition*	New Media (including websites)	Platinum Remi	WorldFest – Houston International Film and Video Festival	2014

Figure 3.17 Animation installation using face detection and recognition, and 3D conversion technology to "teleport" visitors into a virtual city to celebrate the *City's Spring Festival*

using a combination of a face detection and recognition system and 2D-to-3D face conversion technology to "teleport" visitors inside a magical, virtual city. The *Me* section combines cloud computing, motion detection, and augmented reality technology; visitors are able to use their mobile phones to scan and retrieve 10 artifacts that reveal the aesthetic tastes of the Qianlong Emperor and to read artifact-related information.

The *Qianlong C.H.A.O. – New Media Art Exhibition* combines modern technology with traditional artifacts and uses a number of novel technological devices to create a vibrant and lively environment in which visitors "travel" back to the past to enjoy ancient artifacts. Visitors are also provided with an interactive exhibition space in which they can reflect on the varying artistic tastes of different times.

New waves of NPM

In 2013, the NPM launched a series of exhibitions to bring NPM artifacts to various regions of Taiwan: *NPM's Anime Carnival, New Waves of NPM: Chang-hua Traveling Exhibition, New Waves of NPM: Tainan Travelling Exhibition*, and *New Waves of NPM: Songshan Feng-Tian Temple Travelling Exhibition*. For these

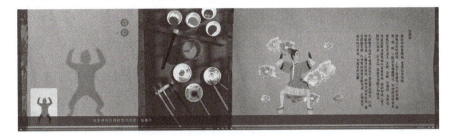

Figure 3.18 The interactive game *Ladies' Fashions,* showcased at the *New Waves of NPM: Tainan Travelling Exhibition*

exhibitions, the relevant artifacts from the NPM's collection were digitized and shown via multimedia devices and films. New forms of digital technology and lively and interactive exhibition methods were also used to enhance the values of the traditional artifacts and to introduce them to people's lives.

The *New Waves of NPM: Tainan Travelling Exhibition* also contained works created by artist Peter Nelson, and works produced through industry-school cooperation. Nelson adopted the perspective of a Western artist to present his works in a "cross-cultural" manner and used 3D modeling programs to transform his landscapes into 3D green ceramics; the resulting contrasts were quite fascinating. In the industry-school cooperation, students created works that were displayed. An example is *Ladies' Fashions,* crafted by students from Shih Chien University, in which visitors were able to interact with a device to experience what it would have been like to pose as a model during the concubine selection process. They were also able to learn about the accessories, clothing patterns, and amusing anecdotes of the ladies from the past, and explore the aesthetic standards of the time.

Conclusion

The NPM has implemented several digital programs in accordance with government policies, focusing on new and different technologies at each stage of development and working hard to achieve the ultimate goal of artifact digitization. Starting from the digital archiving of artifacts and moving through an array of digital applications, NPM artifacts have been given a brand-new look. Achievements such as the construction of rich digital databases and the subsequent development of multimedia audio and videos, high-quality and detailed documentaries, enchanting artifact-themed websites, highly practical e-learning courses, exciting interactive devices, and art exhibitions using new media have become precious artifacts of the NPM, both tangible and intangible. The achievements of the NPM in the area of digitization have been superb and significant. Over the years, its efforts to create diverse forms of digitization have resulted in the production of numerous works and affirmation from the United Nations Educational, Scientific, and Cultural Organization (UNESCO). The International Committee for

Audiovisual and New Technologies of Image and Sound (AVICOM), a committee of the International Council of Museums (ICOM) which maintains strong links with UNESCO, acknowledged that the NPM's digital achievements have far exceeded expectations and subsequently awarded the NPM the unprecedented Grand Prix Award in All Categories.

Although the NPM has rich resources and has laid solid foundations for the digitization of artifacts, it also has the heavy responsibility of facilitating the inter-disciplinary integration of digital technology and the humanities. The NPM is working vigorously to maintain its level of success in the field of artifact digitization and will strive to maximize the value of its digital assets by using new and sophisticated digital technologies in the future to develop its 4G network.

Bibliography

Fung, M. C., and Lin, Q. P. (editor-in-chief) (2012). *Ten years of hard work for a hundred years of connoisseurship: Special issue on National Palace Museum's achievements in digital archiving.* Taipei: National Palace Museum.

Ho, C. H. (2014). An overview of IT business development for the National Palace Museum. *Information Technology News of Government, 318,* 1–15.

Hsieh, C. K., Yang, W. Y., and Su, Y. Y. (in press). 10 golden years of National Palace Museum artifact digitization. *The National Palace Museum Monthly of Chinese Art, 384,* 70–79.

Quo-Ping Lin, J. (editor-in-chief) (2007). *Trends in digital life at the NPM.* Taipei: National Palace Museum.

Quo-Ping Lin, J. (2014). IT-enabled innovative services as a museum strategy: Experience of the National Palace Museum, Taipei, Taiwan. *Digital Heritage and Culture,* 3–20.

Internet resources

Huang, H. I., and Chen, H. Y. (2006). The passing of time, images, and emotions: An interview with director Cheng Wen-Tang, *Taiwan Film Institute: Funscreen Weekly.* Retrieved from http://www.funscreen.com.tw/headline.asp?H_No=37

National Palace Museum. (2011). *The future museum of NPM.* Retrieved from http://www.npm.gov.tw/exh100/3d_npm/

National Palace Museum. (n.d.). *Platform of knowledge for new media art exhibitions.* Retrieved from http://140.92.88.38/NPM/

National Palace Museum. (n.d.). *The digital archives project website.* Retrieved from http://www.npm.gov.tw/da/ch-htm/about03.html

National Palace Museum (n.d.). *NPM media.* Retrieved from http://digital.npm.gov.tw/Article.aspx?Lang=1&Sno=02000151

National Palace Museum. (n.d.). *Website of digital project achievements.* Retrieved from http://www.npm.gov.tw/digital/index1_ch.html

"*Smart moves*" for the government: Creating life with your hands. (n.d.). Retrieved from http://focus.www.gov.tw/subject/class.php?content_id=283

Part II
Organization-related issues

4 Organizational issues in implementing information and communications technology in museum

The case of the National Palace Museum

Tzu-Shian Han and Yi-An Chen

Museums, information technology, and social effects

In the 21st century, the key values of a museum include having a powerful social effect. Digital resources and information technology (IT)-enabled services provided by museums can reach larger audiences than ever before. Museum objects are transformed from being exclusively "within the walls" to online resources that available at any time and anywhere. The Institute of Museum and Library Services (IMLS) has indicated that libraries and museums are expected to cater for a wider range of audiences with more diversity. The preferred ways in which to meet current needs include institutional collaboration, thoughtful "architecture of participation," and successfully applied technology (O'Reilly, 2005). Museums take on the function of a catalyst, coordinating partners with diverse expertise. Audience engagement and experience also become central components of the mission of a museum.

A museum's role is to provide a "flexible, co-created immersive experience that connects individuals with their families and other like-minded people." From the beginning of this century, the term *public value* has gradually become common in museum management. Possibilities beyond the walls of the museum are being recognized (Gurian, 2006; Scott, 2013). It is important for museums to clarify the value they represent in our fast-paced, modern society. Building on the foundations of a solid core value, museums are able to develop practical goals to carry out their missions. Actions such as constantly adjusting museum programs to create public value can be considered tangible methods for delivering social effects.

The National Palace Museum's (NPM's) status as the iconic museum in Taiwan calls for both the government and the museum itself to ensure that the museum is being constantly improved. The NPM has 650,000 objects in its collection; if it exhibited 1,700 objects per season, it would take 100 years for the entire collection to be exhibited. Exhibiting the abundant resources of the NPM is limited due to the lack of space, which represents both a barrier and an opportunity for change. The NPM is obligated to demonstrate powerful social effects within its organizational limits, and it is hoped that the implementation of IT services will bring new life to the museum. To display the museum's content effectively through IT-enabled services, it is essential to build an innovation-enabling organizational culture.

Web 2.0 is a platform provider that allows bottom-up content development processes and provides social ways for audiences to interact with online content (Simon, 2007). Using IT can decrease the time required for data processing and the communication of information. Researchers have also identified IT as an effective tool for improving communication in construction processes, cost control, and project management (Skibniewski and Abduh, 2000). Increasing numbers of organizations have attempted to adopt and implement these new technologies to improve their products, processes, and services (Cleland and Ireland, 2002). Museums devote themselves to the use of digital and IT-enabled services to meet the needs of audiences in our modern society. Museum-related large data, including digitized collections, videos, and visitor information, can obviously benefit from the use of IT tools. Digitization, IT, and IT-enabled services have been introduced into museums for no more than two decades. These new services allow museums to deliver services more efficiently, lavishly, and interactively. This improvement in service is based on both cutting-edge technology and the empathy of developers. As providers of educational and social services, museums are expected by both the government and the public to provide accessible and accountable resources. However, the ever-evolving nature of these modern tools inevitably comes into conflict with museums that retain traditional operational models.

The 2011 Horizon Report–Museum Edition by the New Media Consortium (NMC) covered seven key trends in technology applications for museums (Johnson, Adams, and Witchey, 2011), and outlined their potential for making a significant difference to delivering museum functions such as cross-institutional collaboration, digitization and cataloguing projects, civic and social engagement, seamless cross-device experiences, intensively connected social networks, and data literacy. These features emphasize connection and communication between visitors, museum resources, museum digital resources, other museums, and society in general. The implementation of ICT (information and communications technology) has been shown to improve efficiency and communication within those organizations that have cross-cultural or international backgrounds (Campbell and Uys, 2007; Peansupap and Walker, 2005; Zaidman et al., 2008). Through introducing and refining IT-enabled services, the nature of communication and the integration of IT-enabled tools are expected to elevate the capability of museums to achieve the NMC's expectations.

Successful IT-enabled services can help museums to promote their educational programs, improving public awareness of historical artifacts and sophisticated traditional culture. Given that a museum is a public enterprise that is expected to integrate public participation and knowledge distribution, museums must build an innovation-friendly environment to meet the challenges posed by a constantly evolving society. Figure 4.1 shows the role of organizational culture within the NPM's attempts to deliver ideal IT-enabled services that can successfully transform

Figure 4.1 Organizational culture within the process of IT-enabled services that create social effects

digital content into influential public outreach material. While technology special-ists can readily transform historical treasures into IT-generated content, successful IT-enabled services can only be delivered if there is intense cross-departmental communication. For success, these services need to be recognized not only by service providers, but also by the people who receive them. An organizational culture that encourages communication and collaboration enables better service and provides a foundation for the building up of social effects.

The NPM as an organization for delivering social effects

As the representative museum in Taiwan, the NPM has a fantastic collection of traditional Chinese artifacts. In the 1960s, in contrast to events in communist mainland China, the NPM opened with its exquisite collection inherited from Qing-Dynasty China's royal collections. The wealth of Chinese artifacts held by the NPM made it the main resource for Chinese art history research at the time. The significance of the NPM's selective and comprehensive collection is still rec-ognized today. The NPM is a significant part of the nation's development of its cultural and creative industries and is becoming deeply involved in the creative design industry and the application of IT (NPM, 2013). Political authority con-tinues to have a crucial influence on decision-making in the NPM (Wen, 2011). In addition, its line-department culture is less friendly toward innovation, which is cause for concern regarding the process of change.

Effort has been made to improve the environment of professional museum operations. Regulations and standards for museums are in the process of being established. In September 2014, a draft museum law was passed by the Leg-islative Yuan. This law aims to recognize the professional requirements of the field, provide regulations for private museums, and set standards for best practice. Although the establishment of a museum law is a crucial step in enabling muse-ums in Taiwan to become social and educational organizations that can better fulfill their social mission and functions, it is equally important for museums to improve their organizational cultures and operational models to better incorpo-rate innovation and change.

As an organization with high social expectations and abundant government funding, the NPM needs to constantly improve its function as a museum and implement innovation in a sustainable manner.

The NPM has made many digital implementations in the past decade (Lin, 2007); details of these are described in earlier chapters. The overall goal is obvious: to engage a broader audience, especially younger visitors, by making the move to eliminate geographic boundaries between museum collections and the public through IT-enabled services. IT-enabled services in museums are valued for enabling changes in the way people learn and interact with information. The goal of any innovation or implementation of technology is to have an effective social effect. As Du Plooy (1998) emphasized in discussing a theory of ICT diffusion and implementation, we must conceptualize IT along with its implementation. ICT policies that aim to address socio-economic development should have duality embedded within them if they are to address the process of the adoption of innovation and diffusion of ICT over a country (Du Plooy, 1998). In the same vein, IT-enabled innovative services in museums must be evaluated for their value to the public. Understanding and cultivating the human environment within which IT-enabled services are to be implemented is the foundation of successful IT-enabled innovative services within an organization. However, studies on the NPM have identified problems with several organizational elements, including its leadership, organizational culture, and individual motivation (Chang, 2011; Han, 2011; Lu and Lin, 2011; Pan, 2014; Tong, 2010; Wen, 2011; Yang, 2008).

Identified organizational issues

Political influence

A government line-department is owned by the government and usually operates with less flexibility than a private museum (Lord and Lord, 2009). Public museums in Taiwan, such as the NPM, operate under the direction of line-departments, in a similar way to public museums in France, which are under the control of the central government (Han, 2011). Obvious limitations for museums under government control are political influence and the decision-making process. The NPM is subordinate to the Legislative Yuan, which can cause dilemmas for the NPM when making decisions. As it must follow the directions of the government administration, the museum's vision and goals often change with political party rotation (Wen, 2011). The NPM thus frequently needs to deal with changing decisions at short notice.

The advice given in a report on the organizational evaluation of public museums (Han, 2011) was that national museums in Taiwan should consider establishing a functional board whose members are excluded from belonging to political or other interest groups. A supervision and advisory system of this type would allow museums to be independent of the government and retain their integrity as educational organizations.

Leadership

The NPM's director is part of the cabinet, alternating with the Executive Yuan and appointed through an administrative order from the president. The opaque process of director selection often results in directors having stronger political and academic characteristics than professional museum experience (Han, 2011; Liang, 2001). In addition, because the museum's advisory board takes little part in any decision-making, the visions and goals tend to depend solely on the director's view and risk being biased in their interpretation as the director alternates (Lu and Lin, 2011). When the party of administration changes, projects may be postponed, interrupted, or discontinued. Many resources are thus wasted when the interpretation of the NPM's mission alters completely (Nojima, 2012).

Integration with the government places the NPM's director in a position that requires constant coordination between the museum's leadership and government administrators (McGuire, 2006). Different units within an organization also have different priorities for the implementation of ICT innovations (Charvat, 2003). The power structure of the NPM places the responsibility for decision-making on its director. Directors with different backgrounds can thus make very different decisions; however, a clear and continuous vision from a director would help to lay the foundations for vision-driven innovation.

In the current decision-making process, the uncertainty surrounding program continuity does not occur in certain cases. Examples are Saturday Night at the NPM and the Children's Gallery; both of these programs were planned and implemented under one director and have continued despite much change in leadership (Lu and Lin, 2011). Such continuity relies solely on an intangible consensus among various directors regarding the mission of the museum. Without such consensus existing in written form, project continuity may readily be broken.

Leadership is also a main consideration in implementing innovation-diffusion. Museum directors are dealing with a society that is more complicated now than ever before. The current society presents both opportunities and obstacles for museum leaders. In the case of the NPM, relatively abundant government funding has given the director much scope to make changes. The incumbent of the politically assigned position of director must address the issue of piecemeal planning, gaps in administration, and the waste of resources (Lu and Lin, 2011). The political significance of the NPM is related to national identity. It is thus inevitable that changes in political parties will affect the museum. Strengthening the director's grasp of the museum's mission is a relatively effective way to eliminate the influence of inconsistent leadership (Lu and Lin, 2011).

Organizational structure (line-departments)

The director of the NPM is appointed by the president. Despite the director being responsible for both decision-making and implementation, the selection of the director remains an opaque process. The vision and goals of a museum form the foundations for all of the museum's exhibits and programs. In the NPM currently, the vision is interpreted and the goals articulated according to the director's will, and thus change as the director changes (Lu and Lin, 2011).

The NPM has a relatively conservative process for recruiting museum staff. It follows university regulations and thus has a large proportion of researchers among its staff. The NPM has functioned as a research organization rather than an educational organization for decades. Such organizations do not place stress on communication, thus increasing the difficulty of forming a consensus between individuals and teams. It has been suggested that museums should adopt more flexible recruiting and human resource processes, to obtain the diversity of professional staff that is required to perform the complex duties of a modern museum (Han, 2011).

The NPM has adjusted its organizational structure several times since 2008, to enable better performance of modern functions. In 2006, the NPM's personnel comprised 280 budgeted staff, and 24 contractors. In 2013, the number of budgeted staff had risen to 487, nearly double that in 2006. The significant increase in budgeted staff corresponds to the digitization projects and new visitor services implemented over the past decade. For example, the Department of Education, Exhibition, and Information Services was reorganized in 2008. Curating remains the responsibility of the three research-orientated departments (Tong, 2010). To give the decision-making process more flexibility, it has been advised that national museums in Taiwan should consider establishing a functional board whose members are excluded from belonging to political or other interest groups. Such a supervision and advisory system would allow museums to be independent of the government and retain their integrity as cultural and educational organizations (Han, 2011).

Museum effectiveness

Despite being the most resource-rich museum in the country, the NPM is also affected by this. A clear decline in self-motivated visitors to the NPM has occurred in recent years (Tong, 2010). As the museum has a goal of attracting younger visitors, this decline indicates a gap between museum services and visitor expectations. The NPM must seek ways in which to reduce this disparity. The NPM's digital implementations have been progressing well, and it intends to implement further innovative techniques in its educational and outreach programs. In promoting IT-enabled innovative services, the museum expects to make better use of museum functions and create increased educational value for the public. However, it takes time to reflect this in the actual effects of such organizational changes. According to Tong (2010), despite the efforts made in digitizing the NPM's artifacts, self-motivated domestic visitors continue to decrease, especially in the younger generations. Although the NPM has established abundant high-quality IT services, there is a lack of front-end research into the expectations of and acceptance by the public. It has been suggested that the NPM should carry out visitor research and incorporate the results into its marketing strategy. It has also been noted that the museum does not have a professional marketing manager for coordinating its marketing strategy (Trendgo, 2007).

Organizational communication

A culture of communication is crucial for building an innovative organizational culture, as it helps employees to accommodate organizational changes and find ways through which to achieve goals. Good communication also benefits the establishment of coherent and explicit goals through multi-professional participation, paving the way for a museum to deliver powerful effects. The organizational structure of the NPM has gone through several changes. Chang (2011) observed that the NPM had improved communication within the organization with the help of IT tools. Efficiency and digitization have also proved to be valuable for marketing and organizational cooperation. An example is the exhibition *Diplomatic Credentials Failed to Deliver*, which opened in 2014. The curating of this exhibition was a process that evolved over years, during which the researchers and curators became involved in an IT development process through creating specially designed content for IT-enabled services (Chou, 2014). This evolving operational model demonstrates that the museum was and is aware of the importance of communication between professionals and has accumulated experience from earlier projects. Improvements such as these are triggered by motivated individuals and diffuse throughout project-related teams.

Communication is also important in modern exhibition design that involves innovative changes. The creation of exhibitions with IT-enabled services requires cooperation between curators, educators, and IT professionals. A balance between communication and respect allows professionals to be at their most competent and to produce comprehensive exhibitions effectively. In a similar way, IT projects are considered complex because of the inevitable collaboration required between multiple departments (Charvat, 2003; Ward and Chapman, 2003).

In an organization, employees are, simultaneously, members of multiple discourse systems (Van Dijk, 1997). A discourse system can be defined as a way in which a particular group of people promote their conception of truth or reality according to their ideology. In the case of the NPM, researchers, technicians, civil service personnel, and contractors belong to different discourse systems, and cultural barriers are thus inevitable.

Kwon and Zmud (1987) extended the innovation-diffusion model of Rogers (1995) by including interdependence between organizations. If there is no interaction, differences between community members will be exacerbated. Communication between these diversified communities becomes the most powerful tool for successful cooperation. Ongoing observation of the contributions and efforts of other members is key to developing a shared understanding. Effective communication allows those involved in a project to build trust through continued interaction and to develop common values and a shared understanding. This process can improve the willingness of participants to carry out innovative tasks (Gibson and Manuel, 2003).

Considering the issues outlined above, it is clear that the NPM should develop a tangible and systematic method for incorporating innovation into the organization, to complement what has already evolved. This is a process that should originate from the leadership and unify the organization based on a commonly agreed vision and a communicative culture to achieve more powerful social effects.

Innovation diffusion and change management

Research has indicated that a culture of innovation is key to managing innovation. At the outset of innovative change, there is often vagueness and chaos, requiring a certain amount of endurance, the spirit to try and to learn from mistakes, and the willingness to take risks to gradually reveal the outcomes of innovation. The process of innovation involves disorder and requires adjustment of functions or organizational boundaries, and possibly even adjustments to an organization's structure or environment (Baer and Frese, 2003; Detert et al., 2000; McDermott and Stock, 1999). Innovation demands a certain amount of flexibility and an organization needs to possess such flexibility alongside a tolerance to change.

Successful innovation arises from the pursuit of balanced flexibility-control tensions. Flexibility stimulates creativity and triggers change; enabled employees can thus create innovative outcomes. Control emphasizes order, transforming creativity and ideas into products and services with market value. Within the context of the organization, it is clear that strong leadership and the availability of resources are imperative to the successful development of a community (Brook, 2004). A sustainable and successful community of practice includes the following features: leadership, participation, and the ability to respond to changes in the environment. A delicate balance between stability and change is key to ensuring the sustainability of a community (Stuckey and Smith, 2004).

Diffusion has been defined as the process by which technological innovation and managerial innovation are introduced into work processes and adopted by a specific group or across an entire organization (Bresnen and Marshall, 2001; Green and Hevner, 2000). Rogers (1995) presented an innovation-diffusion model, emphasizing three factors that affect innovation-diffusion: the characteristics of the innovation, communication channels, and the social system. The social system relates to inner and outer organization personnel who are involved in innovation-diffusion, including individuals both within and outside the organization, teams, departments, decision-makers, and the leader (Prescott and Conger, 1995). The interaction and communication channels between these personnel are crucial to the success of innovation-diffusion. Both academic and industry publications have reported the crucial role of complementary human and social environments in the diffusion of innovative tools (Charvat, 2003; Du Plooy, 1998; Rogers, 1995). As differences in cognition and acceptance between individuals in various departments can lead to diverging goals, effective communication is essential for establishing a consensus within the organization.

Both the adoption and the diffusion of ICT are socially constructed processes that require an organization to establish an organizational culture and a behavior model that encourages the adoption of new technologies (Weilbach and Byrne, 2010). When a museum attempts to develop innovative IT-enabled services, it must construct recognition and consensus within its organization. The organization must become one that embraces change and innovation. Such qualities can be found within successful ICT-diffusion organizations. Change management is key to promoting innovation and diffusion within an organization. Ambition and support originating from the leader, cooperation between departments and individuals trained to demonstrate motivation and capacity, a sharing and learning environment, and an open system (Peansupap and Walker, 2005: p. 23) are all possible directions in which the NPM may move to eliminate its organizational barriers.

Innovation-diffusion of IT-enabled services requires change management to encourage individuals within the organization to adopt the new technologies and to offer appropriate training and technical support (Senge, 2014). Research has highlighted the role of senior managers and ICT practitioners in successful ICT implementation, indicating that adoption and implementation by senior managers and ICT practitioners are crucial for achieving the organizational benefits offered by strategic IT interventions (Gardner and Ash, 2003). Senior managers who have a clear understanding of their organization's mission and goals can act as change agents in promoting new ideas and encouraging individuals to adopt them. The application of change management in elementary schools can effectively increase teachers' commitment to the organization via an explicit vision and strategy (Chen, 2006; Fan, 2009). A similar concept can be implemented in a museum setting; however, the more complex employee structure and the variety of modern museum functions should be taken into account during this process. Those in executive roles in a museum should be in consensus regarding innovation and should be capable of applying their influence to all aspects of museum operations to, in effect, create a corporate culture (Falk and Sheppard, 2006).

5. Strategic planning as an effective tool for solving the current organizational issues

Strategic planning is an important aspect of business management and is widely applied in museum administration. It is a management method that incorporates an organization's mission, goals, and objectives (Lord and Lord, 2009). It also represents the most general level of the planning that aims to organize all aspects of a museum's activities into a coordinated direction, articulated as goals to be achieved within the planned period (Anderson, 2012). A strategic plan should be drafted by the director and management staff based on cross-departmental communication, involving all stakeholders and creating a consensus among the museum's staff.

The current barriers existing within the NPM's organization are primarily structural issues. As cited in its annual report, the NPM has developed abundant and high-quality digital and IT-enabled services under the organizational structure of the past decade (Tsaih et al., 2014). However, research has indicated that the current operational structure is insufficient for innovation. While investigating further IT-enabled services to serve the public and meet social expectations, a change should be made to a top-down innovation model that depends solely on leadership. An appropriate and consistent strategy that takes the needs of the public into account is key to having suitable social effects. Such an approach must begin with a visitor-centered vision and continue by considering organizational

Figure 4.2 Strategy implementation model

features and public sector restrictions. Forming a strategic plan is the most efficient method of achieving this, as it can simultaneously incorporate innovative vision, the goals to be achieved, and a change management strategy. The following discussion will show how a comprehensive strategic plan may assist the museum to better incorporate IT-enabled service innovations and to drive its outcomes in terms of having powerful social effects.

Based on a strategy implementation model (Roland Berger Strategy Consultants, 2012), we suggest the approach for the museum that is shown in Figure 4.2. Strong leadership for implementing explicit museum visions and goals is the crucial element in strategic planning and implementation. The strategy should be created through a circular process that involves the entire organization. Rather than the top-down process that is traditional in a museum, it is essential to align strategy creation, execution, and evaluation. Through this circular process, the museum will be able to incorporate front-line feedback into future planning. The model also requires intensive communication between departments, with an overall administration and effectively delivered programs. The fundamental factor in the process is forming an organizational culture of cooperation and communication. A communicative culture that incorporates program outcomes can be expected to assist Taiwan's public museums to perform and unite various duties that aim to deliver powerful social effects.

Building a culture of innovation

Vision

A mission should include program approaches and mission statements, and function to guide planning, service, and activities (Genoways and Ireland, 2003). The mission is the core around which policies should be formed, and policies should be linked to mutually agreed goals. Such goals are then prioritized by the process of strategic planning, which will be effectively directed toward a commonly desired outcome (Lord and Lord, 2009). The museum as an organization must stress its vision and mission in the process of implementing change management. Museum directors are expected not only to be involved with collection, social image, and reporting to the board, but must also be equipped with skills in business management, group building, business insight, and leadership vision. The director is still expected to perform traditional tasks such as fundraising and the maintenance of public relations (Anderson, 2012). Leaders are expected to move outside their usual patterns of leadership and create new patterns within the organization. This requires the capacity to listen openly and non-defensively to different ideas and perspectives, engaging all of the staff, maintaining transparency and momentum, and engendering trust in the process among staff and other cooperate organizations (Anderson, 2012).

Communication allows staff to talk through their assumptions. Commitment usually leads to greater investment in and alignment on direction (Anderson, 2012). Innovation is an issue for top management to address. It is thus especially important for the NPM to implement the process of strategic planning to assist new directors in aligning the museum's mission, goals, and objectives. Adopting IT-enabled innovation services in the NPM is itself an innovative issue, involving the use of change management techniques to foster communication and expectations, create new ways of interaction, and engage as many people as possible in various ways. Such an inside-out approach can make an immediate difference to an organization. It can build a solid foundation on which to develop a greater capacity to serve diverse populations, improve access to services, and proceed to the goal of having social effects.

Planned interventions

The concept of planned interventions to bring about change in individual behavior and team and organizational performance has become popular (Gardner and Ash, 2003). The step in a planned intervention is the framing of the current issues. The power of framing can define an organizational problem, identifying options for solutions that may be found through mission setting, strategic planning, and program development (Chait et al., 2004). This reveals the importance of comprehensive planning and strategy in implementing any innovation.

The director should take responsibility for unifying the museum's organizational resources through the process of strategic planning. Strategic planning and change management have been identified as unifying themes in emphasizing the role of shared understanding during the process (Beckford, 2002). Mature innovation management begins with the selective planning and implementation of innovations, and then becomes a process of continuing learning and improvement (Roland Berger Strategy Consultants, 2012). It has also been shown that the success of business models within a complex ICT-enabled context is not determined by a single variable, but by the management of both planned change and unplanned change that emerges at the people/technology interface (Gardner and Ash, 2003). It is evident from recent research on the NPM that the selection of the NPM's director involves many unpredictable elements and that the organization itself is very different from the usual business models. According to a research report on public museum organizations, publicly owned museums can experience less unpredictable effects by adjusting their current model to give a new organizational structure (Han, 2011). It would thus be preferable for the NPM to apply strategic planning and change management to implement innovative IT-enabled services.

Shared understanding/sense of community

It has been suggested that ICT innovation is usually diffused alongside standard project management phases and informally within informal networks (Jagodic et al., 2009). Rogers (1995) proposed that the diffusion of new ideas occurs in both planned and spontaneous processes. The process of aligning organizational goals is similar to organizational branding, which represents a special contract between an organization and its various stakeholders, and a means of creating a specific organizational culture. Such contracts require consensus to be reached between mid-level managers and must be conveyed comprehensively to front-line employees (Balmer and Gray, 2003).

When an organizational culture is developed, individuals develop their own identities within the community. This provides a motive for individuals to act on behalf of their team to achieve a common goal (Mansour-Cole, 2001). Individuals work to invest in the functions of a community in terms of its development, growth, and creation of meaning, which becomes a process of bonding between community members (Gibson and Manuel, 2003; Mansour-Cole, 2001). Organizational culture has an important role in the implementation of ICT tools (Zaidman et al., 2008). Taking into account the cultural barriers that exist between the various discourse systems in a museum, building a strong organizational culture that embraces innovation will benefit an organization as it attempts to apply new technology. A culture that embraces technology in the community can be built through a shared understanding. A sense of community must be established through encouraging learning. The purpose behind innovation is also crucial. Successful diffusion of technology occurs through identifying the need for that technology and what it is intended to achieve, creating a clear purpose for the implementation of technology (Campbell and Uys, 2007). A planned strategy is thus crucial for continuity and coherence in museum development.

Operational model

Managing a museum is similar to running a business. Although the purpose of a business model is to generate profit effectively, a museum may use a business model to effectively generate mission-driven social effects rather than profit (Falk and Sheppard, 2006). Research has indicated that museums in Taiwan should develop an operating model that is independent of the government adminis-tration. In the context of a national museum's strong reliance on government funding, the lack of operational flexibility, and the abundance of thriving private museums, it is necessary to have museum laws that set operational standards and models (Han, 2011). Traditionally, museums in Taiwan of a moderate scale belong to the government and adopt civil service regulations for both the organi-zation and its personnel. In the case of the NPM, the evaluation of its employees and its organizational structure require examination and adjustment.

The NPM's basic operational model has been in place for decades, ever since museums were first set up in Taiwan. Rather than adopting new operational mod-els, it has been suggested that the museum should carefully scrutinize the features of its current operational structure, and improve the current model by eliminat-ing the obstacles identified (Han, 2011). The process of identifying obstacles can serve as a foundation for strategic planning.

Strategic planning for creating a communicative organizational culture

During the process of innovative change, the museum as an organization must emphasize its vision and mission. Without long-term planning and consistent goals, it is difficult for temporary task-forces to accumulate project experience (Wen, 2011). It is suggested that national museums should draw up human resource plans that are appropriate to their own functions and scale. The range of museum employees required demands specific regulations that include reason-able pay and suitable recruiting processes for museum professionals (Han, 2011).

Strategic planning connects pressing issues and indicates the necessary changes; by clarifying its mission and features, the museum would be able to define its goal to develop a feasible structure within the current environment (Han, 2011). The importance of communication cannot be over-emphasized. The concept of enhancing internal recognition within an organization is called organizational branding, a combination of strategic view, organizational culture, and organi-zational image (Hatch and Schultz, 2003). Rather than a linear distribution of policies, the NPM should endeavor to create an organizational culture that encourages communication between departments, individuals, and professionals. The process of innovation-diffusion requires intense communication in both a formal and an informal structure (Jagodic et al., 2009). A well-developed stra-tegic plan can directly help the museum with both its organizational culture and its corporate image. For decades, the NPM has been transforming itself into a modern museum, in terms of both its facilities and programs. However, adopting change management methods would enable it to create a welcoming environ-ment for innovation.

The director of a museum is responsible for a wide range of resources: col-lections, buildings, people, and funds. Strategic planning allows directors to determine how these resources should be used (Anderson, 2012). Successful inno-vation-diffusion that will benefit the museum requires vision and determination on the part of the director to promote and create an appropriate organizational culture and enable the necessary regulations to be drawn up.

The process of dissemination is usually more efficient with an informal network (Kakabadse et al., 2004). Although some museum employees may be fully aware of the need for IT-enabled innovative services, it is important that such understanding be conveyed to every individual working in the museum. A community must deliver tangible values to its members to create long-term sustainability (Wenger et al., 2002). To unify the museum in aiming at a common goal that emphasizes its mission, tangible values must be delivered to every individual in the museum; such consensus may be achieved through the establishment of a communicative culture.

Strategic planning process to help create meaning

Strategies to increase the potential of individuals and to help them recognize the importance of the organization's mission motivates these individuals to participate in and help to fulfill the organizational vision. Individuals are more willing to commit and contribute to an organization when they embrace its mission. Vision development must include a clear change management strategy. By following an explicit vision and deploying the clear change management strategy, individual organizational commitment will be enhanced (Chen, 2006).

The uptake of technology in a community is significantly affected by the purpose that it achieves (Campbell and Uys, 2007). The creation of meaning for individuals within an organization is an essential tool for articulating purpose. Knox and Bickerton (2003) argued that company brand management is a complex organizational activity, which is not limited to individual products or services, but occurs through managing the relationships between various stakeholders. Brand management is considered to be a systematic procedure in which an organization attempts to create and maintain an improved image and reputation. Company branding can be established through delivering messages to all stakeholders and managing organizational behavior, communication, and symbols (Einwiller and Will, 2002; Muzellec and Lambkin, 2006). Notwithstanding their non-profit status, museums undertake similar pursuits to those of regular companies, such as positive social recognition and providing services to the public. The need to have a common goal for innovation-diffusion is no less important for a museum than for any business enterprise.

Creation of meaning is a process through which the individuals in an organization make sense of the need for adjustments to and reform of the organization's structure, culture, operating procedure, and power base to enable the successful implementation and diffusion of technology (Du Plooy, 1998). The meaning creation process is thus important in shaping the internal motivation for change among individuals within the organization. Recognizing the need for change will form the foundations for establishing a communicative organizational culture.

Establishing a department that is responsible for
change management

The NPM could consider establishing a department that is responsible for the design and implementation of a strategic plan. This would be a higher-level department than all of the other departments and would be responsible for reporting to the director and the Legislative Yuan. The department should include duties such as building a culture of communication and cooperation, overseeing departmental cooperation, encouraging communication, and running cross-departmental meetings. The choice of director for this change management department would be crucial. The incumbent of the position should have responsibility for the continuity of the organization's administration. While possessing a knowledge of museum studies, the head of the change management department should also have a keen understanding of business management. Such cross-domain knowledge would allow the incumbent to assist the museum's director with managing the museum and would minimize negative effects on missions and goals arising from director rotation. The goals and objectives would be implemented on a suitable time line. Senior managers are considered to be potential change agents, who are simultaneously moderators, interpreters, and managers of change in the process of change management (Gardner and Ash, 2003). The training of managers toward a common vision and goal is thus fundamental and should be taken into account when carrying out strategic planning.

Research limitations and directions for further research

This chapter is based on literature review. Organizational issues are drawn from recent case studies of the NPM in Taiwan. Some of the issues identified could have been refined following the publication of this research. In addition, none of the case studies involved an overall survey of NPM staff, with interviews being conducted with selected individuals only. The representativeness of the identified issues should be further scrutinized. Involving the NPM more closely would provide more in-depth observation and advice given by the organization.

There exists no official longitudinal study of visitor satisfaction with the online resources provided by the NPM. Such a longitudinal study is crucial for providing statistical proof of the effectiveness of these IT-enabled services and would complement opinions held within the organization. Wide-ranging research on visitor experiences and organizational recognition among staff are fundamental for the establishment of a strategic plan, which is a process that requires constant adjustment and the involvement of all of the stakeholders within an organization. The limitations of this chapter stem from it relying on literature review, and thus it can only provide general directions and procedures for the museum to consider. The NPM would need to gather more detailed information regarding the operation of the organization and involve as many issues as possible in moving toward an effective strategic plan.

Conclusion

Museums are expected to focus on audience engagement and audience experience as central components of their institutional mission (O'Reilly, 2005). As educational institutes, modern museums are moving toward the implementation of a well-thought-out "architecture of participation" that enables broad-based collaborative engagement between all institutions, audiences, and stakeholders (IMLS, 2009). Through the abovementioned studies, the NPM is aware of the importance of branding and technology, but still suffers from organizational limitations in transforming itself from a temple-like traditional museum to a modern one. While remaining a major preserver of and advocate for traditional Chinese cultural heritage, the NPM must try to overcome its organizational issues to take full advantage of cutting-edge IT and ICT tools in its exhibits and educational programs. A well-developed strategic plan is expected to solve many of these organizational issues through framing policies and approaches for museum development, enabling a degree of consistency in leadership, and building an organizational culture that encourages communication and enables creativity. Such a plan, by strengthening the subjectivity of the museum, would improve the outcomes of cross-institutional cooperation. Such features will benefit the museum in making choices that meet public expectations and further create powerful social effects.

References

Anderson, G. (2012). *Reinventing the museum: The evolving conversation on the paradigm shift*. Lanham, MD: AltaMira Press.

Baer, M., and Frese, M. (2003). Innovation is not enough: Climates for initiative and psychological safety, process innovations, and firm performance, *Journal of Organizational Behavior, 24*(1), 45–68.

Balmer, J. M., and Gray, E. R. (2003). Corporate brands: What are they? What of them? *European Journal of Marketing, 37*(7–8), 972–997.

Beckford, J. (2002). *Quality*. London, UK: Psychology Press.

Bresnen, M., and Marshall, N. (2001). Understanding the diffusion and application of new management ideas in construction, *Engineering Construction and Architectural Management, 8*(5–6), 335–345.

Brook, C. (2004). *Exploring community development in online settings*. Ph.D. Dissertation. Perth: School of Communications and Media, Edith Cowen University.

Campbell, M., and Uys, P. (2007). Identifying success factors of ICT in developing a learning community: Case study Charles Sturt University, *Campus-Wide Information Systems, 24*(1), 17–26.

Chait, R. P., Ryan, W. P., and Taylor, B. (2004). Governance as leadership: Bringing new governing mindsets to old challenges, *Governance Magazine*, BoardSource.

Chang, Kuei-Tzu. (2011). *Organizational change and information technology: A case study of the National Palace Museum*. Master's Thesis, National Chengchi University, Taipei, Taiwan.

Charvat, J. (2003). *Project management methodologies: Selecting, implementing, and supporting methodologies and processes for projects*. Hoboken, NJ: John Wiley & Sons.

Chen, Hsueh-Hsien. (2006). Relationships between the transformational leadership of the principal, the development of a school vision, and the organizational commitment of teachers in Kaohsiung elementary schools, *NTTU Educational Research Journal, 17*(1), 77–106.

Chou, Wei-qiang. (2014, November 25). *IT applied curating of the diplomatic credentials failed to deliver* [Digital Recording]. Taipei: Unpublished recording.

Cleland, D., and Ireland, L. (2002). *Project management – Strategies and implementation* (4th ed.). New York, NY: McGraw-Hill.

Detert, J. R., Schroeder, R. G., and Mauriel, J. J. (2000). A framework for linking culture and improvement initiatives in organizations, *Academy of Management Review, 25*(4), 850–863.

Du Plooy, N. F. (1998). *An analysis of the human environment for the adoption and use of information technology.* Ph.D. Dissertation. University of Pretoria, South Africa.

Einwiller, S., and Will, M. (2002). Towards an integrated approach to corporate branding – An empirical study, *Corporate Communications, 7*(2), 100–109.

Falk, J. H., and Sheppard, B. K. (2006). *Thriving in the knowledge age: New business models for museums and other cultural institutions.* Lanham, MD: Altamira Press.

Fan, Chi Wen. (2009, January). *Study of the relationships among principals' transformational leadership, organization learning, and school's effectiveness in elementary school,* presented at the 2009 International Conference on e-Technology (e-Tech 2009), January 8–10, Singapore.

Gardner, S., and Ash, C. G. (2003). ICT-enabled organizations: A model for change management, *Logistics Information Management, 16*(1), 18–24.

Genoways, H. H., and Ireland, L. M. (2003). *Museum administration: An introduction.* Lanham, MD: Altamira Press.

Gibson, C. B., and Manuel, J. (2003). Building trust: Effective multi-cultural communication processes in virtual teams. In C. B. Gibson and S. G. Cohen (Eds.), *Virtual teams that work: Creating conditions for virtual team effectiveness,* (pp. 59–86). San Francisco, CA: Jossey-Bass.

Green, G. C., and Hevner, A. R. (2000). The successful diffusion of innovations: Guidance for software development organizations, *IEEE Software, 17*(6), 96–103.

Gurian, E. H. (2006). *Civilizing the museum.* London and New York: Routledge.

Han, Pao-teh. (2011). *Research on organizational orientation and business model of National Museums in Taiwan.* Commissioned by Research, Development and Evaluation Commission, Executive Yuan.

Hatch, M. J., and Schultz, M. (2003). Bringing the corporation into corporate branding, *European Journal of Marketing, 37*(7–8), 1041–1064.

Institute of Museum and Library Services. (2009). Museums, Libraries, and 21st Century Skills. Washington DC: IMLS. www.imls.gov/pdf/21stCenturySkills.pdf.

Jagodic, J., Courvisanos, J., and Yearwood, J. (2009). The processes of ICT diffusion in technology projects, *Innovation: Management, Policy & Practice, 11*(3), 291–303.

Johnson, L., Adams, S., and Witchey, H. (2011). *The NMC Horizon report: 2011 museum edition.* Austin, TX: The New Media Consortium.

Kakabadse, A., Bank, J., and Vinnicombe, S. (2004). *Working in organisations.* Brington, VT: Gower Publishing, Ltd.

Knox, S., and Bickerton, D. (2003). The six conventions of corporate branding, *European Journal of Marketing, 37*(7–8), 998–1016.

Kwon, T. H., and Zmud, R. W. (April 1987). Unifying the fragmented models of information systems implementation. In R. J. Boland, Jr. and R. A. Hirshheim (Eds.), *Critical issues in information systems research* (pp. 227–251). Hoboken, NJ: John Wiley & Sons.

Liang, Guang-Yu. (2001). *Introduction to museum organization.* Taichung: Shun-Cheng.

Lin, Q. (2007). *Trends in digital life at NPM.* Taipei, Taiwan: NPM.

Lord, G. D., and Lord, B. (2009). *The manual of museum management.* Lanham, MD: AltaMira Press.

Lu, Wilbur Bing-Yan, and Lin, Pei-Yi. (2011). A case study of National Palace Museum's directors, their roles, and their marketing strategy, *Soochow Journal of Political Science, 29*(1), 179–263.

Mansour-Cole, D. (2001). Team identity formation in virtual teams, *Advances in Interdisciplinary Studies of Work Teams, 8,* 41–58.

McDermott, C., and Stock, G. (1999). Organizational culture and advanced manufacturing technology implementation, *Journal of Operations Management, 17*(5), 521–533.

McGuire, M. (2006). Collaborative public management: Assessing what we know and how we know it, *Public Administration Review, 66*(1), 33–43.

Muzellec, L., and Lambkin, M. (2006). Corporate rebranding: Destroying, transferring or creating brand equity? *European Journal of Marketing, 40*(7/8), 803–824.

National Palace Museum. (2013). *National Palace Museum 2013 Annual Report.* Taipei, Taiwan: National Palace Museum.

Nojima, Tsuyoshi. (2012). *The separation and reunion of the two palace museums.* Taipei, Taiwan: Linking Publishing.

O'Reilly, T. (2005). *What is Web 2.0.* Retrieved on 12/12/2007 from http://www. oreilly. de/artikel/web20. html

Pan, Shih-Chia. (2014, November). *Cross-sector governance applied to e-governance: A case study of the Digital Archives Program conducted by National Palace Museum.* 2014 Social and Public Affairs Conference – Civic Development and Public Management. Symposium conducted at University of Taipei, Taiwan.

Peansupap, V., and Walker, D. (2005). Factors affecting ICT diffusion: A case study of three large Australian construction contractors, *Engineering, Construction and Architectural Management, 12*(1), 21–37.

Prescott, M. B., and Conger, S. A. (1995). Information technology innovations: A classification by IT locus of impact and research approach, *ACM SIGMIS Database, 26*(2–3), 20–41.

Rogers, E. M. (1995). *Diffusion of innovations.* New York, NY: Free Press.

Roland Berger Strategy Consultants. (2012). *The path to successful innovation management.* Roland Berger News Media.

Scott, C. (2013). *Museums and public value: Creating sustainable futures.* Burlington, VT: Ashgate Publishing Company.

Senge, P. M. (2014). *The dance of change: The challenges to sustaining momentum in a learning organization.* New York, NY: Random House.

Simon, N. (2007). Discourse in the blogosphere: What museums can learn from Web 2.0. *Museums & Social Issues, 2*(2), 257–274.

Skibniewski, M. J., and Abduh, M. (2000). *Web-based project management for construction: Search for utility assessment tools.* Proc. INCITE 2000, 56–77.

Stuckey, B., and Smith, J. D. (2004). Building sustainable communities of practice, *Knowledge Networks: Innovation through Communities of Practice*, 150–164.

Tong, Szu-ewi. (2010). *Research on popularizing museum connotations by integrating museum experiences with online resources: An example of the National Palace Museum*. Master's thesis, National Chengchi University, Taipei, Taiwan.

Trendgo. (2007). *Research on the economic effectiveness of the cultural industry – The operational efficiency and output value of national museums in Taiwan*. Taipei: National Taiwan Museum.

Tsaih, Rua-Huan, Lin, James Quo-Ping, and Chang, Yu-Chien. (2014). National Palace Museum and service innovations, *Emerald Emerging Markets Case Studies*, accepted.

Van Dijk, T. A. (1997). The study of discourse, *Discourse as Structure and Process*, *1*, 1–34.

Ward, S., and Chapman, C. (2003). Transforming project risk management into project uncertainty management, *International Journal of Project Management*, *21*(2), 97–105.

Weilbach, L., and Byrne, E. (2010). A human environmentalist approach to diffusion in ICT policies: A case study of the FOSS policy of the South African government, *Journal of Information, Communication and Ethics in Society*, *8*(1), 108–123.

Wen, Sophia S. T. (2011). *The decision-making analysis of National Palace Museum southern branch: A case study*. Unpublished Ph.D. Dissertation. Department of Fine Arts, National Taiwan Normal University, Taipei.

Wenger, E., McDermott, R. A., and Snyder, W. (2002). *Cultivating communities of practice: A guide to managing knowledge*. Boston, MA: Harvard Business Press.

Yang, Chao-Ching. (2008). *The model of brand strategic planning of the Taiwan leisure industry based on branding, brand equity and brand extension strategy – case studies of the bed and breakfast of the Kenting area*. Master's Thesis, National Pingtung University of Science and Technology, Taiwan.

Zaidman, N., Schwartz, D. G., and Te'eni, D. (2008). Challenges to ICT implementation in multinationals, *Education, Business and Society: Contemporary Middle Eastern Issues*, *1*(4), 267–277.

5 Measurement development of service quality for museum websites displaying artifacts

Hsu-Hsin Chiang, Rua-Huan Tsaih, and Tzu-Shian Han

Introduction

Museums all over the world are increasingly using the Internet and digitized information to produce exhibitions and undertake marketing, thanks to advances in and convergence within information and communication technologies (ICT): the Internet, a global telephone system, the TCP/IP (Transfer Control Protocol/Internet Protocol) communications standard, the URL address system, personal computers and cable TV, customer databases, user-friendly free browsers, portable devices (tablet PCs, smartphones), multi-media, cloud computing, and so forth. The National Palace Museum (NPM) in Taipei follows this trend. The NPM has approximately 690,000 ancient Chinese artifacts, which provide precious information about Chinese history and ancient Chinese arts. In the NPM's original interface, photos and explanations could be viewed on Web pages; however, there were no immersive videos allowing visitors to experience the ancient arts, revealing a critical service gap. By adopting advanced ICT, the NPM hopes to render its treasured artifacts accessible, especially to the younger generation, via the Internet, extending beyond the limitations of the physical museum. Advanced ICT can help visitors to view, experience, and interact with treasured arts through cell phones, PCs, tablets, and other mobile devices. Specifically, the NPM has developed the iPalace Video Channel (iPalace), a prototype cloud-based streaming service that provides online video broadcasting on television, Facebook, and YouTube to reveal the beauty of Chinese artifacts to the world (Tsaih et al., 2012).

Before fully launching iPalace, the NPM needs to know how to measure its service quality. The literature shows that service quality is an important determinant of customer satisfaction and behavioral intentions (Ozment and Morash, 1994), and this has been confirmed in website studies (Slywotzky and Morrison, 2001). Museum managers regard customer satisfaction as an integral indicator of the museum experience (Kawashima, 1998; McLean, 1994). Appropriate measurement of the service quality of iPalace is therefore necessary for the purposes of quality management. However, to the best of our knowledge, no suitable method exists for measuring the service quality of a museum website displaying artifacts.

This study addresses this theoretical gap. Specifically, from the service, e-commerce, and museum service literature, this study derives an instrument for measuring service quality, customer satisfaction, and behavioral intentions relating to museum websites displaying artifacts. Through an online survey that applies the derived instrument to the measurement of iPalace and its text-based counterpart, this study identifies the main service quality factors relating to museum websites displaying artifacts. We also conduct exploratory factor analysis, confirmatory factor analysis, discriminant validity tests, and nomological validity tests.

The structure of this chapter is as follows. We first review the service quality, e-commerce, and museum service literature to identify the factors relating to museum websites displaying artifacts, and describe iPalace. Based on the literature review, we propose a suitable instrument and construct, and present the experimental design and procedures. Then, we discuss the background and results of the survey. The theoretical model and the instrument for measuring museum websites displaying artifacts are also refined and verified. Finally, we present a discussion of the findings, along with directions for future work.

Literature review

Museum service

The International Council of Museums (2007) defined a museum as "a non-profit, permanent institution in the service of society and its development, open to the public, which acquires, conserves, researches, communicates, and exhibits the tangible and intangible heritage of humanity and its environment for the purposes of education, study and enjoyment." Museums are service providers that help the public to further recognize the world by taking a closer look at their collections and interpretations of the past and present. However, we are now living in an environment filled with a variety of options for entertainment and leisure. Museums must exert effort to capture consumers' attention and thus fulfill their missions (Hume, 2011; Hume and Mills, 2011). Many modern museum managers are driving a new climate of customer orientation within museum management (Hume, 2011).

Directors of museums, academic institutions, and other stakeholders are now interested in enhancing the museum experience using advanced ICT (Knell, 2003; Marty, 1999; Thyne, 2000). For instance, using Internet technologies, museums can expand their visitor capacity by increasing their core services to include online displays and material, and thus better manage their inventory (Hume and Mills, 2011). Offering services online aimed at raising awareness, enhancing branding, supporting service delivery, and attracting interest are all viable practices.

Here we group the missions (and functions) of a museum into eight categories: collection, preservation, research, exhibition, education, information, propagation, and entertainment. The details are as follows.

- *Collection* means that museums legally acquire relevant physical objects, such as original artifacts, specimens, models, images, data, or species, according to the purpose and nature of the establishment. *Preservation* means museums inscribe, arrange, repair, and preserve their collections. Throughout these processes, museums strive to keep their collections intact, permanently pre-served, and available for research and exhibition.

- *Research* means that museums (1) organize, authenticate, investigate, inter-pret, and maintain their collections; (2) plan and design exhibitions; and (3) explore individual museums' nature, tasks, work methods, and operational management. The purpose of research is to gain the correct knowledge regard-ing the collections and hold attractive exhibitions that are educationally effec-tive. *Exhibition* means that museums display collections, either own or borrow, systematically arranged in themes with a lively presentation. Using objects, or audio and video material, they convey the background to each collection. Exhibition design must therefore use layout to emphasize the exhibits, create a suitable atmosphere, and provide continuity for the underlying story.
- *Education* means that museums share their collections and research with the public, broadening their horizons by guiding them to make good use of the museum facilities through various exhibitions and activities. *Information* means that museums make their collections of material data, research results, laws and institutions, and events available to schools, museums, libraries, and the general public.
- *Propagation* means that museums disseminate their knowledge and display the beauty of their artistic heritage far and wide by issuing and exchanging publi-cations and lending their collections to other museums at home and abroad. *Entertainment* means that museums often become tourist attractions for both domestic and foreign tourists, due to their rich collections, well-designed exhi-bitions, unique cultural atmospheres, and special buildings or activities.

Service quality

As the characteristics of services are intangible and the preferences of custom-ers are uncontrollable, the measurement of service quality is abstract and non-specific (Kaynama, Black, and Keesling, 2011). To enable service providers to measure and improve the quality of their services, service quality models have been developed. However, the early models did not take ICT into consideration because ICT applications were not universal at the time. For instance, Parasura-man, Zeithaml, and Berry (1988) proposed SERVQUAL for assessing service quality, with a disconfirmation model of five factors: "tangibles," "responsive-ness," "reliability," "assurance," and "empathy."

The SERVQUAL model has been criticized on the grounds that perfor-mance assessment alone is more reliable and reasonable than the disconfirmation between expected service and received service (Brady and Cronin, 2001; Cronin and Taylor, 1992; Dabholkar, Shepherd, and Thorpe, 2000; Mentzer, Flint, and Hult, 2001; Page and Spreng, 2002). Another criticism of SERVQUAL is that the five factors proposed are not widely applicable to all industries and are not supported by a number of studies (Abdullah, 2005; Carman, 1990).

In the literature on service quality models for website services, we find that the proposed models are mostly designed for e-commerce websites. Beyond the e-commerce context, other types of website have largely been overlooked (Schaupp, 2010). As artifact-displaying museum websites and e-commerce websites have some similar properties, it is helpful to develop a service quality model for artifact-displaying museum websites by reviewing the relevant literature for e-commerce websites. Liu, Arnett, and Litecky (2000) presented four factors that are critical to website success in e-commerce: "information and service quality," "system use," "playfulness," and "system design quality." Kaynama and Black (2000) introduced E-QUAL, based on the SERVQUAL instrument, for evaluating the service performance of online travel agencies using seven factors: "content and purpose," "accessibility," "navigation," "design and presentation," "responsiveness," "background," and "personalization and customization." Yoo and Donthu (2001) proposed SITEQUAL, which uses four factors, "ease of use," "aesthetic design," "processing speed," and "security," to measure the perceived quality of Internet shopping sites; the model was verified by qualifying college students' actual online purchase experiences, technological advances, and innovativeness. Loiacono, Watson, and Goodhue (2002) developed WebQual™, which contains 12 factors of online service quality: "ease of understanding," "intuitive operations," "informational fit to task," "tailored communications," "trust," "response time," "visual appeal," "innovativeness," "emotional appeal," "online completeness," "relative advantage," and "consistent image," through surveying college students on four types of website: "CDs," "books," "airline reservations," and "hotel reservations." Vidgen and Barnes (2002) assessed an organization's e-commerce capability using five factors: "usability," "design," "information," "trust," and "empathy." Santos (2003) presented a conceptual model of the determinants of e-service quality that divided factors into incubative and active factors. The incubative factors were "ease of use," "appearance," "linkage," "structure and layout," and "content," while the active factors were "reliability," "efficiency," "support," "communication," "security," and "incentives." Parasuraman, Zeithaml, and Malhotr (2005) proposed two models: E-S-QUAL, which uses four factors, "efficiency," "fulfillment," "system availability," and "privacy"; and E-RecS-QUAL, which uses three factors, "responsiveness," "compensation," and "contact." Both models measure the service quality delivered by online shopping websites.

The service quality factors for e-commerce websites can be organized and integrated as shown in Appendix 5.1. There are seven groups: content, usability, interface, system reliability, communication, security, and fulfillment. The details are as follows.

Content refers to the design, presentation, and layout of factual information on a website and the organization of the website's content, which affect whether a visitor finds it easy to read and understand (Loiacono et al., 2002; Santos, 2003). The information provided should be accurate, relevant, and believable (Liu et al., 2000; Loiacono et al., 2002).

• *Usability* is defined as how easy and efficient a website is for visitors to navigate and search (Loiacono et al., 2002; Parasuraman et al., 2005; Santos, 2003; Yoo and Donthu, 2001).

- *Interface* refers to the use of multi-media (including color, graphics, images, and animations) with appropriately sized Web pages that are pleasing to the consumer's eye and avoid being cluttered (Loiacono et al., 2002; Santos, 2003; Yoo and Donthu, 2001). In addition, using a creative and novel approach for a website may cause visitors to feel excited (Loiacono et al., 2002). It is also important to invoke a positive customer experience and reflect the company image (Loiacono et al., 2002).
- *System reliability* is defined not only as the ability to correctly and consistently perform the promised services, but also as the speed of online processing and interactive responsiveness (including downloading, searching, and navigation) (Parasuraman et al., 2005; Santos, 2003; Yoo and Donthu, 2001). Service providers should have sufficient hardware and communications capacity to meet peak demand (Loiacono et al., 2002).
- *Communication* refers to interacting and communicating with visitors to keep them properly informed, effectively comprising technical help, user guidelines, and personal advice available to visitors on the website, enabling them to receive tailored information (Loiacono et al., 2002; Parasuraman et al., 2005; Santos, 2003).
- *Security* is defined as protecting personal information during the service process, by adopting and promoting security and privacy policies and procedures that cause customers to feel safe and secure in dealing with the company (Loiacono et al., 2002; Parasuraman et al., 2005; Santos, 2003; Yoo and Donthu, 2001).
- *Fulfillment* refers to presenting the information that visitors want and allowing them to conduct important business functions over the Web (Loiacono et al., 2002). In other words, it is the extent to which a site's promises are fulfilled (Parasuraman et al., 2005).

In the context of museum services, various structures and factors have been used to build a service quality model. Goulding (2000) argued that the service experience was mediated by a number of sociocultural, cognitive, and psychological orientators, and physical and environmental conditions, all of which had to be seen as interrelated if a high-quality experience was to be provided. Rentschler and Gilmore (2002) indicated that museum service quality factors comprised "museum architecture," "programs," "accessibility," and "communication." Harrison and Shaw (2004) proposed "facility," "service," and "experience," and examined the relationship of these factors with consumer satisfaction and subsequent intentions in the museum context. Saleh (2005) built a service quality model on the basis of the five major factors of the SERVQUAL model ("tangibles," "reliability," "responsiveness," "assurance," and "empathy") plus a "quality of experience" (QOE) factor. To assess the service quality at a cultural, heritage, and educational attraction, the sub-factors of QOE are the learning outcomes of the visit, the authenticity of the displays and crafts, the tranquil and relaxing nature of the encounter, the safe and secure environment of the venue, and the amount of fun and adventure experienced by the visitor. Mey and

Mohamed (2010) developed a model to assess the perceived service quality, satisfaction levels, and behavioral intentions of Malaysian museums. The factors in the model were "museum accessibility," "information sources," "quality of displays/exhibitions," "customer services," "amenities and facilities," and "pricing."

In short, most of the relevant literature includes the native functions of a museum among their service quality factors, such as education (Goulding, 2000; Harrison and Shaw, 2004; Rentschler and Gilmore, 2002; Saleh, 2005), propagation (Goulding, 2000; Harrison and Shaw, 2004; Rentschler and Gilmore, 2002), and entertainment (Rentschler and Gilmore, 2002). The founders, public, and government expect museums to provide the required functions or accomplish their missions. Therefore, museum functions, which are associated with visitor experience, should be included in the service quality model for museum services.

In the context of museum services via the Internet, Campbell and Wells (1996) analyzed museum home page formats and categorized criteria for future assessment according to their function; the categories were "appeal factor," "retention factor," and "revisit factor." "Retention factor" was divided into three sub-factors: "organized format," "quality content," and "personal relevance." Santos (1999) presented a methodology called the website quality evaluation method (QEM) and illustrated it with a case study of typical museum websites for which four main factors for website characteristics and attributes were defined: "usability," "functionality," "site reliability," and "efficiency." Pallas and Economides (2008) introduced MUSEF (the museum sites evaluation framework), a framework for evaluating museums' websites from users' point of view, which used six fundamental evaluation factors: "content," "presentation," "usability," "interactivity and feedback," "e-services," and "technical."

Although the proposed factors for service quality models for measuring museum websites have wide-ranging names and measure different quantities, these items can be classified into the same seven groups for e-commerce websites that are shown in Appendix 5.1. Most museums build their websites as an aid to museum functions. That is, their websites are used to merely advertise or provide information about activities and visiting, rather than substituting for or extending the physical museum in executing its missions and functions. However, the objectives of an artifact-displaying museum website also include furthering some of the museum's missions, such as education, propagation, and entertainment. The existing models for museum websites are thus unsuitable for assessing the service quality of an artifact-displaying museum website.

Customer satisfaction and behavioral intentions

Under the concept of customer orientation, customer satisfaction has been regarded as the most important indicator of any service's survival and success. Measurements of service quality are meaningful only if they are able to indicate whether a service is satisfactory or not (Johns and Howard, 1998). Developing an accurate measurement of customer satisfaction is not easy (Baggs and Kleiner, 1996).

Chu and Choi (2000) stated that poor customer satisfaction leads to unfavorable word-of-mouth communication. Conversely, a customer who is satisfied with a service experience is more likely to engage in positive word-of-mouth communication with others. Customer satisfaction and dissatisfaction directly and indirectly affect customers' future intentions (Oliver, 1980). Additionally, behavioral intentions are considered to be an outcome of overall satisfaction (Bendall-Lyon and Powers, 2004). Building up customer loyalty, so that customers will return requires effort to establish a mutually beneficial relationship between customers and the business (Chen and Gursoy, 2001).

In the website literature, customer satisfaction and behavioral intentions are widely used to assess website success and adoption (Davis, Bagozzi, and Warshaw, 1989; DeLone and McLean, 2003; McKinney, Yoon, and Zahedi, 2002; Seddon, 1997; Venkatesh et al., 2003; Wixom and Todd, 2005). Website satisfaction is defined as the overall indicator of the success of a website. Although the antecedents to satisfaction are well documented in classical contexts (Oliver, 1980, 1997; Szymanski, and Henard, 2001; Yi, 1990), satisfaction in the context of a website has not been subjected to conceptual or empirical scrutiny beyond the e-commerce setting (Schaupp, 2010). Research into the antecedent indicators of satisfaction in the e-commerce context has been carried out (McKinney et al., 2002; Szymanzki and Hise, 2000). However, there have been few empirical studies aimed at identifying the determinants of website customer satisfaction and behavioral intentions (Schaupp, 2010).

In terms of museum services, museum managers also regard customer satisfaction as an integral indicator of the museum experience (Kawashima, 1998; McLean, 1994). In particular, museum marketers are interested in the relationship between customer satisfaction and behavioral intentions such as repeat visits and word-of-mouth communication (Harrison and Shaw, 2001), which significantly affect the number of visitors. Word-of-mouth advocacy has been cited as a key promotional tool for museums and other cultural institutions (DiMaggio, 1986), and indirectly affects the number of visitors. It is thus important for museums to consider customer satisfaction as a primary organizational goal (Harrison and Shaw, 2004). Accordingly, we also assume that customer satisfaction and behavioral intentions are goals of museum websites displaying artifacts.

The iPalace video channel

Table 5.1 shows the strategic service vision of iPalace. The target customer segment is young people who are able to access the World Wide Web, love Chinese heritage, and like watching videos more than reading text. There are two main service concepts for iPalace. The first is to provide an impressive viewing experience of the NPM's artifacts. The key idea is to use the concept of a museum exhibition rather than a warehouse search to organize the videos appropriately and provide an uninterrupted multicasting video service available anytime and anywhere. The second service concept is to make sure that the user interface (UI) is easy to use and retains a profound sense of Chinese culture and aesthetic pleasure.

Table 5.1 The strategic service vision of the iPalace Video Channel

Service Delivery System	Operating Strategy	Service Concept	Target Market Segments
– Fresh and attractive video content 1. Well-defined NPM experiences 2. Appropriate to the NPM's image 3. Easy to use 4. Profound sense of Chinese culture and aesthetic pleasure – Smooth video delivery	– Continual provision of new video exhibitions – Periodic changing of the interface appearance – Effective load balancing – Task-oriented process design – Elastic Web service infrastructure – Multi-task and distributed system architecture	– A video service that smoothly displays the NPM's relics 1. Well-arranged exhibitions 2. Available anytime and anywhere 3. Uninterrupted multicasting – A user interface that is easy to use and has a profound sense of Chinese culture and aesthetic pleasure	– Young people that 1. use Web browsers 2. love Chinese heritage 3. enjoy watching videos

Source: Tsaih et al. (2012)

The operating strategy is to keep the website fresh and attractive to increase customer retention, and to effectively balance loading to display videos smoothly even with a massive worldwide peak demand. Keeping the website fresh and attractive requires continually providing new video exhibitions and periodically changing the interface appearance. For effective load balancing, iPalace requires a task-oriented process design, an elastic Web service infrastructure, peer-to-peer networking, and a multi-task and distributed system architecture. The service delivery system should always smoothly deliver fresh and attracting video content and well-defined NPM experiences.

Customer criteria for embracing iPalace include the reputation of the NPM brand, the dependability and educational value of the content, high-quality video, ease of use and an aesthetic UI, and a stable and smooth Web service that is accessible worldwide and free of charge. In short, being an online media channel of the NPM, iPalace must not only be consistent with the high-quality brand image of the NPM but must also be able to cope with a massive worldwide peak demand.

Research design

Research framework

We propose the model shown in Figure 5.1 for measuring the service quality of museum websites displaying artifacts. As shown in Appendix 5.1, the widely

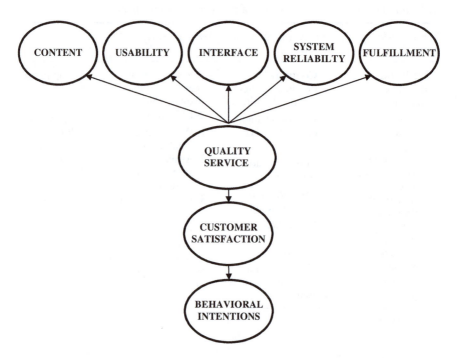

Figure 5.1 The proposed model to describe the relationships between the constructs, service quality, customer satisfaction, and behavioral intentions

adopted service factors in the literature of e-commerce can be grouped into "content," "usability," "interface," "system reliability," "communication," "security," and "fulfillment."[1] In this study, we excluded the factors "communication" and "security" because these were not taken into consideration in the current design of iPalace. The proposed service quality construct for museum websites displaying artifacts thus comprises the following five main factors: "content," "usability," "interface," "system reliability," and "fulfillment."

As shown in Table 5.2, we also assigned some sub-factors to each main factor. Most of these sub-factors are referred to in the literature of e-commerce, while others are new. The new sub-factors are "tele-presence," "education," "entertainment," and "propagation." Here, tele-presence refers to how well the artifacts are presented through multi-media on the website and is classified as a sub-factor of content. Museums care about how well artifacts are displayed through multi-media on their websites. A good tele-presence means that customers feel as if they are at the scene personally and will gaze steadily at the screen when browsing the website.

Education, entertainment, and propagation are museum functions. Visitors expect these museum functions to be fulfilled during their visit and thus most of the museum literature has described these museum functions as indicators of

Table 5.2 Main factors and sub-factors in the service
quality construct

Main Factor	Sub-factor
Content	Information Quality
	Tele-Presence
	Media Quality
Usability	Intuitive Operation
Interface	Innovativeness
	Visual Appeal
	Consistent Image
System Reliability	Accessibility
	Response Time
Fulfillment	Education
	Entertainment
	Propagation

service quality. Accordingly, the museum functions of education, entertainment, and propagation were classified as sub-factors of fulfillment.

Measure development

The questionnaires had three sections. The first section comprised 24 questionnaire items about service quality. These items were based on the proposed service quality construct for museum websites displaying artifacts. As shown in Appendix 5.2, most of the questionnaire items were obtained from the literature; they were then modified to fit the study. Two versions of the questionnaires were developed. That shown in Appendix 5.3 was for a text-based website, specifically the NPM website displaying artifacts through text and images, and that shown in Appendix 5.4 was for a video-based website, specifically iPalace. The questionnaires used the same items, with minor wording differences relating to the use of multi-media in the questionnaire for the video-based website. As shown in Appendix 5.5, the second section comprised four questionnaire items, two to access customer satisfaction and two to access behavioral intensions. The third section collected the following demographic and contact information: gender, age, average daily browsing time, educational level, occupation, location of residence, and email. The statements comprising the questionnaire items were examined and finalized by domain experts and NPM staff members to ensure logical consistency and diction.

A 6-point Likert scale was used in the first and second sections of the questionnaire. The respondents were required to indicate their level of agreement with the statements on a scale ranging from 1 (do not agree at all) to 6 (definitely agree). Chomeya (2010) stated that a 6-point Likert scale had a higher trend toward discrimination and reliability than a 5-point Likert scale.

Survey administration

Convenience sampling was used. The two questionnaires on iPalace and its text-based counterpart were published on open public questionnaire websites. Each respondent had the opportunity to participate in a sweepstake, with a total lucky draw prize value of more than US$666. The respondents could complete one or both of the two questionnaires.

All of the responses were collected within 2 weeks and 337 responses to the text-based version and 387 responses to the video-based version were received. After data screening, three questionable responses were excluded for each version of the questionnaire. The total effective sample was thus 334 for the text-based version and 384 for the video-based version.

Table 5.3 summarizes the overall demographic profile of the respondents. The majority of the respondents were female (64.6 percent) rather than male (35.4 percent). The majority of the respondents were 17–23 years old, comprising 48.5 percent of all respondents, followed by 24–30 years old (30.9 percent). This revealed that most of the respondents were from the younger generation and

Table 5.3 The overall demographic profile of respondents

Measure	Items	Frequency	Percentage
Gender	Male	254	35.4
	Female	464*	64.6*
Age (years)	< 16	10	1.4
	17–23	348*	48.5*
	24–30	222	30.9
	31–40	70	9.7
	41–50	43	6
	51–60	24	3.3
	> 61	1	0.1
Average daily	< 0.5	30	4.2
browsing time	0.5–1	45	6.3
(hours)	1–2	149	20.8
	2–5	343*	47.8*
	> 5	151	21
Educational level	Junior high school (inclusive)	6	0.8
	High school or vocational	17	2.4
	University (college)	450*	62.7*
	Master's degree	216	30.1
	Doctoral degree	29	4
Career	Cultural and creative industries	32	4.5
	Non-cultural and creative	239	33.3
	industries	447*	62.3*
	Student		

* Denotes the highest value in each category.

were thus the targeted users of iPalace. The questionnaire results showed that the majority of the participants spent 2–5 hours per day browsing the Web. Finally, the majority of the respondents had a university education.

Data and analysis

Exploratory factor analysis

To identify service quality factors for museum websites displaying artifacts, we conducted a principal component factor analysis with a varimax rotation. The criterion for extracting the factors was that their eigenvalues had to be higher than 1. Moreover, the factorial loadings had to be greater than 0.5 points. Table 5.4

Table 5.4 Exploratory factor analysis

	Factors			
	1	*2*	*3*	*4*
Fulfillment				
F_3	.778			
F_4	.777			
F_2	.762			
C_4	.704			
F_5	.684			
C_3	.681			
F_7	.654			
F_6	.613			
I_1	.608			
F_1	.565			
Usability				
U_1		.788		
U_2		.770		
C_2		.625		
C_6		.586		
C_1		.540		
C_5		.523		
System Reliability				
R_4			.813	
R_3			.805	
R_1			.782	
R_2			.781	
Interface				
I_4				.760
I_3				.740
I_5				.727
I_2				.646

shows factors extracted for the items. The factor loadings were significant (over 0.5) for all of the items, and there were no cross-loadings. Thus, no item was deleted. However, instead of the five proposed factors (in the proposed construct shown in Figure 5.1), four representative factors accounted for 65.72 percent of the variance. These were relabeled (1) fulfillment, (2) content and usability, (3) interface, and (4) system reliability. The initially proposed content and usability factors were integrated into one factor.

Both of the questionnaire items relating to tele-presence (C_3 and C_4) were classified into the fulfillment factor. One item relating to interface (I_1) was also classified into the fulfillment factor. The C_3 item asked how the user perceived the scene and the C_4 item asked whether the user gazed steadily at the screen when browsing the website. The I_1 item asked whether the interface design was innovative. These three items can be interpreted as museum functions of exhibition that emphasize exhibition layout and the atmosphere. It is thus reasonable to classify them into the fulfillment factor.

Of the four factors, the fulfillment factor explained the largest portion (23 percent) of the total variance. This factor comprised 10 questionnaire items that addressed the museum functions of exhibition, education, entertainment, and propagation. The content and usability factor explained 13.7 percent of the variance. Its six items measured whether the information quality of the website reached a certain level and whether the website was intuitive to use. The system reliability factor accounted for 13.6 percent of the variance. It comprised four items relating to the quality of the system, including accessibility and response time. The interface factor represented 13.3 percent of the variance and comprised three items measuring whether the interface had visual appeal and a consistent image. Table 5.5 summarizes the final main factors and their corresponding

Table 5.5 The main factors and sub-factors of service quality

Main Factor	Sub-factor
Content and Usability	Information Quality Media Quality Intuitive Operation
Interface	Visual Appeal Consistent Image
Reliability	Accessibility Response Time
Fulfillment	Education Entertainment Propagation Exhibition

sub-factors for museum websites displaying artifacts. A sub-factor exhibition was included within the main factor fulfillment.

Confirmatory factor analysis

Figure 5.2 shows the first-order measurement model for service quality of museum websites displaying artifacts. After allowing for three covariances in observed variable error terms (C_3-C_4, U_1-U_2, and R_3-R_4), we obtained an acceptable first-order measurement model, as shown in Table 5.6. All of the items loaded significantly on their designated constructs; as shown in Table 5.7, the item loadings on the corresponding factors ranged from 0.585 to 0.929.

Additionally, as the purpose of this study was to develop an instrument for measuring the service quality of museum websites displaying artifacts, we assumed that there was a second-order factor of overall service quality that explained the four first-order factors. As shown in Figure 5.3, a second-order factor measurement model was therefore developed. This model also exhibited reasonable model fit, as shown in Table 5.8. All four of the first-order factors loaded strongly (> 0.63) and significantly on the second-order factor, confirming that a second-order factor of overall portal quality existed.

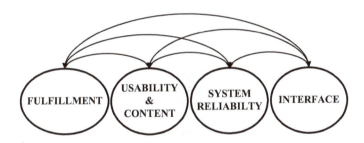

Figure 5.2 The first-order measurement model

Table 5.6 Model fit for the first-order measurement model

Model Fit	Indices	Criteria	Reference
Chi-square per degree of freedom	4.718	< 5	Bollen (1989)
RMSEA	0.072	< 0.08	Jarvenpaa et al. (2000)
CFI	0.918	> 0.9	Bagozzi and Youjae (1988)
GFI	0.875	> 0.8	Doll et al. (1994)
NNFI	0.907	> 0.9	Bentler and Bonett (1980)

Table 5.7 Confirmatory factor analysis

Factor and Item	Loading	CR	AVE
Fulfillment		0.9157	0.5224
F_5	0.779*		
F_4	0.821*		
F_3	0.702*		
F_2	0.737*		
F_1	0.716*		
I_1	0.668*		
C_4	0.71*		
C_3	0.701*		
F_7	0.779*		
F_6	0.588*		
Usability and Content		0.8361	0.4605
U_2	0.676*		
U_1	0.62*		
C_6	0.711*		
C_5	0.645*		
C_2	0.747*		
C_1	0.665*		
System Reliability		0.8579	0.6106
R_4	0.648*		
R_2	0.929*		
R_1	0.904*		
R_3	0.585*		
Interface		0.8611	0.609
I_5	0.752*		
I_4	0.825*		
I_3	0.834*		
I_2	0.703*		

*P < 0.001

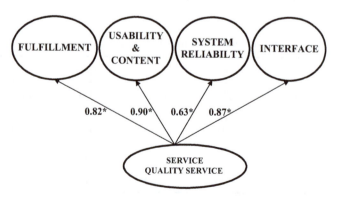

Figure 5.3 The second-order measurement model

Table 5.8 Model fit for the second-order measurement model

Model Fit	Indices	Criteria	Reference
Chi-square per degree of freedom	4.75	<5	Bollen (1989)
RMSEA	0.072	<0.08	Jarvenpaa et al. (2000)
CFI	0.916	>0.9	Bagozzi and Youjae (1988)
GFI	0.872	>0.8	Doll et al. (1994)
NNFI	0.906	>0.9	Bentler and Bonett (1980)

Reliability and validity

We used composite reliability tests to examine the internal consistency of the questionnaire items that measured each service quality factor. Table 5.7 shows that all of the factors exceeded the recommended value of 0.7. The reliability of the scales was therefore deemed to be acceptable.

Convergent and discriminant validity are considered to be sub-categories of construct validity. We therefore tested the convergent and discriminant validity. As shown in Table 5.7, to test the convergent validity of the five factors in the first-order measurement model we calculated the average variances extracted (AVE) for each construct. Except for usability, all of the factors met the recommended minimum level of 0.5. This test has been said to be conservative and to give lower estimates, but can be acceptable when most factors meet the suggested minimum level. The results thus support convergent validity for the first-order measurement model. Moreover, in the second-order measurement model all of the five first-order factors loaded significantly on the second-order factor, with standardized loadings of greater than 0.63. As for the first-order measurement model, this result can be interpreted as an indication of convergent validity for the second-order measurement model.

Discriminant validity implies that one can empirically differentiate one construct from other, similar constructs and can determine what is unrelated to the construct. To test the discriminant validity of the factors, we took a nested model confirmatory analysis approach. For each pair of factors, we first constructed a constrained model in which the covariance between factors was fixed at unity; that is, we assumed that there was no discriminant validity between the factors. We then constructed an unconstrained model by freeing the covariance between the factors. For each pair of factors, there was a significant difference in the chi-square values between the constrained and unconstrained models with one degree of freedom, as shown in Table 5.9. The results indicated discriminant validity among the four factors.

Finally, we examined the instrument in terms of nomological validity. The instrument behaved as expected with respect to other constructs to which it is theoretically related. Previous studies have suggested that if customers receive a

Table 5.9 Test for discriminant validity

	Chi-square Value	df	Chi-square Difference
Unconstrained Model	1146.443	243	
Constrained Model			
(Fulfillment, Usability)	1307.783	244	161.34*
(Fulfillment, Interface)	1277.988	244	131.545*
(Fulfillment, System Reliability)	1334.33	244	187.887*
(Usability, Interface)	1375.955	244	229.512*
(Usability, System Reliability)	1392.286	244	245.843*
(Interface, System Reliability)	1403.941	244	257.498*

* > 3.84

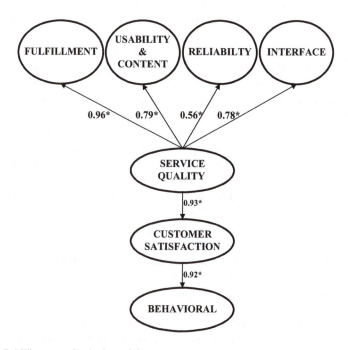

Figure 5.4 The nomological model

high-quality service, they are likely to be satisfied, and that if customers are satisfied, they are likely to revisit. Therefore, as shown in Figure 5.4, we tested a structural model that related service quality to customer satisfaction, and customer satisfaction to behavioral intentions. As shown in Table 5.10, the structural model had a good fit. Moreover, as predicted, it showed that service quality has a positive and significant effect on customer satisfaction, and that customer satisfaction also

Table 5.10 Model fit for the second-order measurement model

Model Fit	Indices	Criteria	Reference
Chi-square per degree of freedom	4.756	<5	Bollen (1989)
RMSEA	0.072	<0.08	Jarvenpaa et al. (2000)
CFI	0.909	>0.9	Bagozzi and Youjae (1988)
GFI	0.848	>0.8	Doll et al. (1994)
NNFI	0.899	>0.9	Bentler and Bonett (1980)

has a positive and significant influence on behavioral intentions. Therefore, the nomological validity of this instrument was demonstrated.

Next, we examined the values of the questionnaire items covered by each sub-factor to identify the reasons behind the differences in the service quality factors. Under fulfillment, we found that all of the items covered by each sub-factor (exhibition, education, entertainment, and propagation) were scored significantly higher for iPalace channel than for the text-based website. Under content and usability, one of the two items covered by information quality was scored significantly higher for iPalace, which was related to whether the information was easy to understand. However, two items covered by intuitive operation were scored significantly lower for iPalace. Two items covered by media quality showed no significant differences between the two websites. Under reliability, two items covered by accessibility also showed no significant differences. Two items covered by consistent image were scored significantly lower for iPalace. Under interface, we found that all of the items covered by each sub-factor (visual appeal, consistent image) were scored significantly higher for iPalace than for the text-based website.

For customer satisfaction and behavioral intentions, we found a significant difference between the text-based website and iPalace, with iPalace scoring significantly higher in both cases for all items.

Conclusions

Contribution

Our research has four main academic contributions. First, the study used a rigorous procedure for establishing an instrument to measure users' perceived service quality of museum websites displaying artifacts. To the best of our knowledge, this is the first instrument for measuring such service quality.

Second, to the best of our knowledge, this study represents the first research into the determinants of user satisfaction and behavioral intentions relating to online museum services displaying artifacts. The results of structural equation modeling showed that user satisfaction and behavioral intentions were dependent on the four identified factors of fulfillment, content and usability, reliability, and interface. Compared with the previously proposed service quality factors for museum websites that merely provide information, fulfillment is especially important. Our findings may serve as a foundation for further exploration into advanced museum websites that involve more complex functions.

Third, video-based museum websites have some advantages and disadvantages compared with text-based museum websites. The t-test results showed that, owing to better performance in the service quality factors of fulfillment and interface, users were more satisfied with iPalace than with the text-based website displaying artifacts. They were also more willing to recommend and reuse the website than users of the text-based website. However, iPalace had a lower performance in system reliability due to the slower response time.

Finally, this study reveals a process for exploring the advantages and disadvantages of a new ICT-enabled service. First, an existing service that has a similar purpose to the new service is identified as a counterpart. A suitable instrument for measuring users' perceived service quality regarding the new service and its counterpart is then developed. A survey experiment is conducted to collect data and to analyze them in the model. By comparing service quality factor performance between the new service and the counterpart, the advantages and disadvantages of the new service can be identified.

Managerial implications

The findings of this study have several implications for museum practitioners. First, through understanding the service quality factors of museum websites displaying artifacts, the museum will have a better knowledge of how to fulfill this function via ICT. This study shows that good performance in each of four identified service quality factors can improve customer satisfaction and behavioral intentions regarding museum websites.

Second, the study shows that curators need to address issues relating to system reliability if they wish to provide a service similar to iPalace. That is, unlike text-based websites, museums must ensure that the servers supplying video-based websites can handle massive peak demand. In addition, the audience needs to have sufficient bandwidth to obtain the video service smoothly.[2]

Unlike traditional Web interfaces, the new metaphorical interface design asks users to expend some effort and time to learn how to operate it. A poor metaphorical interface design will confuse users, reduce the service quality, and give users a poor service experience. Museum managers thus need to take into consideration the possibility of poor effects resulting from an inferior metaphorical interface design.

Research limitations and future research

Our research has the following limitations. We did not consider the two factors communication and security, which are important in e-commerce. In the future, museums may want to collect users' personal information and interact with them. To provide for such museum services, further research should be conducted to develop a measure that takes the factors communication and security into consideration.

We used the developed instrument to measure service quality, customer satisfaction, and behavioral intentions regarding iPalace and its text-based counterpart. In the future, we could apply the instrument to other museum services to verify the authenticity of the instrument and the structural equation model obtained in this study.

Finally, this study relied on the use of cross-sectional and self-reported data obtained from the same source. Common method variance may have affected the validity of our research findings. The procedure used may be sensitive to common method bias, occurring when variance is attributable to the measurement method rather than to the constructs of interest. Further longitudinal studies and collection of data from multiple sources and external respondent are thus recommended to validate our research model in this respect.

Appendices

Appendix 5.1 Groups and factors identified from the e-commerce literature

Literature	Groups						
	Content	Usability	Interface	System Reliability	Communication	Security	Fulfillment
Liu, Arnett, and Litecky (2000)	Information quality	System use	Playfulness	System design quality			
Kaynama and Black (2000)	Navigation		Design and presentation		Responsiveness, Personalization and customization		Content and purpose, Background
Yoo and Donthu (2001)		Ease of use	Aesthetic design	Processing speed		Security	
Loiacono, Watson, and Goodhue(2002)	Ease of understanding	Intuitive operations	Visual appeal, Innovativeness, Emotional appeal, Consistent image	Response time	Tailored Communications	Trust	Informational fit-to-task, Online completeness
Vidgen (2002)	Information	Usability	Design		Empathy	Trust	
Santos (2003)	Content, Structure and layout	Ease of use	Appearance	Reliability, Efficiency	Communication, Support	Security	
Parasuraman, Zeithaml, and Malhotr(2005)		Efficiency		System availability	Responsiveness, Contact	Privacy	Fulfillment

Appendix 5.2 References for questionnaire items

Question No.	Reference
C_1	Barnes and Vidgen (2002)
C_2	Loiacono, Watson, and Goodhue (2002)
C_3	
C_4	
C_5	Collier and Bienstock (2006)
C_6	Collier and Bienstock (2006)
U_1	Barnes and Vidgen (2002); Loiacono et al. (2002); Parasuraman, Zeithaml, and Malhotra (2005)
U_2	Barnes and Vidgen 2002; Liu and Arnett (2000); Parasuraman et al. (2005); Yoo and Donthu (2001)
I_1	Loiacono et al. (2002); Yoo and Donthu (2001)
I_2	Liu and Arnett (2000); Loiacono et al. (2002)
I_3	Barnes and Vidgen (2002); Liu and Arnett (2000); Parasuraman et al. (2005); Yoo and Donthu (2001)
I_4	Loiacono et al. (2002)
I_5	Loiacono et al. (2002)
R_1	
R_2	
R_3	Collier and Bienstock (2006); Liu and Arnett (2000); Loiacono et al. (2002); Parasuraman et al. (2005); Yoo and Donthu (2001)
R_4	Collier and Bienstock (2006); Liu and Arnett (2000); Loiacono et al. (2002); Parasuraman et al. (2005); Yoo and Donthu (2001)
F_1	Goulding (2000); Harrison and Shaw 2004; Rentschler and Gilmore (2002); Saleh (2005)
F_2	Goulding (2000); Harrison and Shaw (2004); Rentschler and Gilmore (2002); Saleh (2005)
F_3	Goulding (2000); Harrison and Shaw (2004); Rentschler and Gilmore (2002); Saleh (2005)
F_4	Goulding (2000); Harrison and Shaw (2004); Rentschler and Gilmore (2002); Saleh (2005)
F_5	Rentschler and Gilmore (2002)
F_6	Goulding (2000); Harrison and Shaw (2004); Rentschler and Gilmore (2002)
F_7	Goulding (2000); Harrison and Shaw (2004); Rentschler and Gilmore (2002)

Appendix 5.3 References for measurement items

CS_1	McKinney, Yoon, and Zahedi (2002)
CS_2	McKinney et al. (2002)
BI_1	Venkatesh et al. (2003)
BI_2	Venkatesh et al. (2003)

Appendix 5.3 The first section of the survey instrument for the text-based version

Factor	Sub-factor	No.	Question
Content	Information Quality	C_1	The information presented on the website is trusted.
		C_2	The information presented on the website is easy to understand.
	Tele-presence	C_3	Browsing the site, I am personally on the scene.
		C_4	Browsing the site, I am gazing steadily at the screen.
	Media Quality	C_5	The pictures are clear.
		C_6	The text is clear.
Usability	Intuitive Operation	U_1	The browsing is simple and intuitive.
		U_2	The operations are easy to learn.
Interface	Innovativeness	I_1	The text-based interface is innovative.
	Visual Appeal	I_2	I always focus on the content.
		I_3	The interface appearance is pleasing to both the eye and the mind.
	Consistent Image	I_4	There is a consistency of style in the Web page design.
		I_5	The design of the interface matches the image of the National Palace Museum.
System Reliability	Accessibility	R_1	I can access the website anytime and anywhere.
		R_2	I can access the website conveniently.
	Response Time	R_3	The pictures and text load quickly.
		R_4	The interface responds quickly.
Fulfillment	Education	F_1	The website makes me have a better understanding of ancient Chinese artifacts.
		F_2	The website makes me feel more enlightened than before.
		F_3	The website makes me feel more creative than before.
		F_4	The website makes me feel more interested in Chinese culture than before.
	Entertainment	F_5	The website entertains me.
	Propagation	F_6	Browsing the website is a substitute for visiting the National Palace Museum.
		F_7	Browsing the website make me feel more impressed about the National Palace Museum than before.

Appendix 5.4 The first section of the survey instrument for the video-based version

Factor	Sub-factor	No.	Question
Content	Information Quality	C_1	The information presented on the website is trusted.
		C_2	The information presented on the website is easy to understand.
	Tele-presence	C_3	Browsing the site, I am personally on the scene.
		C_4	Browsing the site, I am gazing steadily at the screen.
	Media Quality	C_5	The video images are clear.
		C_6	The video's narration is clear.
Usability	Intuitive Operation	U_1	The browsing is simple and intuitive.
		U_2	The operations are easy to learn.
Interface	Innovativeness	I_1	The video-based interface is innovative.
	Visual Appeal	I_2	I always focus on the content.
		I_3	The interface appearance is pleasing to both the eye and the mind.
	Consistent Image	I_4	There is a consistency of style in the Web page design.
		I_5	The design of the interface matches the image of the National Palace Museum.
System Reliability	Accessibility	R_1	I can access the website anytime and anywhere.
		R_2	I can access the website conveniently.
	Response Time	R_3	The video loads quickly.
		R_4	The interface responds quickly.
Fulfillment	Education	F_1	The website makes me have a better understanding of ancient Chinese artifacts.
		F_2	The website makes me feel more enlightened than before.
		F_3	The website makes me feel more creative than before.
		F_4	The website makes me feel more interested in Chinese culture than before.
	Entertainment	F_5	The website entertains me.
	Propagation	F_6	Browsing the website is a substitute for visiting the National Palace Museum.
		F_7	Browsing the website make me feel more impressed about the National Palace Museum than before.

Appendix 5.5 The second section of the survey instrument

Factor	No.	Question
Customer Satisfaction	CS_1	I am satisfied with the browsing experience provided by the website.
	CS_2	I would recommend the website to others.
Behavioral Intentions	BI_1	I intend to revisit the website in the near future.
	BI_2	I will revisit the website in the future.

Notes

1 In the literature of e-commerce, "fulfillment" refers to the expected commercial functions that will be fulfilled when a user visits an e-commerce website. Here, "fulfillment" refers to the expected museum functions that will be fulfilled when a user visits a museum website displaying artifacts.
2 This is an infrastructure constraint that is beyond the control of the museum service provider. The bandwidth requirements of both the server and the customer must be satisfied, as otherwise the service quality received by the customer will be inferior.

References

Abdullah, F. (2005). HEdPERF versus SERVPERF: The quest for ideal measuring instrument of service quality in higher education sector, *Quality Assurance in Education, 13*(4), 305–328.

Baggs, S. C., and Kleiner, B. H. (1996). How to measure customer service effectively, *Managing Service Quality, 6*(1), 36–39.

Bagozzi, R. P., and Youjae, Y. (1988). On the evaluation of structural equation models, *Journal of the Academy of Marketing Science, 16*(1), 74–97.

Barnes, S., and Vidgen, R. (2002). An integrative approach to the assessment of e-commerce quality, *Journal of Electronic Commerce Research, 3*(3), 114–127.

Bendall-Lyon, D., and Powers, T. L. (2004). The impact of structure and process attributes on satisfaction and behavioral intentions, *Journal of Services Marketing, 18*(2), 114–121.

Bentler, P. M., and Bonett, D. G. (1980). Significance tests and goodness-of-fit in the analysis of covariance structures, *Psychological Bulletin, 88*(3), 588–600.

Bollen, K. A. (1989). *Structural equations with latent variables.* New York, NY: John Wiley & Sons.

Brady, M. K., and Cronin, J. J. (2001). Some new thoughts on conceptualizing perceived service quality: A hierarchical approach, *Journal of Marketing, 65*(3), 34–49.

Campbell, H., and Wells, M. (1996). Assessment of museum World Wide Web home page format, *Visitor Studies: Theory, Research and Practice, 9*(1), 216–226.

Carman, J. M. (1990). Consumer perceptions of service quality: An assessment of the SERVQUAL dimensions, *Journal of Retailing, 66*(1), 33–55.

Chen, J. S., and Gursoy, D. (2001). Investigation of tourists' destination loyalty and preferences, *International Journal of Contemporary Hospitality Management, 3*(2), 79–85.

Chomeya, R. (2010). Aggressive driving behavior: Undergraduate students study, *Journal of Social Science, 6*(3), 411–415.

Chu, R. K. S., and Choi, T. (2000). An importance-performance analysis of hotel selection factors in the Hong Kong hotel industry: A comparison of business and leisure travelers, *Tourism Management, 21*(4), 363–377.

Collier, J. E., and Bienstock, C. C. (2006). Measuring service quality in E-retailing, *Journal of Service Research, 8*(3), 260–275.

Cronin, J. J., and Taylor, S. A. (1992). Measuring service quality: A reexamination and extension, *Journal of Marketing, 56*(3), 55–68.

Dabholkar, P. A., Shepherd, C. D., and Thorpe, D. I. (2000). A comprehensive framework for service quality: An investigation of critical conceptual and measurement issues through a longitudinal study, *Journal of Retailing, 76*(2), 139–173.

Davis, F., Bagozzi, R., and Warshaw, P. (1989). User acceptance of computer technology: A comparison of two theoretical models, *Management Science, 35*(8), 982–1002.

DeLone, W. H., and McLean, E. R. (2003). The DeLone and McLean model of information success: A ten year update, *Journal of Management Information Systems, 19*(4), 9–30.

DiMaggio, P. J. (1986). Can culture survive the marketplace? In P. J. DiMaggio (Ed.), *Nonprofit enterprise in the arts: Studies in mission and constraint* (pp. 65–92). Oxford, UK: Oxford University Press.

Doll, W. J., Xia, W., and Torkzadeh, G. (1994). A confirmatory factor analysis of the end-user computing satisfaction instrument, *MIS Quarterly, 18*(4), 453–461.

Goulding, C. (2000). Museum environment and the visitor experience, *European Journal of Marketing, 34*(3–4), 261–278.

Harrison, P., and Shaw, R. (2001). *An empirical investigation of the relationship between satisfaction, intention to repurchase, and intention to recommend infrequently used services,* 9th International Colloquium in Relationship Marketing, Montreal, Canada, 31–45.

Harrison, P., and Shaw, R. (2004). Consumer satisfaction and post-purchase intentions: An exploratory study of museum visitors, *International Journal of Arts Management, 6*(2), 23–32.

Hume, M. (2011). How do we keep them coming? Examining museum experiences using a services marketing paradigm, *Journal of Nonprofit & Public Sector Marketing, 23*(1), 71–94.

Hume, M., and Mills, M. (2011). Building the sustainable iMuseum: Is the virtual museum leaving our museums virtually empty? *International Journal of Nonprofit and Voluntary Sector Marketing, 16*(3), 275–289.

International Council of Museums. (2007). *ICOM definition of a museum.* Retrieved on 20/8/2012 from http://icom.museum/definition.html

Jarvenpaa, S. L., Tractinsky, N., and Vitale, M. (2000). Consumer trust in an Internet store. *Information Technology and Management, 1*(1–2), 45–71.

Johns, N., and Howard, A. (1998). Customer expectations versus perceptions of service performance in the Foodservice Industry, *International Journal of Service Industry Management, 9*(3), 248–265.

Kawashima, N. (1998). Knowing the public. A review of museum marketing literature and research, *International Journal of Museum Management and Curatorship, 17*(1), 21–39.

Kaynama, S. A., and Black, C. I. (2000). A proposal to assess the service quality of online travel agencies: An exploratory study, *Journal of Professional Services Marketing, 21*(1), 63–89.

Kaynama, S. A., Black, C. I., and Keesling, G. (2011). Impact of the Internet on internal service quality factors: The travel industry case, *The Journal of Applied Business Research, 19*(1), 135–146.

Knell, S. J. (2003). The shape of things to come: Museums in the technological landscape. *Museum and Society, 1*(3), 132–146.

Liu, C., and Arnett, K. P. (2000). Exploring the factors associated with website success in the context of electronic commerce, *Information and Management, 38,* 23–33.

Liu, C., Arnett, K. P., and Litecky, C. (2000). Design quality of websites for electronic commerce: Fortune 1000 webmasters' evaluations, *Electronic Markets, 10*(2), 120–129.

Loiacono, E. T., Watson, R. T., and Goodhue, D. L. (2002). WEBQUAL: A measure of website quality, 2002 Marketing Educators, *Conference: Marketing Theory and Applications, 13,* 432–437.

Marty, P. F. (1999). Museum informatics and collaborative technologies: The emerging socio-technological dimension of information science in museum environments, *Journal of the American Society for Information Science, 50*(12), 1083–1091.

McKinney, V., Yoon, K., and Zahedi, F. (2002). The measurement of web-customer satisfaction: An expectation and disconfirmation approach, *Information Systems Research, 13*(3), 296–315.

McLean, F. (1994). Services marketing: The case of museums, *Service Industries Journal, 14*(2), 190–203.

Mentzer, J. T., Flint, D. J., and Hult, G. T. M. (2001). Logistics service quality as a segment-customized process, *Journal of Marketing, 65*(4), 82–104.

Mey, L. P., and Mohamed, B. (2010). Service quality, visitor satisfaction and behavioral intentions: Pilot study at a museum in Malaysia, *Journal of Global Business and Economics, 1*(1), 226–240.

Oliver, R. L. (1980). A cognitive model of the antecedents and consequences of satisfaction decisions, *Journal of Marketing Research, 17*(4), 460–469.

Oliver, R. L. (1997). *Satisfaction: A behavioral perspective on the consumer.* New York, NY: McGraw-Hill.

Ozment, J., and Morash, E. A. (1994). The augmented service offering for perceived and actual service quality, *Journal of the Academy of Marketing Science, 4*(22), 352–363.

Page, T. J., and Spreng, R. A. (2002). Difference scores versus direct effects in service quality measurement, *Journal of Service Research, 4*(3), 184–192.

Pallas, J., and Economides, A. A. (2008). Evaluation of art museums' websites worldwide, *Information Services & Use, 28*(1), 45–57.

Parasuraman, A., Zeithaml, V. A., and Berry, L. L. (1988). SERVQUAL: A multiple-item scale for measuring customer perceptions of service quality, *Journal of Retailing, 64*(1), 12–40.

Parasuraman, A., Zeithaml, V. A., and Malhotra, A. (2005). E-S-QUAL. A multiple-item scale for assessing electronic service quality, *Journal of Service Research, 7*(3), 213–233.

Rentschler, R., and Gilmore, A. (2002). Museums: Discovering services marketing, *International Journal of Arts Management, 5*(1), 62–72.

Saleh, F. A. (2005). The determinants of the quality of the service experience: An empirical study of a heritage park, *University of Sharjah Journal of Pure & Applied Sciences, 2*(2), 75–102.

Santos, J. (2003). E-service quality: A model of virtual service quality dimensions, *Managing Service Quality, 13*(3), 233–246.

Santos, L. O. (1999). *Web-site quality evaluation method: A case study of museums,* 2nd Workshop on software engineering over the Internet (ICSE '99), 2nd Workshop on Software Engineering over the Internet, GIDIS, Department of Computer Science, Engineering School at UNLPam.

Schaupp, L. (2010). Website success: Antecedents of website satisfaction and re-use, *Journal of Internet Commerce, 9*(1), 42–64.

Seddon, P. B. (1997). A respecification and extension of the DeLone and McLean model of IS success, *Information Systems Research, 8*, 240–253.

Slywotzky, A., and Morrison, D. (2001). The rise of the active customer, *Marketing Management, 10*(2), 22–25.

Szymanski, D., and Henard, D. (2001). Customer satisfaction: A meta-analysis of the empirical evidence, *Journal of the Academy of Marketing Science, 29*(1), 16–35.

Szymanzki, D., and Hise, R. (2000). E-satisfaction: An initial examination, *Journal of Retailing, 76*(3), 309–322.

Thyne, M. (2000). The importance of values research for nonprofit organizations: The motivation-based values of museum visitors, *International Journal of Nonprofit and Voluntary Sector Marketing, 6*(2), 116–130.

Tsaih, R. H., Lin, Q. P., Han, T. S., Chao, Y. T., and Chan, H. C. (2012). *New ICT-enabled services of National Palace Museum and their designs.* 17th International Conference on Cultural Economics, Kyoto, Japan.

Venkatesh, V., Morris, M., Davis, G., and Davis, F. (2003). User acceptance of information technology: Toward a unified view, *MIS Quarterly, 27*(3), 425–478.

Vidgen, R. (2002). What's so different about developing web-based information systems?

European Conference on Information Systems (ECIS) Proceedings.

Vidgen, R., and Barnes, S. (2002). An integrative approach to the assessment of e-commerce quality, *Journal of Electronic Commerce Research, 3*(3), 114–127.

Wixom, B. H., and Todd, P. A. (2005). A theoretical integration of user satisfaction and technology acceptance, *Information Systems Research, 16*(1), 85–102.

Yi, Y. (1990). A critical review of consumer satisfaction. In V. A. Zeithaml (Ed.), *Review of marketing* (pp. 68–123). Chicago, IL: American Marketing Association.

Yoo, B., and Donthu, N. (2001). Developing a scale to measure the perceived quality of an Internet shopping site (SITEQUAL), *Quarterly Journal of Electronic Commerce, 2*(1), 31–46.

6 Legal issues regarding innovative museum services in a mobile and cloud computing environment

Examples of copyright and licensing issues for the National Palace Museum

Jerry G. Fong

Introduction

Faced with the formidable popularity of mobile devices and the rapid advances in digital and cloud computing applications, museums and other cultural institutions are beginning to grapple with this fast-developing trend. However, deciding to provide innovative services based on mobile or cloud technology will inevitably entail new challenges, both technological and legal. In Taiwan, the National Palace Museum (NPM) has begun to use digital technology to develop innovative service platforms and related applications. The NPM is also contemplating the deployment of more advanced innovative services to improve both the experiences of visitors and the NPM's services. Before entering into this new environment, the NPM should, in addition to technological considerations, look into the related legal and intellectual property (IP) issues that are closely linked to the use of digitized content.

Advances in digitization and Internet technologies have led to mobile and cloud computing applications being enthusiastically accepted by the general public and various enterprises. Following this trend, museums worldwide have begun to use innovative technologies to support a variety of services, both basic and new. By so doing, the museums hope to attract the general public to visit them more often and to use the innovative services provided by the museums for educational, social, and other purposes.

Given the large number of users of mobile devices, in particular smartphones, major museums around the world have begun to release smartphone and tablet applications (apps) to take maximum advantage of the advances in hardware and software services. Through digital technology, these museums aspire to establish close relationships with the general public and to encourage them to participate actively in a variety of activities offered by the museums. Combining these technologies with the resources of each museum also allows unconventional operational models to be implemented through innovative applications and services.

A number of legal and IP issues, however, are associated with the innovative services offered by the new technology and/or new service platforms. For instance, the general legal principles relating to the provision of content and the various innovative services that adopt new technologies will involve the most basic contractual issues (for instance rights and obligations within a license agreement) and IP. The legal relationship that previously existed between museums and their visitors may now possibly include a third party, such as a service provider, thus forming a triangular relationship involving contractual relationships between a museum and its users, and between the museum and third-party providers. This newly emerging structure requires more issues to be considered than before, such as the rights and obligations of museums, visitors/users, and third-party providers, and ways in which to protect the information available in mobile and cloud computing services; different requirements regarding information security, protection of personal information, and other issues are to be expected vis-à-vis the straightforward legal relationships between conventional content providers and users. For example, a rumor about Apple's iCloud services being hacked and the release of celebrity photos[1] has exposed the complexity and importance of the issues surrounding the adoption of a mobile and cloud computing structure. Accordingly, this article addresses the legal and IP issues relating to innovative services provided by museums and explores how the NPM can best use legal and contractual means to fulfill its goals.

Museum management and services within a mobile and cloud computing structures

The quality of a museum's services is not only a demonstration of the strength of a state and its cultural reputation, but may also be viewed as the primary driver in developing the cultural and creative industries.[2] This developmental role has arisen because today's museums have, in addition to their conventional functions of Research, Enclosure, Conservation, and Exhibition (RICE), the new RICE functions of Recreation, Information, Communication, and Education. That is, in the era of the new economy, the role of museums has moved beyond the fundamentals of cultural storage, research, broadcasting, and development to provide education, tourism, recreation, and so forth.

Museums serving as digital content providers

Although museums were originally created for the purposes of collecting and conservation, in the current Internet age, they have wider responsibilities, such as communicating values and perspectives to the general public, and interpreting cultural meaning through exhibiting their collections. Furthermore, museums today are also tasked with social education and knowledge delivery. Through implementing digital technology and services that use such technology, museums can not only expand the scope of what was conventionally exhibited, but may also provide educational and communication functions via constant interaction with the general public through widely accessible mobile and cloud computing technology.

Following the trend of rapid technology development, hardcopy publications are now available as e-books; radio players and televisions have become cable TVs and streaming services; and the combination of broadband Internet, mobile communications, and cloud computing has resulted in a convergence between telecommunications, cable services, and the Internet. To perfect a digital convergence environment, or to develop and structure a digital content industry, however, it is not sufficient to depend solely on the infrastructure of the Internet and hardware. Sufficient digital content is a prerequisite for developing the cultural industry, and also drives the actions of museums. With their enormous and invaluable collections, and with suitable use of advanced technology, for example in digitizing these collections, museums can transform their role from one of preservation to one of digital content provision and may eventually deliver wider and more powerful service functions.

Accordingly, with respect to mobile and cloud computing structures, today's globally renowned museums tend to be more diverse in presenting their collections, as more newly developed applications and services are being provided[3] to meet the standards of the era of digital convergence. The NPM is no exception.[4]

The NPM has put much effort into moving from a purely digitizing role under the Digital Archive Project to the Cultural and Creative Environment Project with a goal of providing interdisciplinary development of technology and humanity,[5] in which culture and technology converge. By integrating its network of cultural and creative resources, the NPM has also given new life to its cultural heritage through collaborating with design houses and studios to promote the understanding of these cultural and creative resources.[6] The inevitable challenge for the NPM is to work out what it should do to further integrate its accumulated digital resources/creative and cultural content with mobile and cloud computing technology, and further develop innovative services and value-added applications.

Museums serving as digital service platform providers

Due to the diversification of society, the conventional functions of museums, such as archiving, exhibition, promotion, and research, can no longer satisfy society's demands. Today's museums must place more emphasis on functions such as communication, interpretation, interaction, and recreation, and anticipate a role in knowledge and cultural delivery. As the functions of museums have gradually become more complex, the variety of services involving digital content that they provide has led to the concept of museums as platform service providers, which permits better and more efficient communication with the general public.

Influenced by the rapid advances in information technology (IT), the general public expects, with the assistance of mobile technology that establishes communication with museums or gathers relevant information from them, to be able to gain access to the museums when and where they choose. Thus, if a museum is able to take a further step forward and transform a conventional museum website into a digital service platform, and provide mobile and cloud computing services via broadband Internet, the position and role of that museum would be strengthened.[7]

The environment of cloud computing technology and services[8] not only provides numerous medium or small museums that have insufficient resources with more opportunities in terms of survival and growth, but also gives the major museums a new option of providing innovative digital services. Conventional information facilities and services are typically very expensive for small and medium museums. Cloud computing services provided through a third party would not only significantly reduce the cost of such facilities and services, but would also give the museums greater flexibility in deciding whether to increase their storage capacity and broadband bandwidth. Museums can make the most of the inherent flexibility in the cost of cloud computing services and the feature of unlimited access to content, and will eventually be able to cut management costs. In addition, once the digital content has been uploaded into the cloud, or in some situations been formed into a platform that is integrated with resources from other museums, more efficient use can be expected.[9] Via cloud computing services, the functions of data storage, transmission, and cloud back-up[10] can be provided simultaneously, indicating how important cloud computing technology is to the future of museums.

In addition to models in which various museums tread their separate paths, it is worth mentioning the emergence of museum platforms created through digitization of content and the concept of a digital platform. One example is the art platform ArtBabble,[11] established by the Indianapolis Museum of Art. What differentiates ArtBabble from the websites of other museums is that it integrates the digital content of 35 globally renowned museums and cultural institutions,[12] providing the general public with a greater variety of content and choice, furthering its status in the highly competitive world of the Internet. Acting as a platform service provider, it uses Amazon's cloud computing service (AWS) and the operational costs are calculated according to the actual amount of transferred and stored data. This approach has not only reduced the cost associated with the information, but has also provided greater expandability,[13] and has permitted new interpretations of the educational and communication functions of modern-day museums.

Another example is the VertNet platform, which is a biologically oriented museum in the cloud that integrates 63 globally renowned museums, 150 sources, 178 special sources, and 13,254,490 record items.[14] In Europe, the V-musT.net (Virtual Museum Transnational Network),[15] which is another example of virtual museum platform, is established under the auspices of the European Union FP7 Project that strives to develop and integrate the technology and applications of virtual museums. To date, 18 museums from 13 countries are involved in V-musT.net, alongside more than 100 institutional members. The emergence of virtual museum platforms not only provides users with the information they require, but also achieves the modern-day museum functions of conservation, education, communication, and exhibition.

Foreign museums' implementation of innovative services within mobile and cloud computing structures

Since 2009, a wide range of technology services, including those using mobile devices, have been released by globally renowned museums. These museums have collaborated with technology companies to develop free smartphone and tablet applications, promoting these alongside other platform services. By 2012, there were 758 museum-related apps available in the iTunes app store.[16] The main functions of the apps developed worldwide, either independently by the museums or with the involvement of third parties, are guidance and education. GPS positioning and map retrieval functions are used alongside recreational functions to deliver up-to-date news and special museum exhibitions.

The Museum of London, for example, has developed an application called StreetMuseum for iPhone, based on its large collection of photographic works. Using a mobile guidance service, users can display augmented reality (AR) images at particular geographical locations, and thus enjoy a wealth of historical photography at 200 locations in the city of London. The release of the app significantly increased the number of visitors to the museum.[17]

Another example is the free guidance app Explorer,[18] released by the American Science and Historical Museum. Users of the app are allowed to customize it to create ideal routes, through bookmarking their desired content. Visitors' personal devices can then use GPS to accurately determine their position and provide them with directions. During a tour, users can share their thoughts and experiences directly via Facebook, Twitter, other social media, and email. If users are unable to visit the museum in person, there is the option of exploring collections in digital form.

In Taiwan, however, museum-related apps are still in their infancy, with only a limited number being available; the lead development role is being taken by the NPM. For example, the NPM has released a number of mobile apps, such as the NPM Insight app that allows users to explore and enjoy exhibitions using their own mobile devices, to increase the convenience of the visitor experience through developing 3D interactive functions. In addition to information on visiting the NPM, the app also provides weather forecasts, tour schedules, integrated tourism networks and visitor-oriented tourist guidance. Moreover, the app has location positioning functions so that it may offer services such as route planning, virtual 3D AR guidance and related navigation functions. In combination with social media, users are also able to constantly share their experiences with their friends.

In general, the apps developed by museums, either alone or with the assistance of third parties, assist visitors before, during, and after an exhibition to acquire an in-depth understanding of the featured collection and/or the entire archive held by the museum. In addition to providing written, audio, and visual information describing the collections, these apps can also collect user data and feedback to obtain a clearer picture of user preferences and suggestions.

Analyzing the technology application service model adopted by museums reveals that there is frequent use of mobile communication technology, both online and on-site. According to the NMC Horizon Report on new technology, published by the internationally renowned New Media Consortium (NMC) and the Marcus Institute for Digital Education in the Arts (MIDEA),[19] a large proportion of the available museum-related technology relates to mobile devices, location-based services (LBS),[20] and cloud computing services.

To take full advantage of museum-related technology, San Francisco's Museum of Modern Art has redesigned the Web app on its website to satisfy the potential need for future interaction via personal computers or mobile devices. In France, the Louvre Museum has cooperated with app developers to create the museum-exclusive Louvre app for the Apple iOS platform. Users of the Louvre app may view part of the collection from any location and at any time, at no cost. If users wish to view more content via the app, they may pay an additional fee to the Louvre Museum's entire collection.[21]

The Nu.M.E. Virtualized Cultural Collection Program in Italy is a project that combines a cloud computing structure and virtual integration technology, based on the concept of social media. The program virtualizes the Piazza di Porta Ravegnana, an iconic tourist attraction in Bologna, and places this on the Second Life (SL) social media platform for users to access. What differentiates Nu.M.E. from ArtBabble is the cloud computing service platform; the former includes Google Maps, Panoramio, Google Docs, Google Warehouse, and so forth to structure a virtual space within social media, with the benefits of low cost and instant interaction and feedback from users.

Another example can be found in the Getty Museum and the Getty Villa in Los Angeles. In collaboration with Google, these institutions have combined Web apps and mobile apps to enable users to find guidance and relevant information on works of art by simply scanning a work using the camera on their own devices; the app immediately recognizes the work of art and provides the information.[22] In addition, Getty Guide facilities are implemented throughout the museum to allow users to interact freely with the works of art.[23]

The most creative service is found in the Field Museum of Natural History in Chicago.[24] The museum, in collaboration with the University of Chicago Press and a third party, Touch Press, created the Gems and Jewels app that gives access to more than 300 pieces of treasure. The app allows iPad users to access 360-degree views and knowledge of its great variety of content, from diamond mines to pearls in shallow seas, including the chemical compositions of each and every kind of gem, providing users with a totally fresh experience of the convergence of publications and museums.

As shown by these examples of integration between museums and cloud computing structures, with assistance from mobile and cloud computing technology, not only will future services provided by museums be more sophisticated and complete, but they will also be much more convenient for users. Today, users can gain access to specific information whenever and wherever they wish, which is exactly what museums are trying to achieve in the era of the new economy. In the future promotion of innovative services and activities, we should thus be expecting the NPM to follow globally renowned museums by releasing innovative value-added services to attract more visitors and users.

Legal and intellectual property issues for museums adopting mobile services and cloud computing services

Intellectual and legal issues relating to digitization of museum collections

The recent trend among famous museums around the world to combine mobile and cloud computing to provide services effectively strengthens the functions of these museums in terms of education, training, popularizing, and providing applications that go beyond the traditional role of museum collections.

This trend also entails legal issues, which represent significant challenges for these museums. Among all the legal issues, intellectual property and the related contractual issues are the core. Moreover, within the context of IP, copyright is the key issue since it is essential to determine whether digitized collections are protected subject matter under copyright law, or are simply mere duplicates of collections that are already in the public domain.

In principle, if the collections themselves still lie within the period of protection enshrined in copyright law, they are surely protected. However, if the protection has expired, that is, into the public domain, the collections are no longer protected subject matter under copyright law. In this situation, whether the digitized copies of the original can be further protected becomes an issue. In addition, whether the owners of such digitized collections, that is, museums, can claim copyright infringement against any person using the digitized copy of their collections is another thorny issue.

If digitized collections are not protected subject matter under copyright law, such digitized products will not be subject to legal protect and can be freely utilized by any person. In such situation, museums might be hesitated to release their digitized collections willingly. Such consequence also implies that the museums might move in the opposite direction to their mission of enabling the flow of cultural heritage and knowledge.

In order to resolve such dilemma, in addition to copyright law protection, Taiwan lawmakers also adopted other approaches to helping museums and cultural preservation institutions. For example, Taiwan's copyright law provides a unique "plate rights" to any person who arranges or reprints works in the public domain into a new form.[25] Such plate rights, however, are not protected as copyright right per se, but with a shorter and limited duration.[26] Moreover, the lawmakers enacted the Cultural Heritage Preservation Act to provide some extra protection to the preservation institutions. For example, article 69 of the Cultural Heritage Preservation Act states that

> [f]or the purposes of research and promotion, a public antiquities preservation agency (institution) may reproduce and supervise the reproduction of the antiquities under its custody. Third parties may not make any such reproduction except with the permission and under the supervision of the original custodian preservation agency (institution). The regulations governing the reproduction and supervision of antiquities referred to in the preceding paragraph shall be prescribed by the central competent authority.

However, how to distinguish the terms *arrange* or *print* under copyright law and *reproduce* under the Cultural Heritage Preservation Act is still under dispute.

The right to reproduce material might solve the problem of museums lacking the incentive to develop value-added services for cultural heritage assets, by enhancing the protection provided by cultural heritage preservation. Nevertheless, the scope and period of the protection afforded by the cultural heritage preservation policy in the case of *reproduction right* are considered to be much narrower than for *copyright* under copyright law. In addition, the Cultural Heritage Preservation Act also lacks necessary enforcement mechanism to punish any violators. As a result, copyright law is still the most important tool to protect the digitized collections provided by museums and cultural preservation institutions. Therefore, whether the digitized copies, such as scanned images or photographs, are protected under copyright law in Taiwan is still essential for museums and cultural institutions like the NPM.

In order to resolve the protectable issue, it is important to look at relevant cases or laws in other countries, especially in the United States. In fact, before 1991, the substance of copyright law in United States also followed the so-called sweat-of-the-brow doctrine,[27] which gave copyright to any person who invested significant amount of time and resources into their work. However, the United States Supreme Court, in one of the seminal case, *Feist Publications, Inc., v. Rural Telephone Service Co.*[28] made it clear that "sweat of the brow" alone is not the creative spark that is the sine qua non of originality.

In *Feist*, Feist Publishing Co. had copied phone information from Rural Telephone Co.'s telephone listings to include in its own white pages, after Rural had refused to license the information. Rural sued for copyright infringement. The lower courts followed the sweat-of-the-brow doctrine and sided with Rural. However, the Supreme Court ruled that information contained in Rural's phone directory was not copyrightable, and therefore no infringement existed because, without a minimum of original creativity, the information alone cannot be protected by copyright.[29]

Feist ruling not only has major implications for any product that serves as a collection of information or facts, but also has impacts on other fields, such as faithfully reproduction of artistic works by photographing.[30] Such implications were clearly demonstrated in *Bridgeman Art Library v. Corel Corp.* decision.[31] In fact, regarding the protection and use of cultural heritage art, *Bridgeman* is recognized as the most influential legal decision in the area.

In this case, Bridgeman Art Library possessed a large library of photographs of paintings by European masters, as both transparencies and in digital form. The copyright terms on the paintings themselves had expired, but Bridgeman claimed that it owned a copyright on the photographs through licenses with major museums or photographers it hired. Corel Corporation, on the other hand, sold a CD-ROM called "Professional Photos CD-ROM Masters," which contained digitized images of paintings claimed to be owned by Bridgeman. Bridgeman sued Corel for copyright infringement. Corel argued that the paintings in question were in public domain, and Bridgeman couldn't get a copyright on an exact digital copy of a public domain painting. Bridgeman, however, pointed to *Alfred Bell & Co. v. Catalda Fine Arts*, Inc.,[32] which held that reproductions of public domain images can be awarded copyright protection. The trial court found for Corel.

The trial court ruled that exact photographic copies of public domain images could not be protected by copyright in the United States, nor United Kingdom, because the copies lack originality. The court found that despite the fact that accurate reproductions might require a great deal of skill, experience and effort, the key element for copyrightability under U.S. law and other countries is originality, and Bridgeman's digitized photographs lack it.

The court explained that there is "little doubt that many photographs, probably the overwhelming majority, reflect at least the modest amount of originality required for copyright protection." Such elements of originality, according to the court, "may include posing the subjects, lighting, angle, selection of film and camera, evoking the desired expression, and almost any other variant involved."

The court further stated that since "the point of the exercise was to reproduce the underlying works with absolute fidelity, . . . [i]t is uncontested that Bridgeman's images are substantially exact reproductions of public domain works, albeit in a different medium."[33] Since Bridgeman, by its own admission, had performed "slavish copying," the court explicitly held that "[w]hile it may be assumed that this required both skill and effort, there was no spark of originality – indeed, the point of the exercise was to reproduce the underlying works with absolute fidelity. Copyright is not available in these circumstances."[34]

Even though *Bridgeman* was a decision of the United States District Court for the Southern District of New York, it is not a binding precedent on other federal or state courts, but it has nevertheless been highly influential as persuasive authority, and is widely followed by other federal courts. For example, in *Meshwerks v. Toyota*,[35] the Court of Appeals for the Tenth Circuit, cited *Bridgeman v. Corel*, extending the reasoning in *Bridgeman* to cover 3D wireframe meshes of existing 3D objects. The appeals court held that "[t]he law is becoming increasingly clear: one possesses no copyright interest in reproductions . . . when these reproductions do nothing more than accurately convey the underlying image."[36]

In Taiwan, how the courts identify whether a photograph fulfills the requirement of originality is determined by the selection of the theme, the process of lighting and modifying, combinations, and other artistic skills. If "the scenarios arranged for the photography did not entail a representation of the fixed image involving composition, angle, light, speed, or having a choice or adjustment, it does not fulfill the requirement of originality."[37] Such a view adopted by Taiwanese courts is consistent with the views expressed by the Supreme Court of United States in *Feist*. Therefore, whether Taiwan will adopt a similar view as *Bridgeman* is one of the greatest concerns of the NPM and other cultural preservation institutions.

In photographing cultural arts and heritage, the aim is to retain their original look. The question of how such photographs could fulfill the requirement of originality thus becomes an issue when considering enforceable copyright protection of the photographs. This has led to extensive discussion between experts and scholars and the authorities in Taiwan.

For example, on May 26, 2005, the Taiwan Intellectual Property Office (TIPO) held a conference to discuss whether photographs of the items of cultural heritage held by the NPM should be considered photographic works protected by copyright law. The conference did not reach a consensus. On June 28, 2005, TIPO held another conference in the same issue. Although a consensus was again not reached, the majority took a position similar to the *Bridgeman* decision, holding that because the photographs were in essence faithful reproductions of the traditional Chinese paintings, literature, and other heritage in two-dimensional (2-D) format, they should be considered copies of the original and thus fail to satisfy the originality requirement, which is essential to copyright. However, if the subject matter was instead a three-dimensional (3-D) subject, the majority was of the opinion that as the photographers needed to determine angles, composition, lighting, focus, and other considerations and to exercise professional judgment before taking the photographs, this might satisfy the originality requirement. Consequently, photographs of 3-D objects should be protected by copyright.

In summary, as courts in various countries have discarded the concept of "sweat of the brow," the "originality" requirement becomes the essential factor in determining whether copyright exists. Although Taiwanese courts haven't decided any case on this issue, considering the fact that the opinion of the authority, TIPO, is that photographs of traditional Chinese paintings, literature, and other heritage in 2-D format often do not fulfill the originality requirement, NPM can still rely on contracts than to seek remedies under the copyright law system.

Issues regarding the licensing of digitized museum archives

Although there is no consensus in Taiwan on the question of whether digital content, especially photographs produced by museums, is protected under copyright law, in terms of legal practice, museums still can, despite doubts about copyright, clarify their rights, obligations, and relationships with potential users by using contract, especially through licensing agreement.

The best example of using contract, instead of copyright, can be found in the decision of the United States Court of Appeals for the Seventh Circuit in *ProCD, Inc. v Zeidenberg*.[38] Zeidenberg (the defendant) purchased a CD-ROM called Select Phone from the plaintiff; this contained a set of databases compiled by the plaintiff at a cost of over $10 million, plus a software program for searching and querying this database. To recoup its costs, ProCD specifically stipulated in its license agreement that the CD-ROM could not be used commercially. After purchasing a non-commercial version of the CD-ROM, the defendant, in breach of the license agreement, removed the non-copyright-protected telephone number database from the copyright-protected search software, wrote different search software, built his own telephone number search website using the database compiled by ProCD, and provided this database on the Internet for free.

The crux of this case was whether copyright law could preempt contractual stipulations. The Seventh Circuit court referred to the 1991 Supreme Court case of *Feist Publications v. Rural Telephone Service*,[39] in which the Supreme Court held that the telephone directory compiled by Rural Telephone was not copyright-protected due to its lack of originality. In *Zeidenberg,* the Seventh Circuit court, pursuant to the *Feist* case, held that copyright law did not preempt contract law, instead holding that a contract could confer rights among the parties to it, as those rights were not "equivalent to any of the exclusive rights within the general scope of copyright."[40]

The court then held that the license was valid and enforceable as a contract, relying primarily on the Uniform Commercial Code (UCC) sections 2–204 (describing a valid contract) and 2–206 (describing acceptance of a contract). The court held that Zeidenberg accepted the offer by clicking through because Zeidenberg "had no choice, because the software splashed the license on the screen and would not let him proceed without indicating acceptance." As Zeidenberg could have rejected the terms of the contract and returned the software, and failed to do so, the court ruled against Zeidenberg. The court specifically noted that the ability and "the opportunity to return goods can be important" under the Uniform Commercial Code.

Following the *Feist* and *Zeidenberg* decisions, digital content providers have implemented proactive strategies to protect their investments and rights. As a result, instead of relying on copyright laws to protect their investments, they are actively using private contract, such as licensing agreement, to supplement or align relevant copyright law – thereby the dispute regarding whether copyright preempts contracts emerges. For instance, the widely used contracts, such as the "shrink-wrap" agreement or "click-wrap" agreement, provide copyright-like protection for software providers and websites. As increasing numbers of enterprises take a proactive approach by using contracts to govern rights and obligations between the parties involved, this opens the door to "private copyright" on non-copyright objects between the parties.[41]

These decisions have been followed by other court decisions[42] and have been used as arguments in recent cases. For instance, in both *Montz v. Pilgrim Films & Television, Inc.*[43] judged by the Ninth Circuit and *Forest Park Pictures v. Universal Television Network, Inc.*[44] decided by the Second Circuit, the courts ruled that copyright did not preempt implied-in-fact contracts.[45]

In Taiwan, the NPM is using the open data model for digital content relating to its collections. This involves the "right to access" achieves with the purpose of the "reuse of public sector information." Furthermore, the NPM has drawn up different licensing agreements for different products, such as the licensing of publications,[46] images of collections,[47] brand names,[48] and databases, to cover the absence of protection of uncopyrighted digital content. This approach shows that, despite the fact that copyright law and the Cultural Heritage Preservation Act provide extra protection mechanisms, such as plate rights and limiting the reproduction right of the original collections, the NPM is adopting a similar approach as its U.S. counterparties to maximize its protection.

Recommendations to the NPM regarding challenges to the use of digital content

Due to the various legal and IP issues involved in providing innovative services, and the emergence of mobile communications and cloud services, other changes have also been seen in terms of basic contractual relations and what a contract governs. Regarding contractual relations, the previous bilateral museum–visitor relationship has changed to a tripartite one, especially when mobile or cloud services providers are involved.

It has thus become important not only to clarify the rights and obligations of all parties, but also to consider other issues, such as how to ensure the security of personal information in mobile or cloud services, and how to handle the hacking of information stored by third-party providers. Museums need to consider not only their own IT needs, but also the potential legal implications and risks associated with the new technologies and services.

As a provider of digital content through value-added services based on its digital archives, the NPM has made some progress in this area, such as making digital content available for public use (via networks and mobile devices), and involving interested businesses in the development of creative commodities (using the open data model or other licensing models).

However, the current licensing mechanisms used by the NPM mainly operate via applications made on paper; not only is this approach time-consuming and unable to match the rapid flow of data in a digitized environment, but it also differs from the common practice of licensing digital content via the Internet. The NPM should therefore consider setting up a specialized licensing mechanism and platform that can handle standardized licensing activities, saving on administrative time and costs by allowing users to complete an online licensing form, and that can also cater for special cases by permitting the negotiation of licenses relating to trademarks and copyright, thereby providing more convenient and personalized services for individual and business users.

With regard to the protection of digital content on the NPM's website, this currently contains a "Copyright Declaration" link at the bottom of the home page that links to specific declarations regarding copyright protocols for the words and digital archives provided by the NPM. However, the declaration only covers "reasonable usage" and does not specify binding legal consequences for breaching either copyright laws or the declaration itself; neither does the declaration constitute a contract in terms of being an "online licensing agreement."

Although the declaration does not necessarily affect the NPM's rights as the copyright holder, the doubt surrounding the NPM's ability to obtain copyright on certain digital content, such as photographs of traditional Chinese paintings, literature, and other heritage in plain format, and the fact that the NPM is an institution of preservation and cultural archiving, casts serious doubt on whether the "declaration" affords sufficient protection for the contents of the website.[49]

In addition to licensing digital content alone, the NPM can also consider a more flexible licensing strategy. The NPM should in fact pursue trademark licensing more proactively, as licensees and consumers value the NPM's brand name and trademark above others. The NPM should also consider a combined copyright and trademark licensing package to fully utilize the IP protection provided by the law for licensing by negotiation. Moreover, the NPM should also consider protecting its right to digital content through contracts. In terms of issues encountered with third parties regarding reproduction, editing, adaptation, use, and security of information, and those encountered with general users regarding the use of "open data," the existing regulations are incomplete and enhancement is advisable if the NPM wishes to better utilize its digital content.

Conclusion

Given the rapid advances in technology and increased demand from the public for mobile services, the NPM needs to consider, for the purposes of sustainable operation, how to continue to improve its services by adopting the appropriate technology for enhancing internal control, the virtualization/digitization of collections, managing digital assets, introducing innovative services to enhance the basic facilities of the NPM, and monitoring the storage environment of its archives. To enhance the visitor experience, the NPM could consider implementing geographical positioning services, mobile applications, interactive devices, virtual and expanded reality, and the use of social media. In terms of the value-added use of open information, the NPM should consider an integrated database, the licensing of digital assets, and the implementation of more innovative mobile applications.

In the future, as a collector and preserver of treasures from the Chinese culture, the NPM needs to respond to the changes in technology and public demand by providing integrated innovative services, offering additional services related to the exhibition, education, information, communication, and leisure functions of the museum, and incorporating the use of various mobile devices. These measures will increase the mobility of archived information and enhance the value of the NPM's vast archives, further revitalizing the NPM's existing business model by enhancing the visitor experience, narrowing the digital divide, promoting cultural sightseeing, and ultimately promoting the development of the country's cultural industry and becoming a model of this.

While working toward this goal, the NPM should bear legal and IP issues related to the innovated services and technology in mind so that it can avoid potential disputes and achieve its goal of allowing the public to fully explore the treasures preserved in the museum. Without considering legal and IP issues, not only the NPM cannot effective accomplish its goals as a Chinese culture preserver, but the utilization of its digitized collections through licensing arrangement will also be in jeopardy. On the contrary, if the NPM can proactively take IP and contractual design into consideration, it can create a more effective strategy in furthering its services through mobile and cloud platforms. With such advanced services in place, the NPM will definitely attract more visitors to explore and visit its collections, either physically or virtually.

Notes

1 Fan-Er Ai, iCloud bei hai, shi ge yiwai haishi yinmo? [iCloud is hacked! Is it an accident or conspiracy?] CommonWealth, Sep. 2, 2014, http://www.cw.com.tw/article/article.action?id=5060816. For news reports in English, see Daisuke Wakabayashi and Danny Yadron, *Apple Denies iCloud Breach – Tech Giant Says Celebrity Accounts Compromised by "Very Targeted Attack," Wall Street Journal*, Sep. 2014, http://online.wsj.com/articles/apple-celebrity-accounts-compromised-by-very-targeted-attack-1409683803

2 See Qiao-Wen Zheng, Dazao Xin Bowuguantiyan: Guoli Gugong Bowuyuan Gean Yanjiu [Implementing New Museum Experience: The Example of the National Palace Museum], Master Thesis, Institute of Business Administration, National Chengchi University, 2007.

3 I-Ju Tsai and Jiann-Min Yang, *Museum in the cloud: A preliminary study of digital exhibitions of National Palace Museum*, Research Notes in Information Science (RNIS), Volume 12, 2013.

4 Mei-Yi Lee, Bowuguan Xingdong Xuexi Guancha yu Wenti Tantao [Observations on museum mobile learning], Shuwei Diancang yu Xuexi Dianzibao [Digital Archive and Learning Online Newsletter], http://newsletter.teldap.tw/news/InsightReportContent.php?nid=5068&lid=583 (last visited Sep. 21, 2014). The importance of museums using the new technology lies in the concept of making good use of their collections by combining exhibited works with interactive onsite technology, and thus promoting value-added information via digital knowledge spreads and service platforms, and so forth, to fulfill the museums' educational function.

5 Directorate General of Budget, Accounting and Statistics, the Executive Yuan of the Republic of China (R.O.C.), Zhengfu Jiguan Zixun Tongbao [Taiwanese Statistical Data Book], Volume 285, Jul. 2011. The Program of the National Palace Museum Archive lies under the auspices of the iTaiwan project of the Research, Development and Evaluation Commissions, the Executive Yuan of the Republic of China (R.O.C.). The core concept of this is abbreviated to DNA, representing Device, Network, and Application. It applies the Web 2.0 concept in its development of digitized collections, and also expands its use to devices such as smartphones, tablet computers, portable digital gadgets, multimedia devices, and kiosks in conjunction with broadband Internet, optical fiber Internet, and wireless Wi-Fi and WiMAX technology.

6 Currently, the NPM cooperates with design houses and studios within the following structure. 1. The NPM is the provider of content, namely photography and replication archives. 2. The NPM publicly calls for professionals in the cultural and creative industries, allowing more opportunities for cooperation to be generated on a business-to-business basis, and successfully creating new value by developing a series of cultural and creative products based on the museum's collections. 3. The NPM publicly calls for production manufacturers to create the derivative

products. Both the collaboration with the cultural and creative professionals in developing relevant merchandise and the production of the designs chosen by the NPM go through a public bidding process. In some circumstances this process may take the form of a contest, for example the 2013 National Palace Museum 4th National Treasure Derivative Designs Contest.

7 Charles Moad, Edward Bachta, and Rob Stein, *Museums and Cloud Computing: Ready for Primetime, or Just Vaporware?* Indianapolis Museum of Art, USA, http://www.museumsandtheweb.com/mw2009/papers/moad/moad.html (last visited Sep. 16, 2014)

8 The services provided by cloud computing service providers can be grouped into three categories, namely "Software as a Service (SaaS)," "Platform as a Service (PaaS)," and "Infrastructure as a Service (IaaS)." Taking the construction of a physical marketplace as an example, the concept of IaaS can be interpreted as the area of land, PaaS as the buildings on that land, and SaaS as the merchants in those buildings. A wide range of options for museum-related cloud computing services exists from which to select, for example PastPerfect, Argus, TMS/EmBARK, and Archivist Toolkit as IaaS, and PastPerfectOnline, MiniSIS, and MusuemPlus as SaaS.

9 Joe Hoover, *Cloud Computing for Small Museums,* http://discussions.mnhs.org/mnlocalhistory/blog/2011/12/28/cloud-computing-for-small-museums/ (last visited Aug. 20, 2014).

10 Companies capable of providing cloud computing support services include Crash-Plan, Amazon Glacier, and Zmanda.

11 Guo-Ping Lin, Bowuguan Keji Yingyong Qianzhan Fenxi – Cong Horizon Report Tanqi [Museum Techonology Utilization Prospects – Analysis on the Horizon Report], 23 Bowuguanxue Jikan [Museology Quarterly], 2009.

12 Including the Metropolitan Museum of Art, the Museum of Modern Art, the Museo Nacional del Prado, the National Gallery of Art in Washington, DC, the Van Gogh Museum, and other globally renowned museums.

13 The Internet structure of ArtBabble involves all digital content from the museums and cultural institutions stored in the cloud storage spaces provided by Amazon. The webpages are constructed in the Linux-Apache-MySQL-PHP (LAMP) environment, with Drupal as the content management system. The Wowza multimedia system is used for video streaming because the digital content is directly stored in the cloud, allowing users to browse video clips without having to download any contents, which should greatly reduce Internet connection costs.

14 See http://www.vertnet.org, where user may log onto the official webpages of all of the participating museums. See also http://portal.vertnet.org/publishers, where direct information downloads are available by simply selecting a specific museum.

15 See the V-MusT website, http://www.v-must.net/. For a listing of the virtual museums, see http://www.v-must.net/virtual-museums/all.

16 Rua-Huan, Tsai, et al., *New ICT-enabled Services of National Palace Museum and their Designs,* 2012. Of these apps, the main focus is on the 13 iPhone apps and 9 iPad apps designed for renowned museums in the United States, the United Kingdom, and France.

17 M. E. Porter, *Competitive Advantage.* New York, NY: Free Press, 1997.

18 For detailed information, see http://www.amnh.org/apps/explorer.php (last visited Sep. 20, 2013).

19 For the latest version of the report, the NMC Horizon Report, 2013 Museum Edition, see http://www.nmc.org/publications/2013-horizon-report-museum This latest report focused on Bring Your Own Device (BYOD), crowdsourcing, electronic publication, location service, natural user interface, and preservation and conservation technologies. The report was first published in 2010; the

new museum-related technology listed then included mobiles, social media, AR, location-based services, gesture-based computing, and the semantic Web. The 2011 report focused on mobile apps, tablet computing, AR, electronic publishing, digital preservation, and smart objects, while the 2012 report covered mobile apps, social media, AR, open content, the Internet of Things, and natural user interfaces.

20 Location-based services (LBS) on portable devices are widely used by emergency services (E911) and for entertainment information (mapping services, navigation, domestic information, "Find My Friend" functions). Most mobile location services are fairly simple. As smartphone technology gradually advances, along with improvements in broadband and the increasing interest of customers in their surroundings, it is clear that there will be greater demand for mobile location service interactions.

21 For background information on the introduction of the iOS Louvre app, see Apple iTunes, preview of Musée du Louvre, http://itunes.apple.com/us/app/musee-du-louvre/id337339103?mt=8 (last visited Sep. 11, 2014).

22 Maria L. Gilbert, *Connect with Art Using Google Goggles and Our New Mobile Collection Pages!* Jan. 26, 2014, http://blogs.getty.edu/iris/connect-with-art-using-google-goggles-and-our-new-mobile-collection-pages/.

23 Introduction of the Getty Guide, http://www.getty.edu/visit/see_do/gettyguide.html (last visited Jul. 28, 2014).

24 See http://www.fieldmuseum.org (last visited Sep. 15, 2014).

25 Article 79 of copyright law specifically provides that "[f]or a literary or artistic work that has no economic rights or for which the economic rights have been extinguished, a plate maker who arranges and prints the said literary work, or in the case of an artistic work, a plate maker who photocopies, prints, or uses a similar method of reproduction and first publishes such reproduction based on such original artistic work, and duly records it in accordance with this Act, shall have the exclusive right to photocopy, print, or use similar methods of reproduction based on the plate."

26 Under article 79 section 2 of copyright law, the right of "plate right" is a 10-year exclusive right.

27 Under a "sweat-of-the-brow" doctrine, or "industrious collection" doctrine, the creator of a work, even without originality as required by copyright law, is still entitled to have his or her effort and expense protected pursuant to copyright law. Prior to *Feist* decision, U.S. courts recognized such doctrine. As demonstrated in the lower courts decisions in the *Feist* case.

28 499 U.S. 340 (1991). Although the question in *Feist* is whether Rural selected, coordinated, or arranged these uncopyrightable facts, that is, phone listings information, is protectable subject matter of copyright law, the court made it clear that the originality is essential to copyright protection. The Court therefore concluded that "We conclude that the names, towns, and telephone numbers copied by Feist were *not original* to Rural and therefore were not protected by the copyright in Rural's combined white and yellow pages directory. As a constitutional matter, *copyright protects only those constituent elements of a work that possess more than a de minimis quantum of creativity.* Rural's white pages, limited to basic subscriber information and arranged alphabetically, fall short of the mark." (Emphasis added) 499 U.S. 363.

29 Justice O'Conner, delivered the 9:0 opinion of the Court, examined the purpose of copyright and explained the standard of copyrightability as based on originality. The Court held that "[t]he *sine qua non* of copyright is originality. To qualify for copyright protection, a work must be original to the author." (citing *Harper & Row*, pp. 547–549.) Original, as the term is used in copyright, means only that the work was independently created by the author (as opposed to copied from other

works), and that it possesses at least some minimal degree of creativity." *Ib.* 499 U.S. 346.

30 Photography was initially criticized for lacking artistic merit and not copyrightable in the United States. It was not until *Burrow-Giles Lithographic Co. v. Sarony,* 111 U.S. 53 (1884) the United States Supreme Court held that photographs were copyrightable, to the extent of the photograph's original depiction of the subject. The Court distinguished between the subject of a photograph, which, in the case of a person is not copyrightable, and the creative decisions the photographer makes, such as choosing the lighting, posing, and costume of the subject. The Court granted copyright protection only to such *creative* elements of photographs. 111 U.S. at 60.

31 36 F. Supp. 2d 191 (S.D.N.Y. 1999). Actually, the court made two decisions in this case. The first one was applying UK law in deciding the issue, 25 F. Supp. 2d 421 (S.D.N.Y. 1998). The second decision is according U.S. copyright law, after inferred from the provisions of the Berne Convention Implementation Act of 1988 (BCIA), and the absence of U.S. law to the contrary, that Congress had not granted foreign law the power to determine the issue of copyrightability in U.S. copyright actions.

32 191 F.2d 99 (2d Cir. 1951).

33 The court cited *Past Pluto Productions v. Dana,* 627 F. Supp. 1435, 1441 (S.D.N.Y. 1986) (citing *L. Batlin & Son, Inc.,* 536 F.2d at 491)). *Accord, Durham Ind., Inc. v. Tomy Corp.,* 630 F.2d 905, 910 (2d Cir. 1980) and held that "[t]he requisite 'distinguishable variation,' moreover, is not supplied by a change of medium," as "production of a work of art in a different medium cannot by itself constitute the originality required for copyright protection." FN 38 of *Bridgeman.*

34 The court cited Prof. Melville Nimmer's *Nimmer on Copyright,* which stated that there "appear to be at least two situations in which a photograph should be denied copyright for lack of originality." The court held one of those situations to be directly relevant, namely that "where a photograph of a photograph or other printed matter is made that amounts to nothing more than slavish copying." *Nimmer on Copyright,* § 2.08[E][2], at 2–131.

35 528 F.3d 1258 (10th Cir. 2008).

36 The appeals court held, "In *Bridgeman Art Library,* the court examined whether color transparencies of public domain works of art were sufficiently original for copyright protection, ultimately holding that, as 'exact photographic copies of public domain works of art,' they were not." Moreover, the *Meshwerks* ruling also overruled a 1959 case, *Alva Studios, Inc. v. Winninger,* 177 F. Supp. 265 (S.D.N.Y. 1959), in which the district court enforced a copyright claimed on a reproduction sculpture of Rodin's *Hand of God.* The appeal court not only specifically cited the Supreme Court's *Feist* decision in rejecting difficulty of labor or expense as a consideration in copyrightability, but also stated that "[w]e are not convinced that the single case to which we are pointed where copyright was awarded for a 'slavish copy' remains good law."

37 Cf. Taiwan Supreme Court, 92 Tai Shan Zi No. 1424 (2003), 97 Shin Zi Shan I Zi No. 70 (2008), 98 Ming Zu Shu Zi No. 8 (2009).

38 The Federal District Court ruled against the plaintiff (for the full judgment, *see* 908 F. Supp. 640 [W. D. Wis. 1996]), but the Seventh Circuit overruled this decision and made a decision in favor of the plaintiff (*ProCD, Inc. v. Zeidenberg,* 86 F.3d 1447 [7th Cir. 1996]).

39 499 U.S. 340 (1991).

40 ProCD, 86 F.3d at 1449, 1454–1455.

41 Maureen A. O'Rourke, *Copyright Preemption after the ProCD Case: A Market-Based Approach,* 12 Berkeley Tech. L. J. 53, 54 (1997).

42 Lisa Di Valentino, *Conflict between Contract Law and Copyright Law in Canada: Do License Agreements Trump Users' Rights?* (January 4, 2014). Available at SSRN, http://ssrn.com/abstract=2396028.

43 606 F.3d 1153, 1155 (9th Cir. 2010), *reh'g en banc granted,* 623 F.3d 912 (9th Cir. 2010), *rev'd en banc,* 649 F.3d 975 (9th Cir.), *cert. denied,* 132 S. Ct. 550 (2011).

44 683 F.3d 424, 428 (2d Cir. 2012).

45 Michael Palmisciano, *Resurrecting the Spirit of the Law: Copyright Preemption and Idea Protection in Montz v. Pilgrim Films,* 53 B.C.L. Rev. E. Supp. 209 (2012).

46 National Palace Museum Publications and Images Licensing agreement, http://www.npm.gov.tw/zh-tw/Article.aspx?sNo=02000039 (last visited at Aug. 10, 2014).

47 Questions and Answers to National Palace Museum Publications and Images Licensing, http://www.npm.gov.tw/zh-tw/Article.aspx?sNo=02000183 (last visited at Sep. 15, 2014).

48 Procedure of National Palace Museum Brand Licensing agreement, http://www.npm.gov.tw/zh-tw/Article.aspx?sNo=03004037 (last visited at Aug. 10, 2014).

49 Whether the NPM can cite its self-imposed regulations and assert them in litigation is already being questioned. For example, in a case involving the licensing of a graphic and text database built jointly by the NPM and Airiti Inc., the NPM argued that Airiti Inc. breached the license by allowing its clients to use the database after the license had expired, and sought punitive damages of 10 times the royalty received under article 12 of the National Palace Museum Cultural and Creative Products Regulations. However, the Shilin District Court held that Airiti Inc. was only required to pay general damages, because the NPM's regulations were void and null as they went beyond the scope of the Cultural Heritage Preservation Act. For details of the case, see Shilin District Court, 102 Zhi No. 9 (2013) (102 年度智字第 9 號) civil judgment. Note that had the NPM specified such punitive damages in its license agreement, the Court would have held these terms to be enforceable despite the exorbitant amount, but would have been able to impose some deductions. The outcome of this case differed greatly from the current contracting practice of "letting the relevant laws apply on matters not specified in the contract," as the regulations relied on were held to be null and void and thus did not form part of the license.

Bibliography

Ai, Fan-Er. (2014). iCloud bei hai, shi ge yiwai haishi yinmo? *[iCloud is hacked! Is it an accident or conspiracy?].* CommonWealth. Retrieved on 2/9/2014 from http://www.cw.com.tw/article/article.action?id=5060816

Directorate General of Budget, Accounting and Statistics, the Executive Yuan of the Republic of China (R.O.C.). (2011, July). Zhengfu Jiguan Zixun Tongbao *[Taiwanese statistical data book],* 285.

Di Valentino, Lisa. (2014, January 4). *Conflict between contract law and copyright law in Canada: Do license agreements trump users' rights?* Retrieved from http://ssrn.com/abstract=2396028

Gilbert, Maria L. *Connect with art using Google goggles and our new mobile collection pages!* Retrieved on 26/1/2014 from http://blogs.getty.edu/iris/connect-with-art-using-google-goggles-and-our-new-mobile-collection-pages/

Hoover, Joe. *Cloud computing for small museums.* Retrieved from http://discussions.mnhs.org/mnlocalhistory/blog/2011/12/28/cloud-computing-for-small-museums/

I-Ju, Tsai, and Yang, Jiann-Min. (2013). Museum in the cloud: A preliminary study of digital exhibitions of National Palace Museum, *Research Notes in Information Science (RNIS), 12,* 183–188.

Lee, Mei-Yi. (2011). Bowuguan Xingdong Xuexi Guancha yu Wenti Tantao *[Observations on museum mobile learning],* Shuwei Diancang yu Xuexi Dianzibao [Digital archive and learning online newsletter]. Retrieved from http://newsletter.teldap.tw/news/InsightReportContent.php?nid=5068&lid=583

Lin, Guo-Ping. Bowuguan Keji Yingyong Qianzhan Fenxi – Cong Horizon Report Tanqi *[Museum techonology utilization prospects – Analysis on the horizon report],* 23 Bowuguanxue Jikan [Museology Quarterly], 2009.

Nimmer, and Nimmer, Nimmer's. (2007). *Nimmer on copyright.* (2007) § 19D.03 [C][2].

Moad, Charles, Bachta, Edward, and Stein, Rob. (2009). *Museums and cloud computing: Ready for primetime, or just vaporware?* Indianapolis Museum of Art, USA. Retrieved from http://www.museumsandtheweb.com/mw2009/papers/moad/moad.html

The NMC Horizon Report. (2013). *Museum Edition.* Retrieved from http://www.nmc.org/publications/2013-horizon-report-museum

O'Rourke, Maureen A. (1997). Copyright preemption after the ProCD case: A market-based approach, *Berkeley Technology Law Journal, 12*(1), 53–54.

Palmisciano, Michael. (2012). Resurrecting the spirit of the law: Copyright preemption and idea protection in Montz v. Pilgrim Films, *53 B.C.L. Rev., E. Supplement,* 209, 213–214.

Porter, M. E. (1997). *Competitive advantage.* New York, NY: Free Press.

Tsaih, R-H., Lin, Q.-P., Han, T.-S., Chao, Y.-T., Chan, H.-C. (2012). *New ICT-enabled services of National Palace Museum and their designs.* 17th International Conference on Cultural Economics, Kyoto, Japan.

Wakabayashi, Daisuke, and Yadron, Danny. (2014, September 2). Apple denies iCloud breach – Tech giant says celebrity accounts compromised by "Very Targeted Attack," *Wall Street Journal.* Retrieved from http://online.wsj.com/articles/apple-celebrity-accounts-compromised-by-very-targeted-attack-1409683803

Zheng, Qiao-Wen, and Bowuguantiyan, Dazao Xin. (2007). Guoli Gugong Bowuyuan Gean Yanjiu *[Implementing New Museum Experience: The Example of the National Palace Museum],* Master Thesis, Institute of Business Administration, National Chengchi University.

Court decisions

Alfred Bell & Co. v. Catalda Fine Arts, Inc., 191 F.2d 99 (2d Cir. 1951).

Bridgeman Art Library v. Corel Corp., 36 F. Supp. 2d 191 (S.D.N.Y. 1999).

Burrow-Giles Lithographic Co. v. Sarony, 111 U.S. 53 (1884).

Feist Publications, Inc., v. Rural Telephone Service Co., 499 U.S. 340 (1991).

Forest Park Pictures v. Universal Television Network, Inc., 683 F.3d 424, 428 (2d Cir. 2012).

Meshwerks v. Toyota, 528 F.3d 1258 (10th Cir. 2008).

Montz v. Pilgrim Films & Television, Inc., 606 F.3d 1153, 1155 (9th Cir. 2010), *reh'g en banc granted,* 623 F.3d 912 (9th Cir. 2010), *rev'd en banc,* 649 F.3d 975 (9th Cir.), *cert. denied,* 132 S. Ct. 550 (2011).

ProCD, Inc. v. Zeidenberg, 86 F.3d 1447 (7th Cir. 1996)
Studios, Inc. v. Winninger, 177 F. Supp. 265 (S.D.N.Y. 1959).
Shilin District Court, 102 Zhi No. 9 (2013).
Taiwan Supreme Court, 92 Tai Shan Zi No.1424 (2003).
Taiwan Supreme Court, 97 Shin Zi Shan I Zi No. 70 (2008).
Taiwan Supreme Court, 98 Ming Zu Shu Zi No. 8 (2009).

Museum websites

The American Science and Historical Museum, Explorer, http://www.amnh.org/apps/explorer.php

Apple iTunes, preview of Musée du Louvre, http://itunes.apple.com/us/app/musee-du-louvre/id337339103?mt=8

The Field Museum of Natural History in Chicago, http://www.fieldmuseum.org

Introduction of the Getty Guide, http://www.getty.edu/visit/see_do/gettyguide.html

National Palace Museum Publications and Images Licensing agreement, http://www.npm.gov.tw/zh-tw/Article.aspx?sNo=02000039

Questions and Answers to National Palace Museum Publications and Images Licensing, http://www.npm.gov.tw/zh-tw/Article.aspx?sNo=02000183

Procedure of National Palace Museum Brand Licensing agreement, http://www.npm.gov.tw/zh-tw/Article.aspx?sNo=03004037

The VertNet, http://portal.vertnet.org/publishers

The Virtual Museums, http://www.v-must.net/virtual-museums/all

The V-MusT (Virtual Museum Transnational Network), http://www.v-must.net/

Part III
Technology-related issues

7 Developing the cloud services adoption strategy for the National Palace Museum

Hsin-Lu Chang and Kai Wang

Introduction

Cloud computing provides a new platform for enterprises. Its core concept encompasses on-demand access and pay-per-use, which compete directly with traditional desktop or handheld computers. The unique characteristics of cloud computing provide incentives for companies to adopt this new technology. Essentially, the cloud is an enabling force for business evolution that extends beyond technology, allowing companies to re-engineer their corporate strategy more efficiently and effectively. The cloud reduces information technology (IT) costs and offers mobility and collaboration, eliminating the need to maintain a computational infrastructure of operating systems and low-level utilities. The cloud thus makes it easier for companies to implement solutions or combine enabling technologies in response to changing market needs and, to some extent, to reduce or eliminate information latency.

Cloud service technologies thus aim to improve asset utilization, aggregate demand, accelerate system consolidation, improve productivity in the development of applications, provide better responses to urgent client needs and better links with emerging technologies, and more. However, some companies are likely to find that the outcomes of cloud service development differ. A set of resources and capabilities that enables the effective use of cloud service technologies is required, to improve the ability of organizations to develop successful cloud service strategies. Most companies lack a clear picture of what these capabilities are and how they should be built up. Companies also do not know whether they are ready or not to deploy such cloud service technologies. In addition to identifying critical cloud service technologies, therefore, there are many implementation and managerial issues to be addressed, such as assessing the capabilities and readiness of an organization regarding application of these technologies and exploring both the enablers of and barriers to the adoption and diffusion of cloud service technologies.

The National Palace Museum (NPM) has recognized the potential benefits of cloud services for museum education and visitor connection. Cloud services can offer the NPM a different way of organizing and presenting information in multiple levels, perspectives, and dimensions, transforming the museum from a "collection-driven" museum to an "audience-driven" one. However, several issues need to be addressed before cloud services can be implemented in the NPM. First, as the NPM has a relatively conservative attitude toward IT, aligning its functional and operating model with a cloud-based model for the use of IT resources and services will be problematic. Second, ensuring the security of museum objects in the cloud, to prevent the potential loss of control and data, is an important issue. Finally, the NPM needs to address legal issues such as liability, data disclosure, and legislation. To better understand these strategic issues, we will study the adoption of cloud service technologies in the NPM. Our goal is to develop a roadmap for better cloud service management so that the NPM will be able to choose adoption priorities, design diffusion paths, and predict value outcomes.

Potential cloud service applications for the NPM

In 2001, the NPM began a 5-year digital archiving project, with the objective of establishing a complete digitized format for most of the objects in the museum's collection. Through the Internet, users around the world will be able to search for knowledge and information on museum objects. To further this aim, in 2010, the NPM launched a cultural and creative environment project, in line with the government's "i-Taiwan Project – Cultural and Creative Society," to provide an entertaining means of appreciating interdisciplinary cultural creativity through combining cultural and technological elements, developing digital content such as cultural and creative films, marketing these globally via websites, and enhancing the aesthetic literacy of the people. In 2013, the NPM initiated a mobile service project, a sub-project of the overarching Mobile e-Government project, with the goal of providing a mobile tour-guide service. Visitors to the museum can use their mobile devices to obtain real-time exhibition information and design a personalized itinerary. The Web 2.0 concept will be applied to the design of a social platform service, allowing experiences relating to museum objects, exhibition, education, and research to be shared.

Cloud service development may complement these NPM digital projects. We have identified three categories of cloud service that the NPM could consider developing, internal management, open data and value-adding, and experience services (Figure 7.1). For example, infrastructure as a service (IaaS) could provide on-demand storage space and computing capacity for digital archiving. The NPM could also develop platform as a service (PaaS) for video channels and integrated databases. In addition, alternative software as a service (SaaS) could be used in mobile and social platforms.

We now review the relevant cloud service developments in leading museums worldwide. The experiences of these museums can act as a reference for the NPM in developing its own cloud service portfolios.

Cloud-Based Internal Management. The Jewish Women's Archive (JWA) was founded in November 1995. Its mission is to document the lives of American Jewish women from all walks of life and to reach out to the general public and

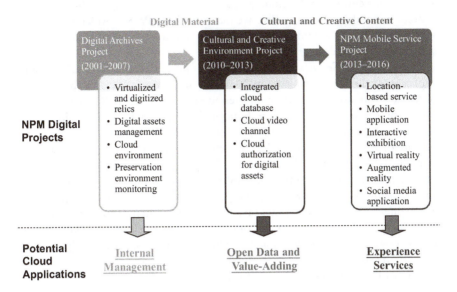

Figure 7.1 NPM digital projects and potential cloud applications

scholars. As this organization has no dedicated IT staff and no in-house expertise, they decided to adopt Amazon's IaaS (so-called Amazon Web Services) for preservation and backup. The money saved in the IT area can be used instead for gathering oral histories and processing them.

Open Data and Value-adding. VertNet (www.vertnet.org) is a searchable online portal that links four distributed vertebrate database networks, which currently comprise 171 collections from 12 countries and 52 additional collections (20 countries) that are committed to participation. Collectively, these networks have successfully demonstrated community data sharing and cooperative data management. VertNet's computing resources are consolidated on the cloud via the Google App Engine PaaS. Under this new model, contributors use a Web-based administrative interface to create accounts, describe their datasets, define usage restrictions and citation information, add contact information, and (later) access information about usage statistics. The data store in the cloud contains the primary data published by all of the contributors as persistently available records, uniquely identifiable by a data store key. Compared with the previous Web portal model, this cloud-based model provides not only a platform on which to store the results of collaboration (such as geo-references and user annotations) associated directly with the primary data they are intended to improve, but also one on which to build innovative applications (e.g., analyses, visualizations, and workflows).

ArtBabble is another example of websites and applications being hosted in the cloud. In late 2008, the Indianapolis Museum of Art created an online video website, called ArtBabble (www.artbabble.org), dedicated to art-related content.

The site runs entirely in the cloud and allows streaming of high-definition video content in a scalable and cost-effective manner. Using PaaS provided by Amazon Web Services, costs are minimized by only paying for the actual bandwidth and storage used monthly.

User Experience Services. The Museum of London introduced a mobile phone application called Streetmuseum in 2010, as part of the opening of the Galleries of Modern London. Streetmuseum uses augmented reality (AR) to give users a unique perspective of old and new London. The app guides users to sites across London where more than 200 images of the capital, taken from the Museum of London's art and photographic collection, can be viewed on-site, essentially offering users a window through time. To give users some historical context, each image is accompanied by a little information about the scene. The museum has also launched a more advanced version of Streetmuseum, called Londinum, which directs users to Roman sites on a map and uses video and audio elements to showcase a 2000-year-old Roman London that users can immerse themselves in. Users are guided around the capital to where they can use a virtual digging tool to unearth artifacts, listen to the sounds of the Roman city, and watch AR scenes of Roman London presented against the modern backdrop.

The research framework

As the NPM began its planning for the adoption of cloud services, the authors were given the task of providing a framework for potential cloud services for the NPM, identifying corresponding readiness factors, and evaluating the effects of these potential cloud services.

The research framework is outlined in Figure 7.2. Based on the discussion in Part II, we propose the following cloud service applications for the NPM:

- **Infrastructure as a Service (IaaS):** The infrastructure of IT, including storage, servers, networks, and other fundamental computing resources, is provided as a service. Potential IaaS for the NPM includes data analytics, data backup/storage/synchronization, disaster recovery systems, cloud storage, cloud servers, and server load balancing.
- **Platform as a Service (PaaS):** Computing platforms and solutions are provided as a service, including the facilities and tools required by application programmers for design, development, and testing. PaaS thus provides a complete development lifecycle environment for users. Potential PaaS for the NPM includes cloud databases, website hosting, and online development platforms.
- **Software as a Service (SaaS):** All types of application, whether these have simple functions such as Web-based email or are software with complex functions, are provided as a service. Potential SaaS for the NPM include internal applications such as software for collaboration, email, office productivity, Web conferencing, and project management. The NPM can also consider using SaaS for external customers, such as those using social networking, Web 2.0, and mobile platforms.

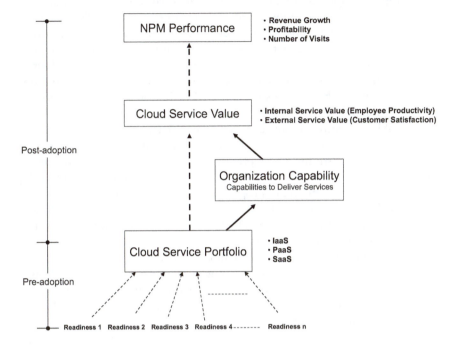

Figure 7.2 Research framework

We have sought to understand the readiness of the NPM for cloud services in each of the service categories above. In the following sections, we outline the readiness factors that affect the adoption of cloud services by the NPM, uncover the set of related cloud service value metrics, and evaluate how these would be affected by organizational capability.

Readiness for cloud services

We began by conducting interviews with Taiwanese cloud service providers to discover how they evaluated the readiness of companies to adopt cloud services. This produced an exhaustive list of readiness factors. We then conducted an interview with the NPM to determine which of these readiness factors were relevant in the museum sector. We identified five major readiness elements, which are summarized as follows.

Safety readiness

Maintaining the safety of collections in exhibition spaces is one of the most important tasks of museum managers (Gilmore and Rentschler, 2002). Priceless collections could be stolen (James, 2000) or destroyed by incidents such as fire (Spafford-Ricci and Graham, 2000). Similarly, a museum's digital collection and online information could be copied or destroyed. There are two aspects of safety that are important for digital collections. The first is regulatory compliance. Museum managers are obliged to consider issues of copyright, in particular before digitizing collections to display in the cloud (Hirtle, Hudson, and Kenyon, 2009). Some artistic works, literary works, musical compositions, or films belong to their authors for a limited period only, whereas others may belong to the public but require "curatorial control," meaning that museums may be able to control the dissemination of their treasures through licensing agreements or digital rights management such as watermarking (Torsen and Anderson, 2010), with the aim of preserving cherished items over time (Smith, 2005). When placing a collection online, a museum should respect its authorship and follow the law of intellectual property carefully, even if the items are "orphan works," collections for which the lawful owner cannot be identified and located after a reasonable search (Brito and Dooling, 2005), or are "publicly accessible" collections to which the public has ready access. The second aspect concerns data security. Online, unscrupulous intent is generally growing; the issue of data security for cloud services is therefore of great concern. Appropriate defensive measures should be put in place. It may be necessary to clarify who is legally responsible for a security attack on a cloud system. How are such attacks dealt with to reduce and limit any damage?

Service readiness

There are two major service readiness issues. The first is service design and management. As an educational organization, a museum provides three core services, education, accessibility, and communication with its users (Gilmore and Rentschler, 2002). Cloud services provide new ways for people to interact with collections, rather than simply viewing exhibitions. Cloud services can also assist with service differentiation in terms of innovative content, the speed and agility of business processes, and variations in exhibition style and spaces (Loebbecke, Thomas, and Ullrich, 2012). In addition, cloud services encourage two-way communications between museums and visitors, and between exhibitions and viewers. In view of the advantages offered by cloud services, the design and management of services on the cloud is important for today's museums.

The second issue to be addressed by museums is the management of service contracts. Many museums source their cloud services from external service providers and thus share the essential risk profile of all outsourcing contracts in terms of opportunistic behavior, shirking, poaching, and opportunistic renegotiation (Clemons and Chen, 2011). As there are multiple cloud providers offering a variety of service options in terms of pricing, performance, and feature sets (Li, Chen, and Wang, 2011), museums in the process of adopting such services should be mindful of contractual issues such as performance, security (including data citizenship and data residence), and legal recourse (Clemons and Chen, 2011).

Environmental readiness

Museums need to consider the competitive landscape and maturity of the cloud market and examine both fully commercial and government-provided cloud services (Kundra, 2011). If cloud markets are not dominated by a small number of players, museums can reduce the risk of vendor lock-in by moving services from one provider to another. The number of adopters within the museum industry may also affect a particular museum's intention to adopt cloud services. As other museums adopt new technologies, a particular museum may become increasingly aware of this and be under pressure to follow suit (Low and Chen, 2011).

Technical readiness

There are three major issues regarding technical readiness. The first is Internet connection quality. Cloud services are generally built and connected via the Internet, suggesting that these services should always be bundled with appropriate connectivity. Cloud computing is a recent IT trend that moves computing and data away from desktop and portable PCs to large data centers. Cloud computing refers both to applications delivered as services over the Internet and to the actual cloud infrastructure, the hardware and software in the data centers that provide these services (Dikaiakos, Katsaros, Mehra, Pallis, and Vakali, 2009). The second issue is virtualization. As cloud computing is a multi-tenant environment for running virtual systems, it provides access to virtual CPUs, memory, storage networks, IP addresses, firewalls, and cataloging capabilities. The implementation of virtualization requires a company to make various changes to virtualize its current equipment and facilitate inner processes (Preimesberger, 2011). Typical requirements of virtualized data centers include the setting up of new tenants, backing up of databases, management of the customization and configurations of tenants, and the obtaining of patches for and newer versions of software. Clearly, there are several important issues related to virtualization that require preparation for those intending to introduce private clouds (Rochwerger et al., 2009). Finally, a cloud infrastructure is often operated solely within a single organization and is managed by that organization or a third party regardless of whether it is located on or off the premises (Dillon, Chen Wu, and Chang, 2010). Self-owned IT will therefore be necessary and some "head room" will be required for managing normal peaks in demand. Infrastructure systems that are able to operate efficiently at reduced loads will reduce the cost of allowing for this head room (Emerson Network Power, 2010).

Organizational readiness

Museums need to consider whether they are ready to migrate services to the cloud. Issues include the availability of capable and reliable managers, the ability to negotiate appropriate service-level agreements, the required technical experience, supportive managerial cultures, and financial stability. Finding ways to meet the dynamically changing needs and expectations of cloud computing is a difficult

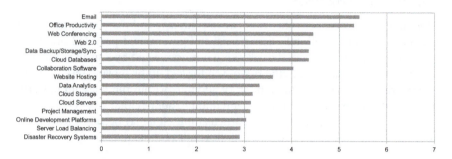

Figure 7.3 Readiness of cloud services for adoption

task for museum professionals (Marty, 2008). Museums that adopt cloud services need to provide appropriate training in implementing and using the associated technology (Subashini and Kavitha, 2011). Museums, like corporations, may be either conservative about or attracted to new knowledge. Building cloud services without a museum culture of pursuing progressiveness will give rise to many obstacles during the process of adoption.

We conducted a survey of IT executives in 155 companies to ascertain the readiness for adoption of various cloud services. We asked the respondents to rate the five categories of readiness factor for each cloud service on a 7-point scale (7 = extremely ready, 1 = not at all ready). Figure 7.3 shows the cloud services ranked by their average readiness scores. We found that the services deemed to be ready for adoption were mostly SaaS and Web-related services such as email, Web conferencing, and Web 2.0.

Measuring cloud service value

As the benefits offered by cloud services can render an enterprise's operations more efficient and improve business value (Aljabre, 2012; Géczy, Izumi, and Hasida, 2012), we can regard cloud service value as the benefits that the cloud brings to the enterprise. After reviewing both research and informal articles on cloud services, we grouped the performance improvements that may be obtained from cloud services into internal and external service value components. Internal service value components focus on improvements in employee productivity and external service value components focus on improvements in customer relationships.

Internal service value

The components of internal service value can be summarized as follows.

Efficiency. Cloud computing can reduce redundancy in hardware and software investment, and lower the cost of maintenance and management. An enterprise can then use the freed-up resources in other investments to increase profits (Aljabre, 2012). Cloud computing also involves utility-style payment, in which enterprises only pay for the resources or services that they actually use (Géczy et al., 2012).

Flexibility. Flexibility allows enterprises to use resources or services more elastically. Cloud computing services can scale capacity up or down depending on the consumer's need (Gartner Report, 2009). These services allow an enterprise to scale services up whenever it needs to and to then relinquish them after the enterprise accomplishes its goal and needs to scale down. This gives enterprises the ability to handle periods of peak demand (Dillon et al., 2010).

Mobility. Mobility allows enterprises more convenient access to resources or services. Cloud computing services are delivered through the Internet, so employees can readily use the information, resources, and services held in the cloud regardless of location. Due to this mobility, cloud computing provides a collaborative environment for enterprises because multiple users can connect to the cloud services at the same time and can run cloud services on different types of operating system (Aljabre, 2012).

External service value

Cloud services are expected to provide the following two benefits.

Innovation. Cloud services allow enterprises to focus on innovation and current business problems without the distractions and costs of building up and maintaining an IT environment (Patil and Klein, 2011). For example, customers may use SaaS solutions to obtain enterprise information from any location, a capability that would be very costly and time-consuming to provide with traditional IT systems (Kundra, 2011). In effect, enterprises can shift their focus from asset ownership to service management. Through collaborating with cloud vendors, enterprises can take advantage of these vendors' innovation engines, by comparing their current services with contemporary marketplace offerings or examining their customer satisfaction scores, overall usage trends, and functionality to identify the need for potential improvements via service innovation.

Collaboration. Cloud services allow the key players in businesses to be brought together easily. For example, Amazon's cloud computing services can help teams, customers, and suppliers to meet, share ideas, and carry out business transactions more effectively and without delay (Aljabre, 2012). Market information is available to business partners through the cloud and collaboration is enhanced. Both business profits and relationships may grow.

In the second part of our survey, we asked the respondents to rate the importance of each value component in terms of the benefits expected or gained from implementing cloud services. Importance was measured on a 7-point scale (7 = extremely important, 1 = not at all important). Figure 7.4 shows the cloud service value metrics (aggregated over the 155 responding companies) that were regarded as being the most important. We found that the metrics deemed to be important were mainly internal service value components such as mobility and flexibility. The underlying causes are discussed in the following section.

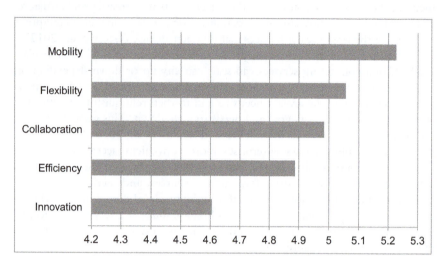

Figure 7.4 Importance ratings for cloud service value metrics

Organizational capabilities affected by cloud adoption

Figure 7.4 indicates the expected effects of adopting cloud services. We propose that these effects will manifest at the level of adopting alternative cloud service applications and, ultimately, at the enterprise level. Cloud service applications are expected to affect three fundamental organizational capabilities, which in turn will affect internal and external service value.

Resource Utilization Capability. Total control of IT resources comes at a price. Software must be installed, configured, and updated. The computational infrastructure of operating systems and low-level utilities must be maintained. Every update to an operating system requires a cascade of subsequent updates to other programs. Adopting cloud services is expected to reduce the effort required to manage IT resources and to enable rapid and continuing fulfillment of demand for IT resources. As IT resources held in the cloud are charged for based on the quantity used and these IT resources are shared across a number of end users, it is expected that better use will be made of the IT resources. This resource pooling may also provide economies of scale at the computing and services levels.

Integration Capability. Integration misalignment occurs when enterprises are not able to coordinate their internal and external resources efficiently. Enterprises often encounter problems with both internal and external integration. Internal integration requires alignment between the existing IT and business models. External integration requires alignment between the internal IT model and the IT models of external parties. As cloud services offer end users advantages in terms of mobility and collaboration, this is expected to facilitate the integration of an enterprise's existing IT model with the cloud-based model of resources and services (Géczy et al., 2012). In addition, software offered as an Internet-based service can be developed, tested, and run on a computing platform of the vendor's choosing. Connectivity between business partners is thus improved.

Service Reconfiguration Capability. Service reconfiguration capability is the ability to identify the needs of a firm's internal or external environment, and to immediately reconfigure the firm's services to meet the changing demands of users and organizations. Cloud environments often have thousands of applications available to rapidly meet specific needs. Companies can usually "try before they buy," allowing them to be more experimental in their approach to solving complex problems. Cloud service vendors normally also provide management tools to allow users to control and modify their subscriptions with ease. The effect of the cloud on the enterprise becomes more measurable, providing opportunities for enterprises to be more proactive regarding service reconfiguration in response to changing environments.

It is expected that improvement in these capabilities will lead to an increase in the performance of adopted cloud services, which will ultimately affect the financial metrics of firm performance.

Assessment of cloud maturity

Based on the results of our survey, we distinguished Best-in-Class companies from Industry Average companies and Laggards. We used service value and organizational capability as performance criteria for classifying each company into these

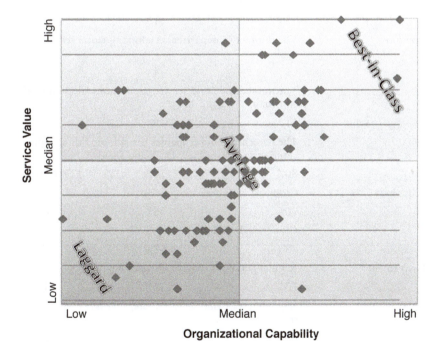

Figure 7.5 Cloud maturity assessment

maturity classes. Best-in-Class organizations demonstrated higher capability and perceived higher value from cloud adoption than their Industry Average and Laggard peers. They scored within the top 24 percent on aggregate performance. Industry Average companies scored within the middle 40 percent on aggregate performance and Laggards within the bottom 36 percent.

The survey results showed that the Best-in-Class organizations shared many characteristics that underpinned their successful adoption of cloud services. Acquiring these characteristics may be the key to the high performance of Best-in-Class organizations. These characteristics, summarized in Table 7.1, may serve as a guideline for best practice and are directly correlated with Best-in-Class performance. For instance, 73 percent of Best-in-Class organizations actively created teams and assigned responsibility to them for maintaining cloud service applications. To ensure that there were sufficient IT resources to support their cloud

Table 7.1 A summary of some characteristics shared by cloud adopters

	Best-in-Class	*Average*	*Laggards*
Resource	The percentage of the IT budget that supports cloud service applications:		
	37%	22%	19%
	Individuals or teams are assigned the responsibility of maintaining cloud service applications:		
	73%	41%	16%
Adoption	The number of departments adopting cloud service applications:		
	5	4	3
	The number of cloud service applications adopted by the company:		
	11	9	7
	The percentage of companies that adopted three types of cloud service (i.e., IaaS, PaaS, and SaaS):		
	80%	70%	68%
Technology	Cloud-to-enterprise integration:		
	90%	55%	24%
	Cloud-to-cloud integration:		
	87%	53%	9%
Management	Regular and consistent performance monitoring:		
	77%	53%	18%
	Alignment of cloud service strategy with overall company strategy:		
	83%	51%	11%
	Full staff training on cloud service applications:		
	70%	45%	18%

services, Best-in-Class organizations invested more than a third of their IT budgets in the cloud (37 percent currently).

Although multiple cloud service applications were used by the adopting companies, the most pronounced differentiator between the Best-in-Class and other organizations was their ability to address the integration challenges posed by cloud computing. Effective strategies for integration, both within the cloud and between the cloud and an enterprise, enable the enterprise to transfer and translate data seamlessly and quickly in real time, which is crucial to business success. Another characteristic that was common among the Best-in-Class was the effort made by the organizations to ensure that cloud service strategies aligned with their overall corporate goals (currently at a level of 83 percent). In addition, 77 percent of the Best-in-Class organizations conducted regular and consistent performance monitoring. As companies begin to move enterprise applications to the cloud, monitoring and management of the performance and availability of applications becomes essential to allow administrators to rapidly identify poor user experiences and correct any problems before these affect the users. Finally, cloud training is necessary because many employees do not feel confident to manage this new IT environment. As shown in Table 7.1, 70 percent of the Best-in-Class organizations were more likely to provide employees with education and training on cloud technology.

Roadmap for implementing cloud-based services

The results of our survey suggest that different services require different levels of effort and that some services are more ready to move to the cloud than others. Based on this analysis, it would appear that the implementation of some cloud service applications may need to be prioritized over others. Figure 7.6 shows

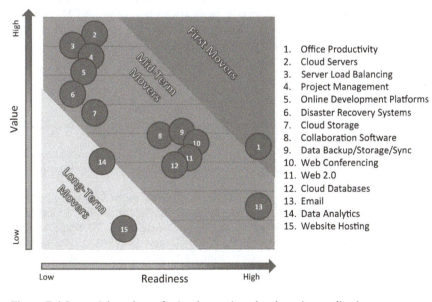

Figure 7.6 Potential roadmap for implementing cloud service applications

which services can be considered to be First Movers, Medium-term Movers, and Long-term Movers. We define First Movers as high-value and ready-for-adoption cloud services, which could be the first to move to the cloud. Office productivity services appear to be the most promising in this respect.

Closing remarks

The insights obtained from this study are applicable to the NPM's focus on the development of cloud services. We identified an implicit set of cloud service applications that the NPM can use to serve internal users and external visitors/customers. Our evaluation (Figure 7.3) suggests that different applications have different levels of readiness for adoption, as the features and functions of the applications may affect their readiness in different ways. A variety of value metrics are proposed to offer the NPM insight into evaluating and positioning those cloud services that are likely to yield the most benefit (Figure 7.4).

Another important insight resulting from our evaluation is that the performance of adopted cloud service applications depends on a combination of specific organizational capabilities. The NPM may evaluate its cloud performance against that of Best-in-Class organizations (Figure 7.5). Regardless of whether the NPM is trying to move its cloud service performance from Laggard to Industry Average, or from Industry Average to Best-in-Class, Table 7.1 provides several actions that may assist with the necessary performance improvements.

Although the data collected in this study were not targeted at the museum sector, they offer both a framework for assessing cloud readiness and maturity, and specific findings that may assist the development of a cloud strategy by museums such as the NPM. We believe that it is important to evaluate the readiness and effects of cloud service applications before the NPM develops its own cloud services. Increased effort could then be directed toward the dissemination and deployment of high-impact and adoption-ready services (Figure 7.6).

References

Aljabre, A. (2012). Cloud computing for increased business value, *International Journal of Business and Social Science*, 3(1), 234–238.
Brito, J., and Dooling, B. (2005). An orphan works affirmative defense to copyright infringement actions, *Michigan Telecommunications and Technology Law Review*, 12(1), 75–113.
Clemons, E. K., and Chen, Y. (2011, January). *Making the decision to contract for cloud services: Managing the risk of an extreme form of it outsourcing*, Proceedings of 44th Hawaii International Conference on System Sciences, 1–10. Kauai, Hawaii.
Dikaiakos, M., Katsaros, D., Mehra, P., Pallis, G., and Vakali, A. (2009). Cloud computing: Distributed Internet computing for IT and scientific research, *Internet Computing, IEEE*, 13(5), 10–13.

Dillon, T., Wu, Chen, and Chang, E. (April 2010). Cloud computing: Issues and challenges, In *Proceedings of 24th IEEE International Conference on Advanced Information Networking and Applications* (pp. 27–33). Perth, Washington.

Emerson Network Power. (2010). *Taking the enterprise data center into the cloud* [White paper]. Retrieved from http://www.emersonnetworkpower.com/en-US/Brands/Liebert/Documents/White%20Papers/scalable-data-center_24567-R11–10.pdf

Gartner Report. (2009). *Gartner highlights five attributes of cloud computing. Gartner press release.* Retrieved from http://www.gartner.com/newsroom/id/1035013

Géczy, P., Izumi, N., and Hasida, K. (2012). Cloudsourcing: Managing cloud adoption, *Global Journal of Business Research, 6*(2), 57–70.

Gilmore, A., and Rentschler, R. (2002). Changes in museum management: A custodial or marketing emphasis, *Journal of Management Development, 21*(10), 745–760.

Hirtle, P. B., Hudson, E., and Kenyon, A. T. (2009). *Copyright and cultural institutions: Guidelines for us libraries, archives, and museums.* Ithaca, NY: Cornell University Library. Retrieved from https://ecommons.library.cornell.edu/bitstream/1813/14142/2/Hirtle-Copyright_final_RGB_lowres-cover1.pdf

James, M. (2000). Art crime, *Australian Institute of Criminology.* Retrieved from http://www.aic.gov.au/documents/9/2/9/%7B9296EF8C-47F0–4B90–95BF-2A4466B5E863%7Dti170.pdf

Kim, W. (2009). Cloud computing: Today and tomorrow, *Journal of Object Technology, 8*(1), 65–72.

Kundra, V. (2011). *Federal cloud computing strategy, the White House, Washington DC.* Retrieved from https://www.dhs.gov/sites/default/files/publications/digital-strategy/federal-cloud-computing-strategy.pdf

Li, Z. J., Chen, C., and Wang, K. (2011). Cloud computing for agent-based urban transportation systems, *Intelligent Systems, IEEE, 26*(1), 73–79.

Loebbecke, C., Thomas, B., and Ullrich, T. (2012). Assessing cloud readiness at continental AG, *MIS Quarterly Executive, 11*(1), 11.

Low, C., and Chen, Y. (2011). Understanding the determinants of cloud computing adoption, *Industrial Management & Data Systems, 111*(7), 1006–1023.

Marty, P. F. (2008). Museum websites and museum visitors: Digital museum resources and their use, *Museum Management and Curatorship, 23*(1), 81–99.

Patil, G., and Klein, R. (2011, June). *The business value of a cloud-based contact center*, Aberdeen Group Report.

Preimesberger, C. (2011). Private vs. Public clouds: The fight has just begun, *eWeek, 28*(10), 24–25.

Rochwerger, B., Breitgand, D., Levy, E., Galis, A., Nagin, K., Llorente, I., . . . Galan, F. (2009). The reservoir model and architecture for open federated cloud computing. *IBM Journal of Research and Development, 53*(4), 1–11.

Smith, M. K. (2005). Exploring variety in digital collections and the implications for digital preservation, *Library Trends, 54*(1), 6–15.

Spafford-Ricci, S., and Graham, F. (2000). The fire at the Royal Saskatchewan Museum, Part 1: Salvage, initial response, and the implications for disaster planning, *Journal of the American Institute for Conservation, 39*(1), 15–36.

Subashini, S., and Kavitha, V. (2011). A survey on security issues in service delivery models of cloud computing, *Journal of Network and Computer Applications, 34*(1), 1–11.

Torsen, M., and Anderson, J. (2010). *Intellectual property and the safeguarding of traditional cultures: Legal issues and practical options for museums*, Libraries and Archives, Geneva, Switzerland: WIPO. Retrieved from http://www.wipo.int/export/sites/www/freepublications/en/tk/1023/wipo_pub_1023.pdf

8 Mobilizing digital museums

Yao-Nan Lien, Hung-Chin Jang,
Tzu-Chieh Tsai, Pei-Jeng Kuo,
and Chih-Lin Hu

Introduction

An important trend among museums worldwide is the digitization and archiving of national cultural heritage in electronic databases for public retrieval through the Internet (Kalapriya, Babu, and Nandy, 2004; National Palace Museum, 2014; Summer Palace, 2014). Due to its long history, the Chinese civilization has a very rich cultural heritage. The National Palace Museum in Taipei is known internationally as an archive for the treasures of Chinese civilization. Since 2001, the NPM has been digitizing and archiving its precious collections. Through the Internet, most of its digital archive is available for public retrieval to fulfill the museum's mission of dissemination and exchange of museum collections for educational, research, and commercial purposes (National Palace Museum, 2014).

After digitization, the next important issue is how best to present its material to the world to achieve the highest level of dissemination of knowledge. Currently, the most popular presentation format for most digital museums is statically structured, HTML-based Web presentation that mimics the presentation of the physical museums. One of the biggest advantages of a digital archive over a physical archive is the flexibility of document retrieval. For example, collections can be arbitrarily classified according to attributes such as time, location, event, etc. Users are able to choose their viewing points for exploring the digital archives to achieve their goals, for either educational or research purpose. For instance, a person researching Chinese porcelain might want to classify porcelain collections by time to study the evolution of porcelain techniques, or by production kilns to compare kiln styles. The rigid format of a physical museum exhibition cannot provide this type of service, whereas a digital museum can easily do so.

It is our long-term mission to develop the necessary technology for enhancing digital museum features to achieve the goal presented above using the available information and communication technologies. This study focuses on the mobilization of the NPM's digital archive using mobile computing and cloud computing technology (Knorr and Gruman, 2008) for the benefit of mobile users.

Analysis of the mobile environment

In recent years, advances in mobile communications and cloud computing, plus the emergence of tablet PCs have led to the daily emergence of many new types of applications. Users of the new equipment, have sparked a new social style. In many developed countries, a large proportion of the population has become heavy users of smartphones or tablet PCs. It is common on commuter trains or buses to see all kinds of people with their heads bent over their smartphones or tablet PCs, quickly moving their fingers over the screen. The population of mobile users has far exceeded that of desktop PC users. This section provides an analysis of the characteristics of the mobile computing environment in terms of hardware, software, and use model, aimed at the supporting of the mobilization of the digital NPM.

Characteristics of the mobile devices

Mobile devices have both advantages and limitations inherent in their human–machine interaction mechanisms, screen sizes, hardware and software capacities, communication bandwidths, and so on, as described below.

- Human–machine interaction capability

  Most mobile devices are equipped with powerful human–computer interaction capabilities, in particular a capacitive multi-touch screen allowing users to use their fingers to manipulate mobile devices. Unfortunately, many devices have neither a mouse nor a keyboard, so their use model is quite different from that of a conventional computer. However, Web pages currently are designed to operate with mouse and keyboard, to the detriment of touch-screen operation; for example, clickable objects on a Web page are usually too small for a finger to tap. Furthermore, it is generally inconvenient to type in much information on a mobile device due to the lack of a keyboard. Web page design for mobile users must thus minimize the need for keyboard typing. The website of the NPM (and many other museums) should be redesigned for this particular type of interaction.

- Screen size

  The screen size of tablet PCs or smartphones is generally smaller than that of regular PCs, approximately 3–5 inches for a smartphone, and 7–10 inches for a tablet PC. These sizes are generally smaller than typical Web pages necessitating constant scrolling up-and-down or left-and-right to browse a full Web page. Furthermore, the font sizes of many Web pages are usually too small for mobile users to view, in particular for far-sighted seniors.

- Limited software and hardware capacities

  It is well known that most mobile computing devices have fewer hardware and software resources, lower processor speeds, less memory, and narrower network bandwidths. In addition, some popular PC software is not available on mobile devices; for instance, Apple Inc.'s iPad does not contains a built-in Flash Player and thus many Flash-based Web pages are not viewable on an iPad. Worse, due to constant innovation in Web authoring tools, Web designers often endow their designs with unnecessary fancy features that inevitably consume more computing resources and create trouble for mobile users.

- Communication bandwidth

  The wireless network bandwidth on a mobile device, delivered via either a cellular network or WiFi, is usually much lower than that of home or office PCs. Additionally, many Web pages may embed unnecessary audio and video streams that consume excessive bandwidth, affecting the performance of mobile devices. Furthermore, as cell phone operators have gradually abolished the "all-you-can-eat" flat-rate tariff model, mobile users now are more sensitive to the amount of data transmitted over wireless networks. Many fancy Web designs may no longer be suitable for mobile users. How to use text-based HTML codes to achieve a more pleasing Web design is an important issue for the NPM.

Behavior characteristics of mobile computing

In addition to the resource constraints described above, the use model and environmental constraints of mobile computing are quite different from those of desktop computing, as outlined below.

- Very short visual attention

  When gazing at the screen, a mobile user may have to pay attention to the surrounding environment simultaneously, resulting in the period of visual attention to the mobile devices being very short. For example, a bus passenger may hold a hanging safety strap in one hand and a smartphone in the other. The information on the mobile device must therefore be presented in a manner that allows the user to grasp the required information instantly and clearly. The design of mobile information presentation faces great challenges in all aspects: color, layout, fonts, frame, hypertext structure, and other arrangements. Most existing Web design styles do not meet the requirements of mobile devices.

- Information pages will be frequently zoomed or scrolled

  Because the screen size of a mobile device is usually very small, and therefore often unable to present a page of information in its entirety, users must frequently zoom in/out and scroll up/down the page of information. Although multi-touch screens make zooming and scrolling operations easy, Web pages are usually not designed to accommodate this requirement.

- Easy to slide and hard to click or tap

  To manipulate a capacitive multi-touch screen using finger gestures, it is much easier to slide than to tap the screen because tapping on a specific area of the screen requires a precise gaze and a precise tap. Gazing increases eyes' tension, while tapping is difficult for large fingers or less conductive fingers. Worse, due to the convenience of mouse-clicking on a conventional computer, most Web pages are designed to be easier to click on than to tap. For example, many checkboxes are usually too small to tap.

Capacity requirements for cloud computing and P2P communication protocols

When traffic in the NPM's web-site services increases, the NPM's server capacity and network bandwidth cannot be scaled up accordingly due to its funding constraint, leading to a decline in service quality. Cloud computing–based services will solve part of this problem. We have been using a cloud platform provided by Chunghwa Telecom to implement a digital video service using NPM content. However, due to network bandwidth limits, it cannot support a large number of concurrent users. The P2P communication paradigm will be substantially useful in increasing the number of concurrent users while maintaining service quality.

Design guidelines for information presentation on mobile devices

The analysis described above shows clearly that the design philosophy of current popular Web sites is not suitable for mobile devices. Through a variety of experiments carried out in this study, we have identified a set of design guidelines for mobile applications, specifically for the digital NPM. The design of a mobile Web page should (Lien et al., 2012)

- make use of the multi-touch screen to compensate for the inconvenience caused by the lack of a mouse and keyboard;
- support the traditional Chinese-style layout (up-down style) including operations such as automatic word splitting (hyphenation);
- support various types of text input (for example, when a user wants to retrieve documents written in Oracle calligraphy, the user must be able to enter Oracle characters);
- size up graphic user interface (GUI) objects, such as check-boxes and radio buttons, to facilitate precise finger tapping;
- allow users to take advantage of multi-touch features to quickly and easily zoom in/out of a Web page (note that some Web pages cannot be zoomed in/out on some tablet PCs);

- allow automatic adjustment of line width to avoid line overflow with a change in font size or zooming (note that ancient Chinese documents are written in a vertical layout);
- provide a context-sensitive automatic-word-completion feature to minimize the need for typing (Automatic word completion is a feature provided by many Web applications and text editors. It involves predicting a word or a phrase that the user wants to type in without the user having to type it in full. Context-sensitive automatic word completion is able to predict a user's input based on the document he or she is reading. For example, when retrieving a document of the Xia or Shang dynasties, if the user types "乾" as the first word of search key, the system can prompt with "乾坤" or "乾卦" but not "乾隆" for the user to choose from. However, if the document to be retrieved is a late Qing Dynasty document, "乾隆" will be prompted to the user. This feature saves users much tedious typing.);
- provide pull-down menus (or similar mechanisms) as much as possible to reduce the demand for text input;
- provide automatic page scrolling with adjustable scrolling speeds (This feature is useful for small screens and long Web pages that lead to frequent page scrolling. For example, many Chinese paintings take the form of long scroll. When expanded, they may be longer than 100 feet. When viewing digitized images of such paintings on a small mobile device, the screen must be constantly and tediously slide with finger. Automatic scrolling would allow users to view the picture more easily.);
- keep information presentation as simple as possible (be user-friendly) (Because a user's visual attention to a mobile device is usually very fleeting, colors, frames, fonts, and other artistic details must be designed to clearly highlight the information of interest, allowing users to instantly capture this information clearly and unambiguously. Complicated information must be appropriately divided and organized using hyperlinks to allow easy navigation of structured information.);
- save bandwidth by avoiding unnecessarily complicated screen pages and using standard script languages such as HTML, CSS, and JavaScript to make pages attractive.

The current popular Web designs use many images or non-HTML tools such as Flash and ActiveX to make Web pages more vivid and attractive. Large images on Web pages may consume considerable bandwidth. Non-standard tools may hinder the viewing of these pages on mobile devices that do not support the required software. On the other hand, the browsers on both the iOS and the Android system support standard HTML, CSS, and JavaScript, which are sufficiently sophisticated to support many artistic designs. Designing Web pages using the standard HTML language suite has many advantages and should be encouraged.

Creating attractive Web pages by using artistic drawings is also very popular. However, artistic drawings are not only time-consuming but also very expensive.

Moreover, they require intensive communication and coordination between Web designers and artists, which is even more of a burden. The use of the standard HTML language suite will reduce or eliminate the participation of artists. Web designers working alone can create and modify Web pages. Not only will productivity be increased dramatically, but design costs will also be significantly reduced.

Prototype systems

We have designed and developed several prototype systems, as described below (Jang et al., 2014; Jang and Lien, 2014; Kuo et al., 2013; Lien et al., 2012).

Qingming painting and Mao Gong Ding inscription graphical exhibition systems

We used two famous collections of the NPM to develop two prototype graphical exhibition systems. The first is the famous painting *Along the River During the Qingming Festival* (Qingming Painting in short), created by Zhang Zeduan during the Northern Song Dynasty. The Qingming Painting documents the real life of the general public in its capital city, Bianjing, which was the most populated city in the world at the time. The preciousness of this painting lies not in the skill with which it was painted or its artistic value, but in its realistic recording of the life-styles of the Northern Song Dynasty. It is a valuable historical record. A small electronic screen cannot display the entire painting, which is painted on a long roll of canvas; users must constantly scroll left/right/up/down and zoom in/out of the screen to view the painting. This may be readily accomplished with a multi-touch screen tablet. However, the process is still very cumbersome because of the length of the Qingming Painting. In our prototype, we used hyperlinks to connect each digital object; these hyperlinks act as an index of knowledge exploration served by a back-end knowledge (meta-data) database. If a researcher wanted to study wagon or boat styles in the Northern Song Dynasty, he or she could easily explore the digitized painting to locate each desired object and tap it to retrieve the meta-data from the back-end database. The design of this system follows the guidelines presented in Part III. A join project between our research team and the NPM was established to populate the system with real meta-data and to evaluate the system in a real-use environment. The Qingming Painting exhibition thus offers not only visual appreciation, but also an educational and research function.

The second prototype used the Mao Gong Ding Inscription exhibition. The Ding, a bowl with three sturdy legs made of copper, was widely used in ancient Chinese dynasties as a ritual vessel and became a symbol of political hierarchy distinguishing the political status of the superiors from subordinates. In addition to its use in worship and ritual ceremonies, the ding was also used to record the meritorious quality of its owner. Such records were often closely related to important events and historical legends, and therefore are of great historical value. The Mao Gong Ding, cast by Mao Gong who was a relative of the emperor of the Zhou Dynasty, features 497 characters in a special calligraphy, called Zhongding-Wen,

Figure 8.1 Mao Gong Ding Inscription exhibition system

engraved on its surface to record a special event. As the government of the time was weak and incompetent, the emperor delegated to Mao Gong a special and powerful political position, similar to that of today's British Prime Minister. To encourage Mao Gong to work hard and love his people, the emperor also gave him various ceremonial gifts. Mao Gong cast the ding to record the event and express his gratitude. We developed a Mao Gong Ding Inscription exhibition system using images of the inscription. Each character in the inscription has an embedded hyperlink linked to its meta-data, which includes not only the relevant explanation, but also the information about the evolution of the character in calligraphy history. A user can study Zhongding-Wen by clicking on any character to gain access to this information. The system is available as a conventional Web site and as an iPad App, as shown in Figure 8.1. To further stimulate users and extend the learning efficiency, we also designed and implemented an edutainment system for each platform, as explained below.

Mobilizing digital museum explorer

The Mobilizing Digital Museum Explorer (MDME) is a ubiquitous media exhibition platform that we have designed to allow mobile users to browse museum artifacts. The MDME can enhance museum services by providing users with an utterly new experience during their museum visit. We used PaaS (Platform as a Service) in cloud computing, allowing users to access museum information at anytime and anywhere. The cloud server for the MDME is able to monitor and analyze user behavior and preferences, and provide personalized information to individual users. We also used Augmented Reality (AR), 3D-imaging, and path-planning technics to give users a brand-new browsing and navigation experience.

The MDME is customized for the NPM, but all of the techniques developed are applicable to other digital museums.

Exhibition platform architecture

The explorer has two components: a cloud service system and a mobile exhibition platform. Figure 8.2 shows the underlying techniques used to build the MDME. Qualcomm Vuforia was used to make AR even more interactive. OpenGL ES was used to generate 3D artifact models. The cloud service was built on the Heroku PaaS. The Ruby on Rails framework renders the code clean and concise. Urban Airship can expedite development and provides cross-platform (iOS, Android, Windows Phone) support.

Cloud service system

Cloud technology is able to provide inexpensive high-performance computing capability and data storage via the Internet. In supporting a mobile digital museum, it is able to reduce the hardware requirements of mobile devices by transferring major computing loads and data storage from mobile devices to cloud servers. We used Heroku's PaaS platform together with Ruby on Rails to rapidly develop a server management interface. Ruby on Rails is based on the MVC (Model, View, and Controller) framework, so the front-end and back-end components can be separated easily. An advantage of this management interface is that administrators can readily synchronize updated data between all of the platforms. Mobile users can pre-load or update information from the cloud server on their way to a museum. When they arrive at the museum, they will be able to read the pre-loaded information offline. Users can also subscribe to specific services provided through the cloud server. When information that has been subscribed to is updated, it can be pushed to the subscribers via a push notification service. Designing the system in this way places most of the responsibility or cost-intensive computation on the cloud server. As a thin client, a mobile device can thus experience smooth browsing and navigation.

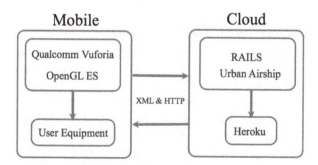

Figure 8.2 Techniques used in the MDME

Data management and XML-based data exchange

With Ruby on Rails, database administrators can use the *scaffold* command to easily create and edit a variety of database tables and management interfaces. Museum staff can then use these tables to create and update digital archive entries for artifacts and exhibitions.

XML-based data exchange between mobile devices and Web pages is easily performed with the Ruby on Rails framework. By using the XML data format, mobile devices are able to exchange data with cloud servers via HTTP Get/Post mechanisms.

Push notification service

Mobile users can subscribe to various services, for example, artifact exhibitions, special events, etc. As each mobile device has a unique device token, that can be used to determine what services have been subscribed to by a specific mobile user, the cloud server can then push personalized information to the individual users using a push notification service once the information subscribed to has been updated.

We implemented a push notification service using the Urban Airship push service library, which supports cross-platform services. When museum staff update data on the cloud server, the system determines the list of users who have subscribed to this updated information and triggers a push notification to them.

Mobile exhibition platform

Rather than using middleware such as PhoneGap, we chose to develop the proposed exhibition platform using iOS native programs, to preserve the native features and interfaces provided by the iOS and to achieve better system performance.

Exhibition floor plan

We used Scroll View to enable users to intuitively switch between floors and zoom in/out of the floor plan. Users are able to check the detailed exhibition information in each exhibition room by tapping the room icon, as shown in Figure 8.3.

Artifact browsing

The platform supports the following innovative features for artifact browsing: asynchronous picture download, intelligent artifact search, interactive 3D artifact model browsing, and AR artifacts.

- Asynchronous picture download: Artifact information is updated through the network. However, this type of information usually involves large image files. Synchronous downloading may slow down information display due to

Figure 8.3 Exhibition floor plan and zoom in/out interfaces

either large image sizes or limited bandwidth. We therefore used an asynchronous operation downloading text before images to speed up information display. In subsequent browsing, the system pre-caches a number of forthcoming images based on the navigation sequence. The experimental results show that asynchronous image downloading is able to make artifact browsing smoother without noticeable lag.

- Intelligent artifact search: We made use of the iOS Search Bar to expedite type-in artifact searches. Once a user has typed in any initial part of a word string, the system uses the embedded "LIKE" function to match the characters against a keyword database, and offers a list of possible matches for the user to choose from without further typing as shown in Figure 8.4.

- Interactive 3D artifact model browsing: This feature offers users an intuitive close-up view of an artifact, which may be physically impossible due to the distance between a displayed artifact and the visitor and to the static nature of physical exhibition with its non-viewable coffin-corners. Users may explore the 3D models by zooming in-and-out, and rotating in all four directions with no coffin-corners. In addition, artifact images are tagged, allowing users to tap them to obtain further information. We used the OpenGL ES library together with the native gesture-recognition function. Figure 8.5 shows interactive 3D artifact model browsing. As the user taps the Buddha's head, the app pops "這是佛像的頭" up.

- AR artifacts: Wikipedia defines AR as a live, direct or indirect, view of a physical, real-world environment whose elements are augmented by computer-generated sensory input such as sound, video, graphics, or GPS data. In this project, we used the Qualcomm Vuforia AR library to generate AR artifact models and tags. Using these models, users can obtain an utterly new experience of the artifacts. Figure 8.6 shows an AR teapot artifact popping out of a plane surface.

Figure 8.4 Artifact search using the Search Bar

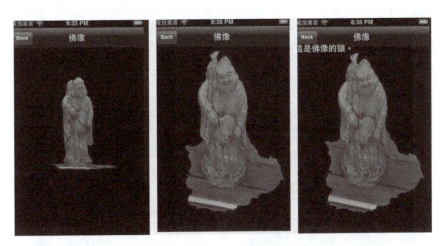

Figure 8.5 Interactive 3D artifact model browsing (zoom in and pop-up)

Figure 8.6 Viewing an artifact using AR techniques

Push notification of a recent special exhibition

The push notification of a recent special exhibition is an example of a personalized push notification service. Figure 8.7 shows a pop-up push notification "NPMApp 有您訂閱的展覽出現了" appearing at the top of a mobile device. The app guides the user to the exhibition page when the user taps the message.

General navigation of artifacts

- Artifact information navigation: We used Table View to enable users to itemize artifact information as shown in Figure 8.8. The information is optionally displayed in either "audio" or "video" mode as shown in Figure 8.9.
- On-the-spot AR artifact direction guide: Even though a museum usually provides vistor with a floor map, they often get lost and cannot find their way quickly toward the artifacts they are interested in. Using OpenGL ES together with a camera, we developed an on-the-spot AR artifact direction guide. By simply tapping the icon of the current location and the icon of the target artifact, the system is able to calculate a route and display it on the screen, together with an arrow pointing toward the target, as shown in Figure 8.10.

Figure 8.7 Push notification of a special exhibition

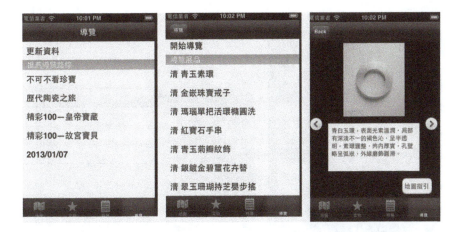

Figure 8.8 Itemized artifact information

Figure 8.9 Alternative displays for artifact information

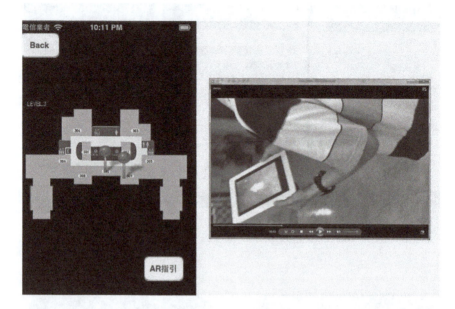

Figure 8.10 Floor plan map and AR direction guide

The arrow is generated by OpenGL ES and is displayed perpendicular to gravity, determined using a gravity sensor (G-sensor). That is, the vector direction of gravity should be normal to the plane the arrow lies in. To simplify the problem, we assumed that the mobile device was placed on the horizontal plane. The system calculates the difference in degrees between the direction of gravity and the horizontal plane. The result is then used to adjust the rotation of the arrow so that it is perpendicular to gravity.

Live voice interactive museum guiding system

Audio interpretations make museum visits more vivid and impressive. Conventional human museum interpreters use analog radio devices, such as walkie-talkies, for this purpose. However, due to the limited number of human interpreters and audio devices, visitors often need to book interpretations in advance. Furthermore, the audio devices used usually only support one-way communication. A visitor wishing to ask a question needs to approach the interpreter and speaks loudly to be heard clearly in a noisy environment.

Taking advantage of recent advances in mobile computing technology, many museums have launched guider apps to solve this problem (Kenteris, Gavalas, and Economou, 2011; Tesoriero et al., 2014). However, the content of these apps is usually fairly static and prepared in advance, and thus allows little improvisation or interaction. Moreover, the memory space and downloading time is usually too small/short to contain/download all of the artifacts archived by a museum. Finally, a user does not need to be next to the displayed artifact while he or she is viewing on such an app. These types of app do not therefore provide a sense of presence when being used.

We therefore propose a new mobile solution to provide live interactive voice interpretation for museums. Human interpreters can use mobile phones to provide interpretations via multi-lingual voice radio channels. The visitors simply subscribe to the channel they want and enjoy their journey. These channels can be bi-directional, in that the subscribers can use the "push to talk" mode to communicate with the interpreter.

The content of an interpretation can be simultaneously recorded and uploaded to the server. Subscribers can then re-play any content they missed or want to hear again. In addition, remote users can subscribe to the channel via the Internet, and feel as if they are participating in the tour.

This innovative museum service is used as follows. A visitor chooses an on-the-air interpretation channel in "live" mode. If no "live" channel is available, the visitor can use the "re-play" mode to download previously recorded interpretations by their interpreter of choice. A snapshot of the app screen is shown in Figure 8.11. On the left is a list of artifacts for the user to choose from. On the right is a list of downloadable interpretation clips by different interpreters at different times.

After re-playing an interpretation clip, a user can write feedback comments and submit a "like" or "not like" opinion to any social network platform. This re-play mode service is also available to Internet users.

WiFi Direct was adopted for implementing the "live" radio channels. WiFi Direct allows mobile phones to communicate directly with each other without any access points (APs). Visitors therefore do not need to subscribe to any 3G/4G/WiFi data services. Moreover, the voice streaming data are directly transmitted from the interpreter's mobile phone to the visitor's. There are thus no server bottleneck problems as seen in conventional streaming services based on central servers.

In the future, P2P (peer-to-peer) technology (Liu et al., 2008) may be adopted in "replay" mode to speed up the downloading of content from the server. As the artifacts that visitors in the same exhibition room are interested in are likely to be the same, some content may be downloaded from nearby users' mobiles that have already downloaded the content, instead of it being downloaded directly from the server. With P2P technology, not only is the loading of the server dispersed among all of the participating users, but users who do not have Internet access can also use the service. Another technology that could be adopted is "location-aware" service technology (Lanir et al., 2013), such as "i-beacon" that can detect users' locations and provide smart services to them.

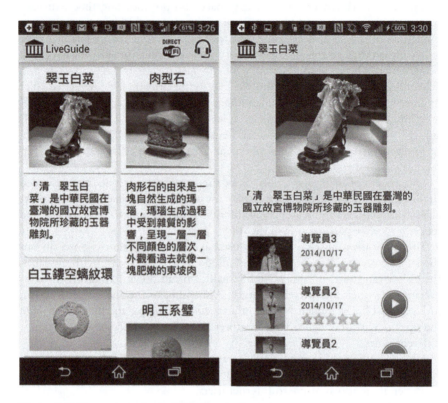

Figure 8.11 Screen snapshots of the "re-play" mode

Edutainment

Edutainment, a buzzword for "learning by entertainment," has long been recognized as an outstanding method of achieving highly efficient learning. However, the creation of such a system has many challenges, requiring many hardware and software resources for its implementation. With their excellent and inexpensive human–machine interaction, multi-media presentations, and mobile computing capabilities, smartphones and tablet PCs are good platforms on which to implement edutainment systems for lively, vivid, and joyful presentation of museum artifacts. We designed a "guessing game" for each of Mao Gong Ding inscriptions and Qingming Painting to stimulate users and enhance their learning efficiency. Through playing these games, users can learn the Zhongding-Wen more efficiently and gain a deeper knowledge of the Qingming Painting. In Mao Gong Ding guessing game, as shown in Figure 8.12, the system iteratively shows an inscription (a character in Zhongding-Wen) on the screen, and provides the user with a number of choices of modern characters. The implementation of these games shows that smartphones and tablet PCs are ideal platforms for

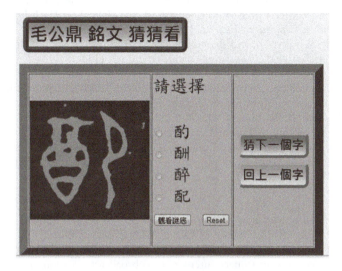

Figure 8.12 Mao Gong Ding Inscription Guessing Game system

edutainment system and that such systems can stimulate users' interest. If greater development resources were available, more sophisticated games for edutainment could be developed.

Concluding remarks

In this chapter, we analyzed the characteristics of the mobile computing environment in terms of hardware, software, and use model with the aim of supporting the mobilization of digital museums and of developing a set of design guidelines using the NPM as a reference. Based on this analysis and the design guidelines, we designed several application prototypes on both the iOS and the Android platforms. We also designed a live voice interactive interpretation system to assist with museum interpretation, in which the interpreter and the audience both use their smartphones. We expect that these technologies will be adopted by the museums around the world.

References

Jang, Hung-Chin, and Lien, Yao-Nan. (2014). *Educational exhibition system and the application of APP on museum mobile learning–National palace museum as an example*, International Conference on e-Commerce, e-Administration, e-Society, e-Education, and e-Technology, Nagoya University, Japan.

Jang, Hung-Chin, Lien, Yao-Nan, Pan, Kuan-Lun, Chen, Wei-Cheng, and Huang, Ching-Chieh. (2014). *Mobilizing Digital Museum Explorer*, International Conference on e-Commerce, e-Administration, e-Society, e-Education, and e-Technology, Nagoya University, Japan.

Kalapriya, K., Venkatesh Babu, R., and Nandy, S. K. (2004). Streaming stored playback video over a peer-to-peer network, *Proceedings of the IEEE International Conference on Communications, 3,* 1298–1302. Paris, France.

Kenteris, M., Gavalas, D., and Economou, D. (2011). Electronic mobile guides: A survey, *Personal and Ubiquitous Computing, 15,* 97–111.

Knorr, E., and Gruman, G. (2008). What cloud computing really means, *InfoWorld,* Retrieved from http://www.infoworld.com/article/2683784/cloud-computing/what-cloud-computing-really-means.html.

Kuo, P. J., Lien, Y. N., Su, W. H., Wang, Y. T., Huang, Y. N., and Chu, W. C. (2013). Mobilizing 3D virtual artifacts exhibition system of National Palace Museum, *Archiving 2013,* 6. Washington, DC.

Lanir, J., Kuflik, T., Dim, E., Wecker, A. J., and Stock, O. (2013). The influence of a location-aware mobile guide on museum visitors' behavior, *Interacting with Computers, 25*(6), 443–460.

Lien, Y. N., Jang, H. C., Tsai, T. C., Kuo, P., and Hu, C. L. (2012). *National Palace Museum exhibition and education system for mobile digital era,* Taiwan Academic Network Conference (TANET 2012). Taipei, Taiwan.

Liu, Jiang-Chuan, Rao, Sanjay G., Li, Bo, and Zhang, Hui. (2008). Opportunities and challenges of peer-to-peer Internet video broadcast, *Proceedings of the IEEE, 96*(1), 11–24.

National Palace Museum. (2014). *U Museum.* Retrieved from http://www.npm.gov.tw/digital/index2_2_1_ch.html

Summer Palace. (2014). Retrieved from http://www.summerpalace-china.com

Tesoriero, R., Gallud, J. A., Lozano, M., and Penichet, V. M. R. (2014). Enhancing visitors' experience in art museums using mobile technologies, *Information Systems Frontiers, 16,* 303–327.

9 Design factors of a mobile museum navigation system

The case of National Palace Museum

Eldon Y. Li and Laurence F. K. Chang

Introduction

Culture is a major motivational factor for tourism and also an important factor in determining tourist destinations. Many countries around the world have made the commitment to combine tourism and culture, design cultural tourism systems, and strengthen activities that promote cultural tourism. Via new technology, culture and tourism are expected to be marketed more effectively. The combination of digital technology and cultural tourism is a growing trend that has important potential in developing business opportunities.

Cultural tourism comprises a major proportion of world tourism demand. According to the World Tourism Organization's survey, 37 percent of international tourist activity is motivated by cultural tourism and the demand for cultural tourism will grow by 15 percent annually. Heritage tourism is a part of cultural tourism. Ryan and Dewar (1995) indicated that heritage tourism is one of the fastest-growing tourism market segments. Museums, national parks, and historical monuments have all seen a gradual increase in the number of tourists, and it has been realized that cultural tourism can bring significant economic benefits to museums and heritage attractions (Ashworth, 2000; Chang and Yeoh, 1999; Cossons, 1989; Richards, 1996; Shackley, 1997).

Successful guided tours are a necessary condition for achieving a high-quality service and may also be the key to the effective management and preservation of cultural heritage; furthermore, they may create prospects for sustainable tourism (Moscardo, 1996). To bring high-quality experiences to visitors, a tour guide must meet the needs of those visitors in exploring the historical artifacts and must also act as a representative of the museum in conveying information, through its studies, collections, displays, educational functions, and leisure functions, to its visitors. The most dynamic interpretive function is undoubtedly a tour guide, available in addition to textual explanations of the artifacts, at all of the contact points between the museum's showpieces and the visitors. A tour guide's clarity of statement, presentation skills, and professional knowledge will not only affect the visitors' understanding of the exhibits and their perception of the museum, but also serve as the key factors affecting the quality of the navigational instructions of the tour guide.

Driven by today's new technology, there is a tremendous change in the way visitors navigate; they are not limited to the transfer of information from pieces of text, but expect more information feedback and two-way communication through human–computer interfaces. Some scholars (e.g., Shen and Liang, 2010) have pointed out that future navigation will change from the current "static" type to a "collection of heavy sensual" type; museums are already beginning to change their navigation types to "semi-static" and will move toward "dynamic" navigation in the future. Dynamic navigation exploits interactive behavior arising from contact with the audience to make exhibits more memorable, through providing a profound recreational experience to visitors and further enhancing the recreational functions of the museum.

Due to the mature technological environment, digital concepts have gradually expanded the types of exhibit available to visitors. For the public, the museum is no longer a place where static artifacts are on display, but where they may experience a variety of sensory stimuli in an integrated experience (Chesapeake Bay Maritime Museum, 2014). Tourists are no longer passively content with pre-arranged tours, but navigate more selectively. How to embed a mobile museum navigation system (MMNS) into a smartphone to encourage tourists to use such a system, rather than traditional voice navigation, and increase their learning experience thus needs to be investigated.

According to the "2011 Survey of Taiwanese Wireless Network Usage" report, 50.73 percent of Taiwanese people own smartphones and one-third of the population uses smartphones to surf the Internet. The survey had 3,553 respondents who were more than 12 years old, already owned a smartphone, and would purchase a new smartphone in the future. Of these 3,553 respondents, 59.32 percent (2,107) used their smartphone to access the Internet. Of these 2,107 people, 89.20 percent regularly used their smartphone to access the Internet. In the past, mobile Internet usage was low for Taiwanese people, but the market for mobile phones to be used to access the Internet has dramatically grown during the past few years.

This study used visitors of the National Palace Museum in Taiwan as research participants. We first derived 7 design guidelines with 38 influence factors based on a review of the literature and an analysis of personal digital navigation systems in various domestic and foreign museums. An analytic hierarchy process (AHP) was then used to rank those influence factors to provide a reference for building a smartphone mobile navigation system. The specific objectives of the research were as follows. We expect the results to provide smartphone navigation system design guidelines for system developers and to become the basis for the planning of museum exhibitions.

1   Collect the desired and required functions of a museum navigation system from previous studies, and current museum navigation systems.
2   Analyze the status of navigation systems for museum operations
3   Investigate the influence factors that affect tourists' use of navigation systems from an expert point of view
4   Determine the priority of those influence factors

Relevant studies

Museum navigation

In a museum, "navigation" carries the meanings of "guide" and "interpretation." As guide, it has the important role of providing instruction on museum operations, giving guidance and inspiration and indicating directions for viewing beautiful artifacts. As interpretation, its role is to provide a meaningful arrangement of museum exhibits for educational purposes, presenting these to visitors so that they may absorb knowledge through personal participation.

Tilden (1957) proposed six principles of interpretation for exploring the relationship between museums and visitors.

1   Any interpretation that does not somehow relate what is being displayed or described to something within the personality or experience of the visitor will be sterile.
2   Information, as such, is not interpretation. Interpretation is revelation based on information, but they are entirely different things. However, all interpretation includes information.
3   Interpretation is an art, which combines many arts, whether the materials presented are scientific, historical, or architectural. Any art is in some degree teachable.
4   The chief aim of interpretation is not instruction, but provocation.
5   Interpretation should aim to present a whole rather than a part and must address itself to the whole man rather than any phase.
6   Interpretation addressed to children (say up to the age of 12) should not be a dilution of the presentation to adults, but should follow a fundamentally different approach. To be at its best, it will require a separate program.

Recently, Yorke Edwards described interpretation as a series of services, including information, guiding, education, entertainment, propaganda, and inspiration (Edwards, 1982). In an information service, interpretation must be able to provide both information on appropriate display themes and an interesting message. This information directly contributes to the enriching of visitor experiences. Guiding services can help people to avoid feeling lost at the beginning of a visit to an unfamiliar environment and can provide a complete description of the history and facilities of the location. In an educational service, interpretation allows people from different backgrounds and of different ages to interact with exhibits. It acts as a catalyst by not only providing people with the right information, but also by inducing a thirst for knowledge. Good interpretation can also provide people with a pleasant, relaxed, and wonderful experience by achieving the goals of an entertainment service. In a propaganda service, interpretation can be seen as a way of improving public image and seeking public support, increasing the level of mutual understanding between the people and a museum. Furthermore, for local people good interpretation may evoke pride in the natural or cultural heritage of their area.

In summary, navigation can be viewed as a process of interpretation; it can make things better understood or give something special significance (Edson and Dean, 1994).

Museum navigation systems

Navigation can be simply divided into the following six categories according to differentiation by media vehicle.

1   Guides

Guides provide interpretation directly to tourists, either throughout the visit or through regular guided tours at set times and set locations. Guided tours provide high levels of interaction with tourists, with highly flexible and elastic arrangements.

2   Brochures

Using brochures for museum navigation can reduce the space occupied by explanation boards; not only can the brochures provide extra information or pictures, but they can be taken home after the visit.

3   Video clips

Due to the need to set up display equipment, video clips are not widely used. However, they provide good sound and light effects and lively animation, and thus readily attract the attention of visitors. An advantage lies in combining television features with special multi-media effects.

4   Computer kiosks

The general reason for including a kiosk in an exhibition is to provide advisory services or an overall introduction. Because a computer can hold and present a wealth of information, an exhibition kiosk can provide a more detailed and diverse explanation of each of the themes of the exhibition. Visitors may even participate in interactive games at the kiosk or perform a self-learning assessment of their knowledge relating to the exhibition.

5   Voice

Voice navigation can be provided through various carriers, such as cassette recorders, MP3 players, or specially designed equipment. The voice content can be played throughout the exhibition, on demand, or at regular intervals.

6   Briefing slides

Using slides to provide exhibition information may be seen as a type of video or voice navigation. However, slides are usually presented in a conference hall or briefing room rather than in the exhibition, to give enough space for a large number of visitors and groups of visitors. Groups of visitors can also book the briefing room for a video navigation or multimedia introduction.

Table 9.1 The shortcomings of common museum navigation systems

Type of System	Shortcomings
Guides	High human resources cost
	High job training cost
	Inconsistent quality of personnel
	Difficulty in assembling an entire group of visitors at a certain location in the exhibition at the same time
	Live interpretation tends to cause congestion in visitor traffic along the exhibition route
Brochures	High cost of printing
	Cannot be reused
	Environmentally unfriendly
Video clips	High production cost
	The length of a typical video restricts the amount of information that can be included
Computer kiosks	High hardware cost and high maintenance cost
Voice	The expense of producing the voice content dominates the overall cost.
	Frequent use leads to the equipment becoming damaged and increases maintenance costs.
	Lack of interaction with user
	Image information is hard to express due to the purely aural format.
	When exhibition themes change frequently, voice navigation is often not ready in time.
Briefing slides	Services cannot be provided for individuals, as briefings have be at set times.

Each of the six navigation modes has its own advantages, but there are also shortcomings, listed in Table 9.1. To overcome those shortcomings, the current study aimed to identify the key impact factors through investigating all of the possible design factors discussed in the literature that might influence the success of a museum navigation system.

Design factors for a mobile museum navigation system

We collected and reviewed the research data and literature, at home and abroad, that was related to navigation systems, exhibition spaces, and culture and creation. We also considered scenarios using the latest smartphone applications and the promotional requirements of the museum. We attempted to list all of the factors that might affect whether visitors will use an MMNS and developed a hierarchical architecture of the design factors for an MMNS.

Infrastructure

Signal stability: In a digital learning study performed in a museum, Schwabe and Göth (2005) found that a system must have the ability to respond in a timely manner, whether the venue is indoors or outdoors. Signal stability is thus very important for an MMNS.

Coverage: Wireless network signal coverage is a key indicator for competitive digital environments and development opportunities (Intel, 2005a; ITU, 2007). The level of wireless network signal coverage provided by the museum will thus affect the museum's opportunities and capabilities for using information technology.

Ubiquitousness: In addition to the coverage and signal stability of a wireless network, whether visitors are able to roam between hot spots is also a critical indicator of the adequacy of the infrastructure and service competitiveness.

Broadband connection speeds: Intel (2005a) held that to support the promotion of wireless services, the network bandwidth must be able to meet demand. Because the museum's navigation system contains a wealth of audio and video content, the infrastructure must be able to provide sufficient bandwidth to ensure that the navigation system operates properly.

Near-field detection: Context-aware technology, which can help visitors with learning that is not limited by place and time, and near-field detection technology can work together in the museum's navigation facilities to provide visitors with a more realistic and rich navigation experience (Chen and Huang, 2012). Context-aware technology also provides visitors with an interactive experience with the exhibits and freedom of choice during the visit (Huang, Wang, and Sandnes, 2011).

Compatibility: An open wireless network environment may involve many different brands of device and different operating systems. Thus, whether a wireless network environment is compatible with a variety of terminal equipment is a key factor of an Internet service (Intel, 2005b).

Security: Security mechanisms for information infrastructure are able to ensure that data can be securely transmitted on the Internet and prevent leakage of confidential information from mobile Internet devices (Intel, 2005b). Furthermore, to provide users with more secure protection, mobile navigation application services must have safety certification.

Human–computer interface

Information richness: Information quality plays a key role in the success of a website (Liu and Arnett, 2000). There is a very rich cultural knowledge contained within a museum's collection. If that cultural knowledge can be delivered by media vehicles with the ability to pass on a wealth of information, exhibits can show the full content, thus reducing vagueness in the information and enhancing the accuracy and richness of the information.

Information presentation: How to present museum exhibit information appropriately on handheld devices is a major challenge. On the one hand, the information must be easy to read, so it must use large fonts on the device's screen, producing low-density information; on the other hand, it must provide as much rich information as possible on the limited screen, and must therefore rely on an explicit order for the information (Ziefle, 2010).

Icon design: An icon is an abstract symbol of text and information. To avoid mistakes and the confusion of users, icons for navigation should not be too complicated to allow users to easily identify them (Horton, 1994).

Screen menu design: With a navigation system on a limited screen space, insufficient detail in the information shown is likely to cause users to become lost. The mobile navigation system must therefore make good use of the scroll function and consider the appearance of the information when designing the system interface (Jones et al., 2005). For mobile phones, Beck, Han, and Park (2006) proposed a design concept menu containing sub-menus to provide users with highly efficient operation within the space limitations of the mobile phone screen.

Multi-language support: The museum navigation system must be capable of supporting several languages, to assist foreign tourists to visit and interact with the museum (Cui and Yokoi, 2012).

Search function: In terms of information system use, information-seeking behavior can be divided into searching and browsing (Marchionini, 1997). In addition to allowing browsing, a complete mobile navigation system should also have a search function.

Content design

Timeliness: Bailey and Pearson (1983) proposed 39 indicators associated with information systems for assessing user satisfaction, including the correctness of the information, timeliness (output timeliness), reliability, completeness, relevance, and accuracy. Of these, the timeliness of an information system is key to its success or failure (DeLone and McLean, 1992).

Interactivity: Museum visitors spend an average of 30 seconds at an exhibit (Cone and Kendall, 1978). The use of mobile Internet devices in the museum can create a seamless environment for visitors to explore within. The visitors can explore via creative thinking before coming to the museum, then experience the exhibits in the museum, and continue their individual research after leaving the museum. In designing an interactive function, care must be taken to avoid treating the handheld device merely as a mini workstation; instead, the design should be based on a model that can change the system of interaction with visitors to assist with learning, collaboration, or teaching (Hsi, 2003).

Locational notification: The interests, background, experience, and so on of each museum visitor may differ greatly and they may therefore have different needs. The design of a navigation system should take into account the actual needs of the visitors and permit flexible adjustment. Ghiani et al. (2009) proposed a multi-device navigation system with location-aware technology that allows users to obtain more detailed information or other services; the system also provides individual or multi-player games via a big screen, to enrich the museum visit journey. Through this multi-device environment, visitors can hold the navigation device while moving around freely and at any time can connect to a nearby desktop computer with a big screen.

Browsing history: A history function can give users access to recently visited pages, favorite pages, and bookmarks at any time and may use different colors to distinguish clicked from never-clicked hyperlinks, allowing users to store specific page addresses for future use. This function allows users to tell if they have visited a particular page and to revisit their use of the website (or navigation system) (Rosenfeld and Morville, 2007).

Information download/pre-download: Wang, Su, and Hong (2009) proposed a campus navigation system that combined indoor RFID and outdoor GPS position detection. When users are outside the navigation area, they can use the Internet to navigate the campus via the system. A pre-download mechanism can be used to reduce waiting times and browse scenes more smoothly. When users carry their mobile device into the scene, the system automatically determines their path of movement, pre-downloads the required information so that the users do not need to wait, and then provides seamless navigation.

Site map: A site map is usually used to show website content with a top-down architecture. It provides an overview of the website and allows users convenient access to the website content they want. The site map can be graphical or a series of text links, so that users can link directly to a specified Web page. In addition, the site map can direct a search engine to important pages, so is useful in search engine optimization (Rosenfeld and Morville, 2007).

User experience

Satisfaction: Bailey and Pearson (1983) pointed out that user satisfaction may significantly affect the use of an information system and its success rate; thus, an MMNS should be designed to improve user satisfaction as much as possible.

Utilization: McLean (1993) believed that learning is an individual behavior with its own tempo in a museum and thus the learning model of each visitor is different. A museum exhibition should provide diversified learning modes and content for all types of visitor, to increase the number of people visiting the exhibition. Similarly, the museum navigation system should also provide users with a variety of exhibition modes to increase the utilization of the system.

Ease of use: Davis (1989) demonstrated that the usefulness and the ease of use of an information system had a strong positive correlation with the use of the system. Museum navigation systems should therefore be designed to allow visitors easy access at any time to the information they need, and this goal should be achieved in as simple a way as possible.

Personalization: Yang (2009) suggested that a museum navigation system with a recommendation function can provide an adaptive navigation mechanism to attract visitors and increase the length of time an exhibition is viewed. An MMNS can provide personalized information services to permit individual control in accordance with users' needs.

User needs: Museum navigation aims to provide instructions, answers to inquiries, contact, participation, commentary, and other functions based on individual visitor needs. The navigation system must therefore meet visitors' needs, coordinate with route planning, and meet the demands of personal navigation design (Tseng, 2005).

Service

Professional knowledge: In providing professional services, people with the appropriate professional knowledge are the core of a service company, because they directly influence the quality of the services, the price, and the company's image. Guides are thus required to have suitable expertise for providing services and presenting information to visitors. Similarly, an MMNS needs to contain the appropriate professional content to offer to visitors to browse (Ellis and Mosher, 1993).

Service attitude: Parasuraman, Berry, and Zeithaml (1991) revealed that regardless of the type of service company – insurance companies, hotel services, or repair services – customers want a more personalized service and a closer relationship with the service provider. Relationship building is an intensive process that must provide immediate and reliable responses that demonstrate empathy. Museum staff must therefore be able to listen attentively to visitors talking about how to use the navigation system and maintain a positive attitude when teaching them how to operate the system.

Quick response: Johns and Clark (1993) indicated that the process of travelers visiting a museum has five stages: preview, transportation, entry, service experience, and leaving. During the service experience, desk staff must be able to solve problems or answer various queries regarding ticketing, and even provide entertainment suggestions for visitors.

Service customization: Customers want to have a more personalized service and a closer relationship with service providers (Parasuraman et al., 1991). Williams et al. (2005) indicated that providing services with a customized theme helped to improve the potential value of those services. Therefore, museum staff who provide customized services according to the needs of different types of visitors will be able to enhance the value of a navigation service.

Service proactiveness: Museums should choose exhibition themes carefully to effectively develop new audiences and attract visitors. Fronville (1985) explored marketing tools for analyzing various activities provided by museums, such as school visits, seminars, travel guides, videos, and books, in terms of their effectiveness in marketing, and found that these activities significantly enhanced the effectiveness of marketing. Museums should therefore provide regular information about activities through the museum navigation system.

Promotion: Chen (1998) believed that museums should actively use new marketing methods and tools to effectively and appropriately spread their message to their target market. He categorized seven marketing methods: database marketing, channel marketing, event/theme marketing, joint promotion, Internet marketing, marketing, publications marketing, and promotion. Of these, promotion had a significantly positive effect on financial indicators.

Exhibition space

Space saving: The arrangement of a museum's exhibition spaces, in terms of circulation, may be roughly divided into the following types: linear, radial, random, and open. Different circulation arrangements are appropriate for different themes and several types of arrangement can be combined in accordance with the requirements (Matthews, 1991). If a museum's exhibition space is limited, visitors can be allowed to preview the exhibition and related content through an MMNS. Such a system can thus provide a more flexible way of managing visitor circulation.

Visitor routing: Bitgood (1994, 1995) found that museum visitors had specific behaviors, typically goal-oriented moving, being attracted to an exhibition or item that is tagged with a description, being attracted by an open door, and following the existing direction of movement. If none of these behavior options were observed, visitors tended to follow a right-turn circulation. Therefore, in designing an exhibition, visitors' behavior and preferences should be taken into account to create the most appropriate circulation route for the exhibition. Recommending a particular route to visitors through an MMNS may contribute to a positive visitor experience.

Exhibition information: Hung (2007) found that if there was no buffer space between an exhibit and the associated descriptive text, the position of the exhibit description was not obvious, or the description was placed at the end of an exhibit showcase, the description was often ignored or the visitor moved on to the next exhibit. In other words, if exhibit information was placed in the path of the visitor and directly facing him or her, the proportion of visitors who paused to read it increased. An MMNS is an excellent method of displaying exhibit information, with a clear screen and minimal distance from the visitor.

Direction signs: To avoid visitors adopting a "missing" or "ignore" visit behavior, or even a wayfinding behavior, a clear direction needs to be indicated to them, particularly at a crossroads formed by the arrangement of exhibits and where there are path choices in an exhibition space. Huang (2007) revealed that inappropriate content and placement of direction signs was an important factor affecting circulation in the National Palace Museum and also an important reason for wayfinding behavior. An MMNS must therefore be able to clearly indicate the best direction on a screen.

Cultural and creative

Knowledge provision: Kravchyna and Hastings (2002) found that the information needs of visitors in a museum website included recent exhibitions, museum collections, news about special events, museum instructions, digital images of collections, research required, contact information, gifts for purchase, ticket information, etc. The application of information technology in museum exhibitions should not focus purely on the technology itself: it is important to provide an integrated, new entertainment concept for exhibition information and knowledge.

Aesthetics: Aesthetics often receives little attention, even from media producers, but plays a key role in the field of website design. Aesthetics does not just involve creating images required by the website publisher and to comply with the website's style, but must also support the presentation of website content and functionality, and thus encourage the target audience to browse (Thorlacius, 2002, 2007). The design of an MMNS must thus involve aesthetic concepts.

Creativity: After interviewing 1,200 visitors, Marty (2008) found that up to 87.4 percent of museum visitors looked forward to learning more about a museum through its navigation system. From this perspective, the value of the museum lies not only in managing collections, but also in providing a place in which to share knowledge with the public (MacDonald and Alsford, 1991).

Humanities: Reynolds, Walker, and Speight (2010) found that hand-held navigation devices offered visitors a variety of imaginative views of exhibition spaces and exhibits, and provided additional information for enhancing the user's knowledge of and interest in the exhibitions. Museum exhibitions can help visitors of different ages to understand and appreciate the great cultural achievements that the exhibits represent and to acquire the skills, attitudes, and knowledge associated with the exhibits (DCMS, 2014).

Research design and methodology

There are many factors that affect whether tourists will use an MMNS. Due to personal, subjective opinions and the personal acceptance of such a system by tourists, opinions may differ widely regarding how to design an effective MMNS that takes these factors into consideration. This study collected from relevant studies a comprehensive list of impact factors that may affect the design of an effective MMNS, and used an analytic hierarchy process (AHP) to determine the weights and rankings of those factors, with the aim of evaluating the importance of the various impact factors and the design dimensions.

The work in this study can be divided into five steps:

1　Explore impact factors and the overview of an MMNS. Review the literature on design factors that affect the use of an MMNS and analyze these with reference to past and present MMNSs.
2　List all possible impact factors. Review the relevant literature and aggregate the factors to explore all possible factors.
3　Build a hierarchical structure. Develop a hierarchical architecture based on the above factors.
4　Calculate factor weights. Construct an AHP questionnaire, collect and integrate the results from expert groups, and calculate the factor weights.
5　Discussion and suggestions. Use the results of the weight calculations to inform the discussion. The results should provide a reference source and recommendations for agencies involved in the future design of an MMNS.

Analytic hierarchy process

The AHP was developed in 1971 by Thomas L. Saaty, an American scholar at the University of Pittsburgh. Saaty (1980) edited the AHP approach and published it in a book. The AHP is mainly applied to decision making and problem solving under conditions of uncertainty that have multiple criteria; the problems are influenced by a number of factors that may be tangible or intangible, qualitative or quantitative, and may affect each other. The AHP is readily adapted by academic research units, because of its simplicity and practical value. It is commonly used to solve priority determination, resource allocation, resource planning, prediction of results, risk assessment, generation of alternatives, choice of the best solution, decision making, conflict resolution, performance measurement, and optimization problems, and ensuring the stability of a system during its design.

The AHP approach involves simplifying a complicated problem so that decision-makers can readily make an appropriate decision, for example when solving an unstructured economic, social, or management science issue. First the decision-makers set the overall goal for the issue, develop secondary-level goals contributing to the overall goal, and iteratively develop the next sub-level (third-level) goals that contribute to the previous ones (secondary-level goals) until the most detailed level of goals is reached. The goals in the final level are called impact factors. Next, the impact factors are pairwise compared using nine scaled question items, eigenvectors are calculated as the weight needed to evaluate each factor, and the higher-level goals are prioritized by ranking the sum of sub-factor weights for each. Finally, the decision-makers make their decision based on the priorities thus revealed.

AHP analysis process

According to Saaty's (1980) proposal, the AHP analysis process for decision-making is as follows.

Model the research problem as a hierarchy

Establish a hierarchy for the current complex research issue. Although there is no specific procedure or rule for constructing the hierarchy, the highest-level element of the structure is the final goal of the research issue; the lowest-level elements are the most detailed items used to assess the research issue; elements with similar importance with respect to the final goal are organized on the same level; there should be no more than seven elements within the same level of the hierarchy; and each element in the same level of the hierarchy is independent of the others.

Design a questionnaire and form a pairwise comparison matrix

The principle of pairwise factor comparison involves comparing the influence of pairs of subordinate elements, those on the same level and below a particular superior element, on the superior element. The scale used for comparison

Table 9.2 Nominal scale used in the AHP

Scale	Definition	Description
1	Equally	The two comparisons have the same importance or make the same contribution to the superior element.
3	Moderately	Moderately preferred to the other element according to experience or judgment
5	Strong	Strongly preferred to the other element according to experience or judgment
7	Very strong	Very strong tendency to dominate over the other element
9	Extremely	Extremely certain that one element dominates over the other
2, 4, 6, 8	Intermediate judgment values	Whenever you need a compromise between two neighboring judgment scales

Source: Saaty (1980)

of elements is usually a nominal scale, comprising the response categories for each question item (i.e., equally, moderately, strong, very strong, extremely), plus four intermediate response categories that lie between the five categories above, giving a total of nine categories (see Table 9.2). A research issue with N factors requires $N(N-1)/2$ comparisons to be performed to create a pairwise comparison matrix.

Estimate consistency

This step involves investigating whether there is any inconsistency among the pairwise comparisons and whether any contradictions exist in the results of the comparison. In AHP research, the consistency of all comparison results must be tested and the consistency index (C.I.) calculated. The formula for the consistency index is defined as follows, where λmax is the maximum eigenvalue of the matrices and n is the number of assessment factors:

$$\text{C.I.} = \frac{\lambda\text{max} - \text{n}}{\text{n} - 1}$$

When C.I. = 0, the pairwise comparisons have been judged consistently; larger C.I. values indicate greater inconsistency. Saaty suggested that as long as C.I. ≤ 0.1, the consistency of the pairwise comparison matrix can be considered acceptable; otherwise, the responses to the pairwise comparison questionnaire are determined to be invalid.

The consistency ratio (C.R.) is another indicator for judging whether the responses are adequate for the research problem. C.R. is the ratio of C.I. to the corresponding random index (R.I.), where R.I. is the average C.I. of randomly generated pairwise comparison matrices; different numbers of leaf elements result in different values of R.I. (see Table 9.3). Saaty (1980) suggested that if the number of leaf elements is 3, the C.R. should be less than 0.05, if the number of leaf elements is 4, the C.R. should be less than 0.08, and a C.R. of less than 0.1 is usually acceptable if the number of leaf elements is more than 5. Otherwise, the decision will not be adequate.

$$C.R. = \frac{C.I.}{R.I.}$$

Calculate priority vectors

Place the measurements resulting from the pairwise comparison of n elements in the upper triangular matrix of the full pairwise comparison matrix (Matrix A); the value of each measurement might be $1/9, 1/8, \ldots, 1/3, 1/2, 1, 2, 3, \ldots,$ 8, 9 (see Table 9.4). To the lower triangular matrix, assign the reciprocal of the

Table 9.3 Random Index

N	1	2	3	4	5	6	7	8	9	10	11	12	13	14	15
R.I.(n)	0.00	0.00	0.58	0.90	1.12	1.24	1.32	1.41	1.45	1.49	1.51	1.48	1.56	1.57	1.58

Table 9.4 An example of the factors preparedness questionnaire

	Ratio Scale											
FACTOR	Extremely preferred (9:1) 8:1	Very strongly preferred (7:1) 6:1	Strong preferred (1:5) 4:1	Moderately preferred (3:1) 2:1	Equally preferred (1:1) 1:2	Moderately preferred (1:3) 1:4	Strong preferred (1:5) 1:6	Very strongly preferred (1:7) 1:8	Extremely preferred (1:9)	FACTOR
F_A			✓							F_B
F_A				✓						F_C
F_A						✓				F_D

upper triangular matrix, that is, $a_{ij} = \dfrac{1}{a_{ji}}$. The complete pairwise comparison matrix is thus:

$$A = \begin{bmatrix} 1 & \cdots & a_{1j} \\ \vdots & \ddots & \vdots \\ 1/a_{i1} & \cdots & 1 \end{bmatrix}.$$

To determine the priority of each element in a level of the hierarchy, the eigenvalue method, which is commonly used in the field of numerical analysis, is applied to the comparison matrix to calculate the eigenvector and the eigenvector is taken to be a priority vector. If the eigenvector does not sum to one, normalize the eigenvector to obtain the priority vector. The order of the priority vectors represents the relative importance of each factor. The formula for eigenvalues in the priority vector is:

$$w_i = \frac{\left[\prod_{j=1}^{n} a_{ij} \right]^{\frac{1}{n}}}{\sum_{i=1}^{n} \left[\prod_{j=1}^{n} a_{ij} \right]^{\frac{1}{n}}}.$$

Determine the overall priority of the alternatives

Not only must the priorities of the factors in each level of the research problem hierarchy be determined, but a best solution also has to be chosen from among the alternatives. A pairwise comparison matrix of problem goals and alternatives is constructed for calculating the priorities of alternatives. Finally, the overall priority of an alternative is calculated by multiplying its priorities with respect to each criterion by the priority of the corresponding criterion and summing the results.

Demographics

This study investigated the factors that affect the success of an MMNS using the AHP. We used an AHP questionnaire to interview experts in the domain, comprising five people from each of the following categories: system development companies experienced in museum navigation systems, senior volunteer docents, academic staff, and visitor representatives; a detailed list is given in Table 9.5. Wherever possible we conducted face-to-face interviews, but also carried out email interviews with experts who were too busy to participate in a face-to-face interview; in those situations, we described the research issue and question items clearly via email. Data collection took place between May 1, 2012, and June 10, 2012.

Table 9.5 Interviewee list

Expert category	Respondents
Industry expert	Industry Expert 1 (Company A),
(from museum navigation systems development companies)	Industry Expert 2 (Company B),
	Industry Expert 3 (Company C),
	Industry Expert 4 (Company D),
	Industry Expert 5 (Company E).
Senior volunteer docents	Senior Volunteer 1,
(in Taiwan's National Palace Museum)	Senior Volunteer 2,
	Senior Volunteer 3,
	Senior Volunteer 4,
	Senior Volunteer 5.
Academic staff	Academic Staff from:
(scholars from colleges and researchers from government)	(1) Dept. of Information Engineering,
	(2) Dept. of Information Engineering,
	(3) Dept. of Information Engineering,
	(4) Dept. of Business Administration,
	(5) Dept. of Cultural Affairs, Taipei City Government.
Visitor representatives	Visitor Representative 1,
(to Taiwan's National Palace Museum)	Visitor Representative 2,
	Visitor Representative 3,
	Visitor Representative 4,
	Visitor Representative 5.

Reliability and validity

In the AHP approach, researchers use a consistency test to check for reliability. Accordingly, C.I. and C.R. were calculated to verify consistency in this study, with reference to Saaty's (1980) suggestion that the C.I. values should be less than 0.1. Table 9.6 gives the C.I. values for each impact dimension by respondent and shows that the responses from all 20 experts in this study have good consistency.

Saaty (1980) further suggested using reference C.R. values to check for consistency between respondents. This study had seven factors in the infrastructure dimension, so the C.R. values for each respondent in this dimension should be less than 0.1. There were six factors in the human–computer interface dimension, the content design dimension, and the service dimension, so the respective C.R. values should be less than 0.1. There were five factors in the user experience dimension, so the respective C.R. values should be less than 0.1. There were four factors in the exhibition space dimension and the cultural and creative dimension, so the respective C.R. values should be less than 0.8. All of the responses in this

Table 9.6 Consistency Index

Respondents \ Design Criteria	Infrastructure	Human–Computer Interface	Content Design	User Experience	Service	Exhibition Space	Cultural and Creative
Industry Expert 1	0.07	0.1	0.1	0.09	0.1	0.034	0.06
Industry Expert 2	0.03	0.02	0.07	0.08	0.09	0.06	0.01
Industry Expert 3	0.1	0.087	0.082	0.086	0.06	0.034	0.07
Industry Expert 4	0.043	0.03	0.02	0.03	0.02	0.054	0.05
Industry Expert 5	0.02	0.02	0.025	0.023	0.03	0.01	0.053
Senior Volunteer 1	0.065	0.071	0.091	0.08	0.098	0.06	0.062
Senior Volunteer 2	0.1	0.084	0.09	0.079	0.071	0.02	0.028
Senior Volunteer 3	0.07	0.09	0.07	0.03	0.07	0.03	0.069
Senior Volunteer 4	0.09	0.08	0.043	0.06	0.062	0.02	0.07
Senior Volunteer 5	0.06	0.08	0.09	0.04	0.1	0.03	0.066
Academic Staff 1	0.1	0.07	0.07	0.071	0.063	0.034	0.071
Academic Staff 2	0.08	0.01	0.01	0.01	0.01	0.01	0.01
Academic Staff 3	0.1	0.1	0.09	0.1	0.1	0.03	0.07
Academic Staff 4	0.09	0.06	0.1	0.09	0.09	0.01	0.02
Academic Staff 5	0.09	0.09	0.085	0.1	0.087	0.023	0.07
Visitor Representative 1	0.047	0.1	0.1	0.08	0.1	0.055	0.069
Visitor Representative 2	0.1	0.098	0.093	0.1	0.076	0.056	0.065
Visitor Representative 3	0.092	0.1	0.1	0.09	0.09	0.05	0.66
Visitor Representative 4	0.1	0.1	0.08	0.06	0.084	0.034	0.043
Visitor Representative 5	0.08	0.06	0.1	0.078	0.08	0.05	0.06

study complied with the theoretical constraint on consistency, indicating that this study had good reliability (see Table 9.7)

In terms of validity, all of the factors identified in this study as being associated with MMNSs have been explored in the relevant literature and via current navigation systems operating in museums. We also carried out interviews with industry experts, senior volunteer docents, academic staff, and visitor representatives. This

Table 9.7 Consistency ratio values

Respondents	Infrastructure	Human–Computer Interface	Content Design	User Experience	Service	Exhibition Space	Cultural and Creative
Industry Expert 1	0.053	0.081	0.081	0.080	0.081	0.038	0.067
Industry Expert 2	0.023	0.016	0.056	0.071	0.073	0.067	0.011
Industry Expert 3	0.076	0.070	0.066	0.077	0.048	0.038	0.078
Industry Expert 4	0.033	0.024	0.016	0.027	0.016	0.060	0.056
Industry Expert 5	0.015	0.016	0.020	0.021	0.024	0.011	0.059
Senior Volunteer 1	0.049	0.057	0.073	0.071	0.079	0.067	0.069
Senior Volunteer 2	0.076	0.068	0.073	0.071	0.057	0.022	0.031
Senior Volunteer 3	0.053	0.073	0.056	0.027	0.056	0.033	0.077
Senior Volunteer 4	0.068	0.065	0.035	0.054	0.050	0.022	0.078
Senior Volunteer 5	0.045	0.065	0.073	0.036	0.081	0.033	0.073
Academic Staff 1	0.076	0.056	0.056	0.063	0.051	0.038	0.079
Academic Staff 2	0.061	0.008	0.008	0.009	0.008	0.011	0.011
Academic Staff 3	0.076	0.081	0.073	0.089	0.081	0.033	0.078
Academic Staff 4	0.068	0.048	0.081	0.080	0.073	0.011	0.022
Academic Staff 5	0.068	0.073	0.069	0.089	0.070	0.026	0.078
Visitor Representative 1	0.036	0.081	0.081	0.071	0.081	0.061	0.077
Visitor Representative 2	0.076	0.079	0.075	0.089	0.061	0.062	0.072
Visitor Representative 3	0.070	0.081	0.081	0.080	0.073	0.056	0.733
Visitor Representative 4	0.076	0.081	0.065	0.054	0.068	0.038	0.048
Visitor Representative 5	0.061	0.048	0.081	0.070	0.065	0.056	0.067

process enabled the accurate assessment of the research issues and, as a result, the study has good content validity and good expert validity.

Analysis and discussion

Synthesizing the judgment of criteria (design dimensions)

After completing the consistency check on the responses collected in the expert interviews, we calculated the eigenvalue as a weight of each design dimension for every respondent and ranked the design dimensions by the average weights of

Table 9.8 The relative weights of each design criteria dimension

Respondents \ Dimension	Infrastructure	Human–Computer Interface	Content Design	User Experience	Service	Exhibition Space	Cultural and Creative
Industry Expert 1	0.112	0.225	0.272	0.139	0.049	0.114	0.094
Industry Expert 2	0.083	0.155	0.115	0.028	0.054	0.186	0.379
Industry Expert 3	0.101	0.101	0.140	0.236	0.268	0.032	0.122
Industry Expert 4	0.156	0.385	0.260	0.021	0.091	0.054	0.033
Industry Expert 5	0.161	0.349	0.239	0.029	0.066	0.084	0.072
Senior Volunteer 1	0.173	0.320	0.039	0.072	0.059	0.110	0.227
Senior Volunteer 2	0.230	0.101	0.199	0.090	0.075	0.043	0.262
Senior Volunteer 3	0.032	0.116	0.155	0.073	0.039	0.316	0.269
Senior Volunteer 4	0.039	0.087	0.114	0.362	0.058	0.146	0.194
Senior Volunteer 5	0.064	0.305	0.261	0.061	0.100	0.049	0.160
Academic Staff 1	0.227	0.060	0.110	0.038	0.073	0.173	0.319
Academic Staff 2	0.170	0.202	0.140	0.058	0.069	0.195	0.166
Academic Staff 3	0.060	0.227	0.233	0.109	0.051	0.177	0.143
Academic Staff 4	0.228	0.098	0.211	0.085	0.080	0.038	0.260
Academic Staff 5	0.083	0.155	0.115	0.028	0.054	0.186	0.379
Visitor Representative 1	0.325	0.174	0.125	0.065	0.032	0.099	0.180
Visitor Representative 2	0.378	0.165	0.096	0.031	0.043	0.121	0.166
Visitor Representative 3	0.304	0.170	0.196	0.102	0.061	0.058	0.109
Visitor Representative 4	0.050	0.170	0.205	0.099	0.065	0.228	0.183
Visitor Representative 5	0.169	0.203	0.138	0.060	0.068	0.196	0.166
Average Weight	0.157	0.188	0.168	0.089	0.073	0.130	0.194
Ranking	4	2	3	6	7	5	1

each dimension. These values are given in Table 9.8. The respondents assessed the dimensions differently, based on their personal experience and knowledge, and the ranking of each dimension therefore also differed between the respondents. Overall, the results showed that the most important criterion was the cultural and creative dimension (0.194), the second was the human–computer interface (0.188), the third content design (0.168), followed by infrastructure (0.157), exhibition space (0.130), user experience (0.089), and service (0.073). In the experts' view, service was the design dimension that would least affect the successful design of an MMNS.

Synthesizing judgment of the sub-criteria (design factors)

The judgments were broken down into the sub-criteria of our research problem, in the sequence infrastructure, human–computer interface, content design, user experience, service, exhibition space, and cultural and creative.

Infrastructure

Seven design factors were used to categorize the infrastructure dimension; Table 9.9 gives the factor weights for those seven factors for each respondent.

Table 9.9 The factor weights within the Infrastructure dimension

Infrastructure / Respondents	Signal Stability	Coverage	Ubiquitousness	Broadband Connection Speeds	Near-field Detection	Compatibility	Security
Industry Expert 1	0.069	0.211	0.039	0.042	0.074	0.051	0.514
Industry Expert 2	0.161	0.161	0.161	0.139	0.139	0.161	0.079
Industry Expert 3	0.277	0.113	0.142	0.265	0.082	0.046	0.075
Industry Expert 4	0.390	0.261	0.153	0.092	0.054	0.026	0.024
Industry Expert 5	0.354	0.240	0.104	0.159	0.068	0.031	0.045
Senior Volunteer 1	0.079	0.212	0.028	0.052	0.064	0.055	0.510
Senior Volunteer 2	0.256	0.171	0.152	0.108	0.190	0.076	0.048
Senior Volunteer 3	0.200	0.330	0.079	0.085	0.141	0.040	0.125
Senior Volunteer 4	0.413	0.228	0.157	0.045	0.098	0.033	0.026
Senior Volunteer 5	0.138	0.082	0.136	0.144	0.037	0.096	0.367
Academic Staff 1	0.207	0.331	0.072	0.087	0.142	0.038	0.124
Academic Staff 2	0.243	0.176	0.104	0.114	0.097	0.087	0.179
Academic Staff 3	0.084	0.023	0.052	0.064	0.045	0.224	0.510
Academic Staff 4	0.096	0.110	0.062	0.098	0.041	0.220	0.373
Academic Staff 5	0.080	0.126	0.220	0.040	0.372	0.098	0.064
Visitor Representative 1	0.190	0.343	0.057	0.042	0.082	0.055	0.232
Visitor Representative 2	0.342	0.181	0.056	0.031	0.042	0.089	0.258
Visitor Representative 3	0.172	0.175	0.034	0.211	0.054	0.089	0.265
Visitor Representative 4	0.251	0.305	0.061	0.080	0.151	0.040	0.112
Visitor Representative 5	0.264	0.042	0.113	0.097	0.079	0.041	0.364
Average Weight	0.213	0.191	0.099	0.100	0.103	0.080	0.215
Ranking	2	3	6	5	4	7	1

The average weight of each factor indicated its relative importance to the infra-structure dimension. The ranking with respect to the importance of the seven fac-tors, in sequence, was security (0.215), signal stability (0.213), coverage (0.191), near-field detection (0.103), broadband connection speed (0.100), ubiquitous-nous (0.099), and system compatibility (0.080). The domain experts generally considered security to be the most important factor within the infrastructure dimension affecting the success of an MMNS, with signal stability and coverage having a similar level of importance. Compatibility was considered to be of the lowest importance (the lowest average weight), but some of the academic staff believed that compatibility was also of considerable importance.

Human–computer interface

Six design factors were used to categorize the human–computer interface dimen-sion; Table 9.10 gives the factor weights for these six factors for each respon-dent. The average weight of each factor indicated its relative importance to the

Table 9.10 The factor weights within the human–computer interface dimension

Respondents	Information richness	Information presentation	Icon design	Screen menu design	Multi-language support	Search function
Industry Expert 1	0.064	0.441	0.248	0.15	0.031	0.066
Industry Expert 2	0.061	0.368	0.143	0.143	0.143	0.143
Industry Expert 3	0.052	0.105	0.34	0.144	0.073	0.285
Industry Expert 4	0.102	0.368	0.254	0.162	0.068	0.045
Industry Expert 5	0.1	0.381	0.256	0.158	0.064	0.041
Senior Volunteer 1	0.093	0.058	0.046	0.402	0.252	0.149
Senior Volunteer 2	0.061	0.309	0.276	0.121	0.133	0.101
Senior Volunteer 3	0.243	0.428	0.133	0.084	0.063	0.049
Senior Volunteer 4	0.167	0.087	0.08	0.054	0.384	0.228
Senior Volunteer 5	0.082	0.436	0.16	0.157	0.061	0.104
Academic Staff 1	0.063	0.276	0.282	0.127	0.148	0.104
Academic Staff 2	0.133	0.333	0.172	0.138	0.109	0.114
Academic Staff 3	0.243	0.425	0.048	0.133	0.092	0.06
Academic Staff 4	0.067	0.23	0.274	0.095	0.233	0.1
Academic Staff 5	0.05	0.36	0.067	0.127	0.164	0.232

(Continued)

Table 9.10 (Continued)

Respondents \ Human–Computer Interface	Information richness	Information presentation	Icon design	Screen menu design	Multi-language support	Search function
Visitor Representative 1	0.194	0.402	0.192	0.084	0.06	0.069
Visitor Representative 2	0.409	0.273	0.064	0.032	0.053	0.17
Visitor Representative 3	0.231	0.335	0.254	0.073	0.034	0.073
Visitor Representative 4	0.242	0.426	0.047	0.133	0.084	0.07
Visitor Representative 5	0.16	0.293	0.38	0.07	0.044	0.053
Average Weight	**0.141**	**0.317**	**0.186**	**0.129**	**0.115**	**0.113**
Ranking	3	1	2	4	5	6

human–computer interface dimension. The ranking in terms of the importance of the six factors, in sequence, was information presentation (0.317), icon design (0.186), information richness (0.141), screen menu design (0.129), multi-language support (0.115), and search function (0.113). The domain experts deemed that in the human–computer interface dimension, it was first necessary to focus on the design of information presentation to design a successful MMNS. The average weight of the information presentation factor placed it significantly ahead of the others, as this was most important for attracting tourists to use the system. The next most important considerations were icon design, information richness, and screen menu design. Multi-lingual support and search function were much less important.

Content design

Six design factors were used to categorize the content design dimension; Table 9.11 gives the factor weights for these six factors for each respondent. The average weight of each factor indicated its relative importance to the content design dimension. The ranking in terms of importance of the six factors, in sequence, was timeliness (0.242), locational notification (0.224), interactivity (0.213), site map (0.148), information download/pre-download (0.094), and browsing history (0.079). The top priority in the content design dimension, according to the domain experts, was to make it possible for visitors to receive real-time information. The weights of timeliness, locational notification, and interactivity were high, above 0.2, indicating that these three factors dominated over site map, information download/pre-download (0.094), and browsing history in the content design dimension.

Table 9.11 The factor weights within the content design dimension

Content Design Respondents	Timeliness	Interactivity	Locational Notification	Browsing History	Information Download / Pre-Download	Site Map
Industry Expert 1	0.114	0.518	0.123	0.088	0.104	0.053
Industry Expert 2	0.252	0.297	0.143	0.102	0.149	0.058
Industry Expert 3	0.154	0.126	0.293	0.115	0.255	0.057
Industry Expert 4	0.160	0.250	0.382	0.101	0.064	0.043
Industry Expert 5	0.149	0.253	0.379	0.112	0.060	0.047
Senior Volunteer 1	0.311	0.327	0.044	0.055	0.095	0.168
Senior Volunteer 2	0.082	0.077	0.322	0.061	0.278	0.180
Senior Volunteer 3	0.303	0.124	0.182	0.055	0.069	0.266
Senior Volunteer 4	0.137	0.310	0.346	0.101	0.062	0.044
Senior Volunteer 5	0.300	0.220	0.240	0.102	0.052	0.086
Academic Staff 1	0.299	0.126	0.183	0.059	0.078	0.255
Academic Staff 2	0.253	0.211	0.214	0.084	0.099	0.139
Academic Staff 3	0.311	0.327	0.044	0.055	0.095	0.168
Academic Staff 4	0.072	0.056	0.470	0.152	0.039	0.211
Academic Staff 5	0.082	0.039	0.460	0.130	0.056	0.233
Visitor Representative 1	0.365	0.294	0.173	0.030	0.055	0.083
Visitor Representative 2	0.418	0.220	0.130	0.034	0.049	0.149
Visitor Representative 3	0.488	0.207	0.054	0.034	0.088	0.129
Visitor Representative 4	0.229	0.175	0.096	0.061	0.097	0.343
Visitor Representative 5	0.353	0.104	0.195	0.054	0.042	0.252
Average Weight	**0.242**	**0.213**	**0.224**	**0.079**	**0.094**	**0.148**
Ranking	1	3	2	6	5	4

User experience

Five design factors were used to categorize the user experience dimension; Table 9.12 gives the factor weights for these five factors for each respondent. The average weight of each factor indicated its relative importance to the user experience dimension. The ranking in terms of importance of the five factors, in sequence, was ease of use (0.287), satisfaction (0.224), utilization (0.195), user needs (0.184), and personalization (0.110). The domain experts believed that ease of use was the most important consideration within the user experience dimension; if visitors felt that the system was easy to use, they would be

Table 9.12 The factor weights within the user experience dimension

Respondents \ User Experience	Satisfaction	Utilization	Ease of Use	Personalization	User Needs
Industry Expert 1	0.284	0.120	0.470	0.062	0.064
Industry Expert 2	0.306	0.195	0.187	0.124	0.187
Industry Expert 3	0.471	0.229	0.100	0.100	0.100
Industry Expert 4	0.095	0.155	0.451	0.060	0.239
Industry Expert 5	0.099	0.162	0.420	0.066	0.252
Senior Volunteer 1	0.189	0.048	0.139	0.089	0.535
Senior Volunteer 2	0.106	0.071	0.487	0.096	0.240
Senior Volunteer 3	0.147	0.363	0.264	0.094	0.132
Senior Volunteer 4	0.413	0.054	0.161	0.210	0.161
Senior Volunteer 5	0.399	0.042	0.114	0.159	0.285
Academic Staff 1	0.235	0.075	0.208	0.076	0.407
Academic Staff 2	0.228	0.183	0.300	0.115	0.174
Academic Staff 3	0.157	0.383	0.264	0.084	0.112
Academic Staff 4	0.106	0.071	0.487	0.096	0.240
Academic Staff 5	0.056	0.239	0.095	0.391	0.218
Visitor Representative 1	0.417	0.265	0.194	0.076	0.048
Visitor Representative 2	0.144	0.201	0.493	0.105	0.058
Visitor Representative 3	0.156	0.442	0.268	0.087	0.047
Visitor Representative 4	0.178	0.423	0.234	0.068	0.098
Visitor Representative 5	0.288	0.180	0.395	0.049	0.089
Average Weight	**0.224**	**0.195**	**0.287**	**0.110**	**0.184**
Ranking	2	3	1	5	4

encouraged to reuse the system. In the domain experts' view, personalization had the lowest priority within the user experience dimension, because adjusting the navigation system based on visitors' preferences is cumbersome, and most tourists visit infrequently.

Service

Six design factors were used to categorize the service dimension; Table 9.13 gives the factor weights for these six factors for each respondent. The average weight of each factor indicated its relative importance to the service dimension. The

Table 9.13 The factor weights within the service dimension

Respondents \ Service	Professional Knowledge	Service Attitude	Quick Response	Service Customization	Service Proactiveness	Promotion
Industry Expert 1	0.036	0.336	0.172	0.258	0.099	0.099
Industry Expert 2	0.086	0.272	0.316	0.232	0.039	0.055
Industry Expert 3	0.101	0.314	0.282	0.094	0.084	0.126
Industry Expert 4	0.101	0.382	0.250	0.160	0.064	0.043
Industry Expert 5	0.104	0.386	0.236	0.173	0.062	0.039
Senior Volunteer 1	0.273	0.269	0.172	0.157	0.088	0.041
Senior Volunteer 2	0.138	0.431	0.214	0.084	0.088	0.046
Senior Volunteer 3	0.271	0.340	0.162	0.083	0.095	0.049
Senior Volunteer 4	0.279	0.398	0.121	0.102	0.052	0.047
Senior Volunteer 5	0.076	0.162	0.112	0.167	0.405	0.078
Academic Staff 1	0.265	0.282	0.149	0.197	0.065	0.042
Academic Staff 2	0.165	0.340	0.224	0.136	0.078	0.056
Academic Staff 3	0.270	0.279	0.175	0.157	0.078	0.041
Academic Staff 4	0.087	0.271	0.326	0.222	0.039	0.056
Academic Staff 5	0.088	0.270	0.324	0.221	0.037	0.061
Visitor Representative 1	0.230	0.264	0.322	0.047	0.089	0.047
Visitor Representative 2	0.279	0.293	0.222	0.105	0.056	0.045
Visitor Representative 3	0.268	0.377	0.146	0.071	0.094	0.044
Visitor Representative 4	0.273	0.329	0.171	0.070	0.097	0.059
Visitor Representative 5	0.202	0.339	0.281	0.084	0.054	0.041
Average Weight	**0.180**	**0.317**	**0.219**	**0.141**	**0.088**	**0.056**
Ranking	3	1	2	4	5	6

ranking in terms of importance of the six factors, in sequence, was service attitude (0.317), quick response (0.219), professional knowledge (0.180), service customization (0.141), service proactiveness (0.088), and promotion (0.056). The domain experts believed that service attitude represented the most important factor within the service dimension. The service attitude of museum staff determines visitor satisfaction after visitors have asked museum staff for help with an operational problem in the navigation system. Minor considerations were quick response, professional knowledge, service customization, and service proactiveness. The promotion factor was assessed as having the lowest weight of all six factors, as visitors do not care about what type of promotion channel is used for the navigation system.

Exhibition space

Four design factors were used to categorize the exhibition space dimension; Table 9.14 gives the factor weights for these four factors for each respondent. The average weight of each factor indicated its relative importance to the exhibition space dimension. The ranking in terms of importance of the four factors, in sequence, was visitor routing (0.333), direction signs (0.214), exhibition

Table 9.14 The factor weights within the exhibition space dimension

Exhibition Space / Respondents	Space Saving	Visitor Routing	Exhibition Information	Direction Signs
Industry Expert 1	0.110	0.408	0.211	0.271
Industry Expert 2	0.096	0.368	0.368	0.168
Industry Expert 3	0.104	0.332	0.390	0.174
Industry Expert 4	0.098	0.503	0.159	0.240
Industry Expert 5	0.160	0.467	0.277	0.095
Senior Volunteer 1	0.053	0.308	0.132	0.506
Senior Volunteer 2	0.070	0.285	0.315	0.330
Senior Volunteer 3	0.131	0.395	0.202	0.272
Senior Volunteer 4	0.119	0.220	0.201	0.460
Senior Volunteer 5	0.280	0.116	0.516	0.087
Academic Staff 1	0.155	0.193	0.606	0.046
Academic Staff 2	0.175	0.355	0.269	0.201
Academic Staff 3	0.120	0.418	0.191	0.271
Academic Staff 4	0.079	0.288	0.307	0.327
Academic Staff 5	0.146	0.415	0.346	0.093
Visitor Representative 1	0.246	0.575	0.117	0.062
Visitor Representative 2	0.553	0.148	0.054	0.245
Visitor Representative 3	0.103	0.488	0.157	0.251
Visitor Representative 4	0.511	0.209	0.177	0.102
Visitor Representative 5	0.438	0.163	0.320	0.079
Average Weight	**0.187**	**0.333**	**0.266**	**0.214**
Ranking	4	1	3	2

information (0.266), and space saving (0.187). The domain experts determined the visitor routing factor to have a major influence within the exhibition space dimension, with route planning being of high importance. How to quickly and accurately direct a visitor using an MMNS, whenever that visitor enters an unfamiliar space, is an important consideration in the future design of an MMNS.

Cultural and creative

Four design factors were used to categorize the cultural and creative dimension; Table 9.15 gives the factor weights for these four factors for each respondent. The average weight of each factor indicated its relative importance to the cultural and

Table 9.15 The factor weights within the cultural and creative dimension

Cultural and Creative / Respondents	Knowledge Provision	Esthetics	Creativity	Humanities
Industry Expert 1	0.654	0.053	0.164	0.130
Industry Expert 2	0.375	0.125	0.375	0.125
Industry Expert 3	0.399	0.174	0.111	0.316
Industry Expert 4	0.462	0.134	0.103	0.301
Industry Expert 5	0.116	0.458	0.240	0.185
Senior Volunteer 1	0.429	0.161	0.085	0.325
Senior Volunteer 2	0.065	0.373	0.249	0.313
Senior Volunteer 3	0.540	0.067	0.252	0.142
Senior Volunteer 4	0.201	0.094	0.191	0.514
Senior Volunteer 5	0.433	0.293	0.077	0.197
Academic Staff 1	0.457	0.205	0.051	0.287
Academic Staff 2	0.342	0.159	0.205	0.294
Academic Staff 3	0.431	0.159	0.086	0.324
Academic Staff 4	0.082	0.368	0.242	0.308
Academic Staff 5	0.151	0.075	0.265	0.509
Visitor Representative 1	0.519	0.166	0.244	0.072
Visitor Representative 2	0.171	0.077	0.231	0.521
Visitor Representative 3	0.625	0.059	0.209	0.107
Visitor Representative 4	0.154	0.082	0.494	0.270
Visitor Representative 5	0.348	0.064	0.139	0.449
Average Weight	0.348	0.167	0.201	0.284
Ranking	1	4	3	2

creative dimension. The ranking in terms of the importance of the four factors, in sequence, was knowledge provision (0.348), humanities (0.284), creativity (0.201), and aesthetics (0.167). The domain experts believed that the reason why visitors use an MMNS is that they want to obtain more knowledge and thus intangible value arising from that knowledge, from the system; knowledge provision was therefore given a very high weighting in the cultural and creative dimension.

Relative weights of the criteria and their sub-criteria

In this section, we summarize all of the weights of the criteria and their sub-criteria in Table 9.16, for reference.

Table 9.16 Relative weights of the criteria and their sub-criteria (The numbers in brackets represent the importance rankings.)

Design Dimensions/Criteria		Design Factors/Sub-criteria	
Dimension	Weight	Factor	Weight
Infrastructure	0.157 (4)	Signal Stability	0.213 (2)
		Coverage	0.191 (3)
		Ubiquitousness	0.099 (6)
		Broadband Connection Speeds	0.100 (5)
		Near Field Detection	0.103 (4)
		Compatibility	0.080 (7)
		Security	0.215 (1)
Human–Computer Interface	0.188 (2)	Information Richness	0.101 (3)
		Information Presentation	0.317 (1)
		Icon Design	0.186 (2)
		Screen Menu Design	0.129 (4)
		Multi-language Support	0.115 (5)
		Search Function	0.113 (6)
Content Design	0.168 (3)	Timeliness	0.242 (1)
		Interactivity	0.213 (3)
		Locational Notification	0.224 (2)
		Browsing History	0.079 (6)
		Information Download/ Pre-download	0.094 (5)
		Site Map	0.148 (4)
User Experience	0.089 (6)	Satisfaction	0.224 (2)
		Utilization	0.195 (3)
		Ease of Use	0.287 (1)
		Personalization	0.110 (5)
		User Needs	0.184 (4)

Service	0.073 (7)	Professional Knowledge	0.180 (3)
		Service Attitude	0.317 (1)
		Quick Response	0.219 (2)
		Service Customization	0.141 (4)
		Service Proactiveness	0.088 (5)
		Promotion	0.056 (6)
Exhibition Space	0.130 (5)	Space Saving	0.187 (4)
		Visitor Routing	0.333 (1)
		Exhibition Information	0.266 (2)
		Direction Signs	0.214 (2)
Cultural and Creative	0.194 (1)	Knowledge Provision	0.348 (1)
		Aesthetics	0.167 (4)
		Creativity	0.201 (3)
		Humanities	0.284 (2)

Conclusion and recommendations

This study explored the relevant literature and current museum navigation systems to compile a set of design factors. It constructed a hierarchical structure for those factors via an AHP pairwise comparison questionnaire to address the research problem and synthesized judgments of the importance of each design factor and dimension provided by 20 participants from four groups of domain expert: industry experts, senior volunteer docents, academic staff, and visitor representatives. According to this synthesis, the four top-ranking dimensions were cultural and creative, human–computer interface, content design, and infrastructure. Overall, the domain experts attached more importance to the cultural and creative dimension, then the human–computer interface, followed by content design and then infrastructure.

Within the cultural and creative dimension, knowledge provision was ranked as the most important sub-criterion. The experts all agreed that knowledge provision was the most influential of the design factors. The experts deemed that visitors use a mobile navigation system during visit to a museum because they wish to obtain valuable knowledge, both tangible and intangible, from the system and hope that this knowledge will enrich their journey even after the visit is over. The major role of the navigation system is to act as a docent to interpret and deliver knowledge relating to exhibitions for visitors to the museum. Accordingly, system developers must pay attention to enriching knowledge relating to exhibits and exhibition themes in an MMNS rather than concentrating on the functionality of the system.

The human–computer interface was also critical in influencing the success of an MMNS; information presentation and icon design were the major sub-criteria within this dimension. The experts believed that when deciding to purchase or use an object, most people will intuitively judge whether they like the object, whether it is appropriate for them, and whether they intend to use the object at the first glance, before understanding the implied value of the merchandise in depth. Accordingly, information presentation directly affects whether an MMNS will be accepted. Additionally, icons are not only more attractive than text descriptions, but are also understood more clearly and are easier to accept. An analogy is traffic signals along the road; few of these use words, mostly delivering information through illustrations. For these reasons, information presentation and icon design are important considerations.

In this study, the word *content* in content design means the functionality, presentation, and arrangement of system functions in an MMNS, which are crucial to a software system. Of the factors within the content design dimension, timeliness was the most important. The domain experts viewed a visit to a museum as a dynamic moving flow of watching, with visitors watching different exhibits during different time slots. Accordingly, exhibition information delivered to visitors must be displayed in real time and accurately correspond to the item the visitor is viewing. In addition, in a wide exhibition space, it is not easy for visitors to correctly judge their location and even more difficult to locate an exhibit far away from them. Visitors rely on a location sign in an exhibition hall, or a location-aware MMNS, to inform them. Moreover, interactivity allows visitors to operate the MMNS more flexibly and thus they may use the system to freely explore the exhibitions. Locational notification and interactivity are therefore important considerations.

Although the infrastructure dimension was only ranked fourth, there is no doubt that the system environment and infrastructure are crucial to a smartphone mobile application. Within the infrastructure dimension, security and signal stability were assessed as the important factors by the domain experts. To prevent user resistance to a system, it must not only improve the way in which users communicate with it, but also address any safety issues that users might be concerned about. In addition, the domain experts believed that the most attractive service will offer users stability and the convenience to use the system wherever they are.

The contributions of this study include not only an up-to-date summary of the relevant literature and an analysis of current museum navigation systems, but also a focus on the elements accompanying the system itself, such as museum staff and promotions, and addressing of the modern trend toward smartphone applications. We expect the research findings to provide design criteria for system developers and to act as a reference guide for museum staff. We also believe that our findings comprise a useful reference for scholars.

References

Ashworth, G. J. (2000). Heritage, tourism and places: A review, *Tourism Recreation Research, 25*(1), 19–29.

Bailey, J. E., and Pearson, S. W. (1983). Development of a tool for measuring and analyzing computer user satisfaction, *Management Science, 29*(5), 530–545.

Beck, J., Han, S. H., and Park, J. (2006). Presenting a submenu window for menu search on a cellular phone, *International Journal of Human–Computer Interaction*, *20*(3), 233–245.

Bitgood, S. (1994). Designing effective exhibits: Criteria for success, exhibit design approaches, and research strategies, *Visitor Behavior*, *9*(4), 4–15.

Bitgood, S. (1995). Visitor circulation: Is there really a right-turn bias, *Visitor Behavior*, *10*(1), 5.

Chang, T. C., and Yeoh, B. S. (1999). New Asia–Singapore: Communicating local cultures through global tourism, *Geoforum*, *30*(2), 101–115.

Chen, C. C., and Huang, T. C. (2012). Learning in a u-Museum: Developing a context-aware ubiquitous learning environment, *Computers & Education*, *59*(3), 873–883.

Chen, Z. X. (1998, December). Market research and audience development, In *New directions for the New Century: Proceedings of the Conference on Museum Marketing* (pp. 88–110). Taipei: National History Museum.

Chesapeake Bay Maritime Museum. (2014). Retrieved on 30/9/2014 from http://www.stmichaelsmd.org/pages/MaritimeMuseum

Cone, C. A., and Kendall, K. (1978). Space, time, and family interaction: Visitor behavior at the Science Museum of Minnesota, *Curator: The Museum Journal*, *21*(3), 245–258.

Cossons, N. (1989). Heritage tourism – trends and tribulations, *Tourism Management*, *10*(3), 192–194.

Cui, B., and Yokoi, S. (April, 2012). Promote visitor interactions by smart devices in museum learning scenario, *Computing Technology and Information Management (ICCM), 2012 8th International Conference, IEEE*, *1*, 376–379.

Davis, F. D. (1989). Perceived usefulness, perceived ease of use, and user acceptance of information technology, *MIS Quarterly*, *13*(3), 319–340.

DeLone, W. H., and McLean, E. R. (1992). Information systems success: The quest for the dependent variable, *Information Systems Research*, *3*(1), 60–95.

Department for Culture, Media and Sport (DCMS). (2014). *The Learning Power of Museums ~ A Vision for Museum Education*. Retrieved on 30/9/2014 from http://dera.ioe.ac.uk/4551/2/musuem_vision_report.pdf

Edson, G., and Dean, D. (1994). *The handbook for museums*. London, UK: Routledge.

Edwards, Y. (1982). An overview of interpretation. In G. W. Sharpe (Ed.), *Interpreting the environment* (2nd ed., 2–27). New York, NY: John Wiley and Sons.

Ellis, B., and Mosher, J. S. (1993). Six Ps for four characteristics: A complete positioning strategy for the professional services firm CPA's, *Journal of Professional Services Marketing*, *9*(1), 129–145.

Fronville, C. L. (1985). Marketing for Museums: For profit techniques in the non profit world, *Curator: The Museum Journal*, *28*(3), 169–182.

Ghiani, G., Paternò, F., Santoro, C., and Spano, L. D. (2009). UbiCicero: A location-aware, multi-device museum guide, *Interacting with Computers*, *21*(4), 288–303.

Horton, W. K. (1994). *The icon book: Visual symbols for computer systems and documentation*. New York, NY: John Wiley & Sons.

Hsi, S. (2003). A study of user experiences mediated by nomadic web content in a museum, *Journal of Computer Assisted Learning*, *19*(3), 308–319.

Huang, Y. P., Wang, S. S., and Sandnes, F. E. (2011). RFID-based guide gives museum visitors more freedom, *IT Professional*, *13*(2), 25–29.

Hung, C. C. (2007). *Museum visit access design: Case study of the National Palace Museum display space.* Unpublished master's thesis, Department of Fine Arts, National Taiwan Normal University, Taipei, Taiwan.

Intel. (2005a). *Intel digital community framework whitepaper.* Intel.

Intel. (2005b). *Core technologies for developing a digital community framework.* Intel.

ITU. (2007). *ITU digital opportunity index.* ITU.

Johns, N., and Clark, S. L. (1993). Customer perception auditing: A means of monitoring the service provided by museums and galleries, *Museum Management and Curatorship, 12*(4), 360–366.

Jones, S., Jones, M., Marsden, G., Patel, D., and Cockburn, A. (2005). An evaluation of integrated zooming and scrolling on small screens, *International Journal of Human–Computer Studies, 63*(3), 271–303.

Kravchyna, V., and Hastings, S. (2002). Informational value of museum Web sites, *First Monday, 7*(2), doi:10.5210/fm.v7i2.929

Liu, C., and Arnett, K. P. (2000). Exploring the factors associated with Web site success in the context of electronic commerce, *Information & Management, 38*(1), 23–33.

MacDonald, G. F., and Alsford, S. (1991). The museum as information utility, *Museum Management and Curatorship, 10*(3), 305–311.

Marchionini, G. (1997). *Information seeking in electronic environments* (No. 9). New York, NY: Cambridge University Press.

Marty, P. F. (2008). Museum websites and museum visitors: Digital museum resources and their use, *Museum Management and Curatorship, 23*(1), 81–99.

Matthews, G. M. (1991). *Museums and art galleries: A design and development guide.* Oxford: Butterworth Architecture.

McLean, K. M. (1993). Planning for people in museum exhibitions, *The Association of Science and Technology Centers,* 1. Washington, DC.

Moscardo, G. (1996). Mindful visitors: Heritage and tourism, *Annals of Tourism Research, 23*(2), 376–397.

Parasuraman, A., Berry, L. L., and Zeithaml, V. A. (1991). Understanding customer expectations of service, *Sloan Management Review, 32*(3), 39–48.

Reynolds, R., Walker, K., and Speight, C. (2010). Web-based museum trails on PDAs for university-level design students: Design and evaluation, *Computers & Education, 55*(3), 994–1003.

Richards, G. (1996). Production and consumption of European cultural tourism, *Annals of Tourism Research, 23*(2), 261–283.

Rosenfeld, L., and Morville, P. (2007). *Information architecture for the World Wide Web* (3rd ed.). Sebastopol, CA: O'Reilly Media, Inc.

Ryan, C., and Dewar, K. (1995). Evaluating the communication process between interpreter and visitor, *Tourism Management, 16*(4), 295–303.

Satty, T. L. (1980). *The analytic hierarchy process.* New York, NY: McGraw Hill.

Schwabe, G., and Göth, C. (2005). Mobile learning with a mobile game: Design and motivational effects, *Journal of Computer Assisted Learning, 21*(3), 204–216.

Shackley, M. (1997). Saving cultural information: The potential role of digital databases in developing cultural tourism, *Journal of Sustainable Tourism, 5*(3), 244–249.

Shen, E. S., and Liang, C. C. Y. (2010). Research of interactive exhibition design for the web-based virtual reality museum, *Journal of Educational Media and Library Sciences, 37*(3), 275–298.

Thorlacius, L. (2002). A model of visual, aesthetic communication focusing on Web sites, *Digital Creativity, 13*(2), 85–98.

Thorlacius, L. (2007). The role of aesthetics in web design, *Nordicom Review, 28*(1), 63–76.

Tilden, F. (1957). *Interpreting our heritage*. Chapel Hill, North Carolina: University of North Carolina Press.

Tseng, Y. C. (2005, December). Experienced Wireless - The Case Studies of the Museum Digital Guide. Paper presented at 2005 Digital Design Conference. Taichung, National Taichung University of Science and Technology.

Wang, C. S., Su, Y. H., and Hong, C. Y. (2009). A 3D virtual navigation system integrating user positioning and pre-download mechanism, *World Academy of Science, Engineering and Technology, 40,* 172–176.

Williams, D. A., Wavell, C., Baxter, G., MacLennan, A., and Jobson, D. (2005). Implementing impact evaluation in professional practice: A study of support needs within the museum, archive and library sector, *International Journal of Information Management, 25*(6), 533–548.

Yang, T. T. (2009). *Lifestyle-oriented recommendation system*. Unpublished master's thesis, Department of Industrial Design, National Cheng Kung University, Tainan, Taiwan.

Ziefle, M. (2010). Information presentation in small screen devices: The trade-off between visual density and menu foresight, *Applied Ergonomics, 41*(6), 719–730.

10 Investigating security mechanisms for ICT-enabled services of the National Palace Museum

Fang Yu

Introduction

Originality and content play a significant role in the service economy, as people tend to have greater mental than material needs with respect to increasing the quality of life. As a result, Taiwan's cultural and creative industries are set to boom. For instance, the National Palace Museum (NPM) in Taipei, Taiwan, with its extensive collection of high-quality Chinese artifacts spanning thousands of years, has been asked by the government to build a cultural and creative platform for promoting cooperation and exchange between academics and the cultural and creative industries. In addition, rapid advances in information and telecommunications technology (ICT) have resulted in ICT-enabled services becoming a reality as people, organizations, systems, and heterogeneous devices are able to be linked more efficiently at a lower cost than ever before. In response to these ICT advances and the accompanying wave of globalization, the NPM has devoted considerable effort in recent years to completing the Digital Archives Project and increasing its cultural influence (National Palace Museum, 2010).

By adopting advanced ICT and new media, the NPM intends to extend itself beyond the museum's physical boundaries, ensuring that its treasured artifacts and educational resources reach the younger generation and the world stage. The NPM thus wishes to participate in the 4th Phase Taiwan E-Government project by providing services via portable devices to increase the level of interaction between young people and the NPM. From an academic perspective, the NPM's service is evolving to become customer oriented, innovative, and ICT enabled. One way to meet the evolving needs of customers (especially those of the younger generation) and to generate leverage from these innovations is for the NPM to use appropriate ICT applications to provide online, real-time, interactive services. Through ICT-enabled services, the NPM can conquer the limitations of time, space, human resources, and so forth, and improve its efficiency and competitiveness.

In this chapter, we investigate techniques for hardening ICT-enabled services for the cultural and creative industries, addressing the security mechanisms of clouds and webs relating to services providing digital content. It is essential to reduce the security risks involved in adopting new ICT technologies to allow full advantage to be taken of new services and innovations. We direct our attention to the research on and mechanisms for system-level protection, application-level protection and content-level protection, with the joint aim of providing a sound security environment for ICT-enabled services. The techniques presented here not only provide a solid security mechanism for clouds and webs used for ICT-enabled services for the cultural and creative industries, but can also be used in other security contexts.

System-level protection: a reliable cloud platform

The first part of this project involved the development of a reliable cloud platform, addressing performance and security issues for the fundamental hardware structure. We adopted a Linux Kernel-based Virtual Machine (KVM) as the hypervisor for building a cloud environment on top of a Linux system. The hypervisor provided a full-virtualization environment that emulates hardware, including CPU(s), network interfaces, and mother-board chips. The KVM allowed heterogeneous operating systems to be installed in Virtual Machines (VMs) within a homogeneous environment. There were two directions for our research, dynamic resource allocation and a virtual introspection system, together forming a reliable cloud environment.

Dynamic resource allocation

In this section, we describe how to allocate and cluster VMs dynamically, achieving load balance for task demands. The main concept involves coping with task demand overloading through building an elastic cluster of VMs to share the workload. A cluster is a set of identical VMs. Unlike requests handled by a single machine, requests are distributed in balance to each machine in the cluster. In addition, the size of the cluster dynamically increases to keep the average load of all of the VMs within the cluster below an acceptable bound (one low enough to provide a high-quality service).

We use the iPalace Video Channel (Tsaih, Lin, Han, Chao, and Chan, 2012) as an example Web service for illustrating the proposed approach. The iPalace Video Channel is a recently launched ICT-enabled service of the NPM that aims to provide users around the world with new experiences linked to exploring the beauty of Chinese artifacts through the multicasting of NPM video collections online. Video-based services require a higher standard of service quality and more development resources than text-based Web services. To meet the high standard of service quality and cope with the potential peak demand, the iPalace Video Channel needs to be built on an elastic and adjustable cloud platform.

Figure 10.1 proposed by Yu, Wan, and Tsaih (2013) shows an elastic architecture for the iPalace Video Channel service. Here they use the DC collection, the main service of the iPalace Video Channel, as an example to illustrate how we can deploy a cluster of VMs to tackle task demand overload. Initially, there

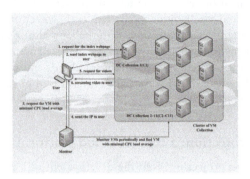

Figure 10.1 An elastic architecture for the iPalace Video Channel service

is only one VM operating. We set up an auxiliary VM to monitor the workload of all of the VMs in the cluster for each task demand. The monitor periodically checks the CPU workload of all of the VMs that are running and reports the VM with the lowest CPU workload. If this workload is below an acceptable bound, the next new task will be directed to this VM. If the CPU workload exceeds the acceptable bound (as will also occur for other VMs), we increase the size of the cluster by cloning/invoking a new VM to join it and direct the next new task to this VM. We can use this elastic cluster mechanism to achieve load balancing of task demand. The monitor also gathers other status information periodically from each running VM, including the average CPU load, the number of received and sent packets per second, the number of requests, and the average number of connections. We use this information to adjust our load balancing strategy. We describe the load balancing steps in detail in the following, using the DC collection as the target task. A cluster of VMs is used (instead of a single machine) to respond to DC collection requests. There are six steps in the process of delivering the service, as outlined below.

1   A user sends a service request to DC Collection 1 (DC C1).
2   DC C1 responds by providing the webpage of the iPalace Video Channel service to the user.
3   Before access to the videos is permitted, the user device directs the monitor to determine which VM will build the connection. The VM is selected on the basis of our heuristic, that is, that with the lowest workload over the past few minutes or a newly invoked VM.
4   The monitor sends an XML file back to the user, which provides all of the information required to build the connection with the selected VM.
5   The ensuing user request is directed to the VM according to the XML file.
6   The selected server receives the request and provides the video service.
7   We periodically monitor the VMs, select that with the smallest load, and update the XML file for the next task.

Algorithm monitor_handler( )	*Algorithm* monitor *(hostname[ ], log, BOUND)*
1. **define** DURATION, BOUND;	1. **init** load[ ]= init_load (hostname[ ]);
2. **init** hostname[ ], log;	2. monitor_VMs (hostname[ ], load[ ], log);
3. **while** *true*:	3. minhost = select_min(hostname[ ], load[ ]);
4. set_xml(monitor(hostname[ ], log,BOUND));	4. **if**(load[minhost] > BOUND)
	5. new = create_VM();
5. time.sleep(DURATION);	6. minhost = new;
	7. update(hostname[ ], new);
	8. **return** minhost;

The pseudo codes are shown as above. There are two control variables, BOUND and DURATION. BOUND is an upper bound on the value of the average CPU load that determines the ability of a VM to accept more tasks. It also determines when to add a new VM to increase the size of the cluster, which has an effect on service quality. DURATION defines the interval between the monitoring of VMs and determines the frequency with which the monitoring procedure is executed. The smaller the DURATION, the more often the VM selection is updated. As we distribute requests by looking up the selected VM, all of the requests arriving within the period of DURATION will be assigned to the currently selected VM. If requests suddenly increase within DURATION, it is possible for the selected VM to experience overflow. One way of improving this approach is to monitor VMs on receipt of requests, with the trade-off of a potential run-time delay.

The array hostname is used to record the names of the VMs in the cluster. It is set to one VM by default. When a new VM is created (monitor(), lines 5–7), the hostname is updated with this new VM. When calling the procedure monitor_VMs(), we connect all of the VMs listed in the hostname and collect their status information, such as the average CPU load over 1 minute from / proc/loadavg (saved in load[ ]). We also collect other data related to the CPU and network status of each VM in the log through three Unix commands, uptime, iostat, and netstat, and the requests per second (collected from the Apache's server status). Uptime provides the current (logged) time, how long the system has been running, how many users are currently logged on, and the system load average for the past 1, 5, and 15 minutes. Iostat is used to monitor system input/ output device loading through observing active devices in relation to their average transfer rates. It also reports CPU and device utilization. Netstat provides information about the Linux networking subsystem, for example, a list of open sockets. The information (log) is used to evaluate and adjust our load balancing strategy.

The strategy presented involves selecting the VM with the lowest average CPU load to take all incoming requests before the next monitoring process

(DURATION). If the CPU load of this VM exceeds the threshold that we set (BOUND), we invoke/clone a new VM to share the workload. A new VM is required because exceeding the threshold in the VM with the lowest average CPU load implies that all of the other VMs are also exceeding the threshold. The new VM has the same ability to handle user demands as the original VM. By calling the procedure set_xml(), we update the XML file with the IP of the selected VM. Incoming requests will be directed to the new VM specified in the XML file without any additional monitoring. By using this method, we prevent run-time overheads.

We believe that the core issue of the load balancing of servers providing data streaming, addressed in this part, is both generalizable and applicable to a much broader range of information/service systems. We extend this mechanism in the next section to address security concerns.

Virtualization introspection system

Many people have had their PCs compromised through computer worms, viruses, spyware, or botnets. As VMs run in the cloud with all information exposed to the VM manager, cloud providers should be able to provide VMs with additional system-level protection (compared with PCs) to detect or prevent VMs being compromised through modern malicious attacks. It is also essential to protect the kernel/hypervisor of the cloud platform, as an intruder can gain rights to attack the hypervisor from a VM and thus compromise all of the VMs running in the cloud, such as occurred in the well-known cloudbuster attack (Elhage, 2011).

In this second section, we focus on the development of a Virtualization Intro-spection System (VIS) that protects VMs and the hypervisor from security threats through monitoring VM states and intercepting suspicious system calls or abnormal VM behavior via termination (shutting down the VM) or isolation (migrating the VM to a honeypot so that it can work normally without causing damage to the hypervisor or other VMs). The results have been published in part in (Lee and Yu, 2014).

The VIS monitors the run-time status and behavior (such as system calls) of VMs, and checks static images (i.e., the QEMU in the KVM) via QEMU monitors for the integrity of guest VMs. If the VIS detects abnormal behavior or changes, it can terminate or isolate the potentially malicious VM, or send the request to the common VM manager, for example, OpenStack (2013) or Open-Nebula, to take the action required. A system overview of the VIS (Lee and Yu, 2014) with OpenStack is shown in Figure 10.2.

The dashed red line indicates the flow of an attack triggered by a guest VM to gain root privileges for the KVM kernel (and thus for the other VMs). This type of attack was first identified by N. Elhage and demonstrated at DEFCON 2011 (Elhage, 2011). The VIS checks the integrity of the QEMU images of guest VMs, is able to detect the attack after the QEMU image has been modified, and terminates (or migrates) the guest VM before it gains root privileges to prevent potential damage.

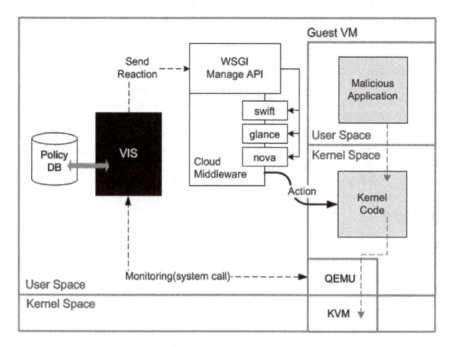

Figure 10.2 System architecture of the Virtualization Introspection System

Characterizing and detecting attacks

A major challenge is how to characterize malicious behavior. To prevent a known attack, we propose a straightforward solution: replay the attack on a VM and observe and characterize its behavior. We used the characterization of the observed behavior as an attack signature for detecting malicious behavior in VMs. An attack signature must provide sufficient information to distinguish malicious behavior from normal behavior. This raises the issue of how to characterize the observed behavior. We propose using finite automata to characterize malicious behavior. An attack signature is an automaton that accepts all of the observed behavior of the malicious VM. A word (e.g., a sequence of system calls) that is accepted by an attack signature is identified as malicious behavior. Our previous work on automata construction techniques (Yu, Bultan, Cova, and Ibarra, 2008; Yu, Bultan, and Ibarra, 2011) could be extended to this context.

Although an identified malicious behavior (one accepted by an attack signature) is a true attack (completeness), this approach is not sound and may return false negatives for unknown attacks. We can address this by collecting as many attack signatures as possible and using them (as a blacklist) to identify malicious attacks. As soon as the VIS detects malicious behavior in a VM, it can terminate that VM. Alternatively, we can apply the same idea but collect normal signatures from VMs that can be trusted and use these normal signatures (as a whitelist) to identify good behavior in a sound manner. For a VM that has (grey) behavior that are accepted neither by normal signatures nor attack signatures, we can migrate the VM to a honeypot so that the VM still operates normally but is physically isolated from the other VMs.

In addition to attacks targeting the host, some attacks target VMs with the aim of compromising them and taking control from the outside. The VIS detects such attacks by checking the integrity of the VM kernel images. The VIS also logs system calls that are directed to VMs from outsiders. Again, one can replay a known attack on a VM and collect its attack signature, that is, host an outsider to compromise a VM, log and characterize the information about the compromised VM during the process, and then use it as a blacklist for identifying outsiders' malicious behavior. Similarly, one can build a whitelist and direct grey system calls to a VM that has been migrated to a honey pot. We summarize the research steps below.

1   Develop a prototype VIS system for the cloud, including online migration.
2   Collect attack (normal) signatures by replaying modern attacks (standard services) on VMs.
3   Build the rules for the detection and prevention of malicious behavior.

Compared with traditional VM monitors, for example, OpenStack and Open-Nebula, the VIS (Lee and Yu, 2014) addresses security concerns and provides an extensible security framework (through the addition of attack signatures) to protect the host and guest VMs from known (or unknown) attacks. A similar architecture for securing the cloud through monitoring VMs was proposed by Padmanabhan and Edwin (2011). The VIS improves on this by incorporating additional detection rules and prevention mechanisms. Compared with security tools using active monitoring, for example, Lares (Payne, Carbone, Sharif, and Lee, 2008) and SecVisor (Seshadri, Luk, Qu, and Perrig, 2007), the VIS adopts both whitelist and blacklist mechanisms along with online migration and honeypots. As a result, the VIS is able to provide sound and complete system-level protection.

Application-level protection on the server side: Verifying Web application security

After developing a sound environment for hosting services, we shifted our focus to the provision of sound applications. In this part we first discuss how to provide application-level protection on the server side through the detection of patching vulnerabilities in Web applications. Web applications have become crucial in commerce, entertainment, and social interactions, but are notorious for security vulnerabilities that can be exploited by malicious users. In the Common Vulnerabilities and Exposures (CVE) list (which documents computer security vulnerabilities and exposures), Web application vulnerabilities have occupied the first three positions for several years. The percentage of these three Web application vulnerabilities increased from 3 percent of all reported vulnerabilities in 2001 to 45 percent in 2006 and was steady at around 35 percent for the following 3 years. For every three reported vulnerabilities, one falls into this category. Although much research has been carried out on securing Web applications, these vulnerabilities still threaten many Web applications.

The main concept behind our application-level protection is the application of advance symbolic string verification techniques and tools to secure Web applications. In our previous research (Yu, Alkhalaf, and Bultan, 2011; Yu, Alkhalaf, Bultan, and Ibarra, 2014; Yu, Bultan, and Ibarra, 2009; Yu, Bultan, and Ibarra, 2011), we developed several automata-based string analysis techniques for verifying string manipulation programs and evaluated our approach against open-source Web applications (Yu and Tung, 2014). In Yu, Alkhalaf, and Bultan (2011), we investigated abstract string verification, with the objective of developing string abstraction techniques to reduce the cost and adjust the precision and performance of our symbolic reachability analysis. In Yu, Bultan, and Ibarra (2011), we proposed automatic sanitization synthesis to effectively patch vulnerabilities detected in the applications. In particular, we investigated the use of multi-track automata to model the relationships between inputs. By combining these techniques, we can provide a solid and sound security mechanism for Web applications for the cultural and creative industries.

Due to its importance in security, string analysis has been widely studied. One influential approach is grammar-based string analysis, which statically calculates an over-approximation of the values of string expressions in Java programs (Christensen, Møller, and Schwartzbach, 2003) and has also been used to check for various types of errors in Web applications (Minamide, 2005; Wassermann and Su, 2007; Yu et al., 2008). Several recent string analysis tools use symbolic string analysis based on DFA encoding. Some of these are based on symbolic execution and use a DFA representation to model and verify the string manipulation operations in Java programs (Shannon, Hajra, Lee, Zhan, and Khurshid, 2007). HAMPI (Kiezun, Ganesh, Guo, Hooimeijer, and Ernst, 2009) is a bounded string constraint solver. It outputs a string that satisfies all of the constraints or reports that the constraints are unsatisfiable. Note that this type of bounded analysis cannot be used for sound string analysis, whereas the string analysis techniques we present in this paper are sound. Symbolic verification using automata has been investigated in other contexts (e.g., Bouajjani, Jonsson, Nilsson, and Touili, 2000). In this work, we focus specifically on the verification of string manipulation operations, which is essential for detecting and preventing Web-related vulnerabilities. Other work has used abstraction techniques on automata (Bouajjani, Habermehl, and Vojnar, 2004), whereas we proposed abstractions in Yu, Bultan, and Hardekopf (2011) that were based on string values and relationships between string variables. These abstractions allow useful heuristics based on the constants and relationships for the input program and the property. It is critical that vulnerabilities are not only discovered quickly, but are also repaired quickly. There has been previous work on automatically generating filters for blocking bad input (Costa, Castro, Zhou, Zhang, and Peinado, 2007), although this has focused on buffer-overflow vulnerabilities that differ from the string vulnerabilities we investigated. In Castro et al. (2007), the generation of filters was carried out from the starting point of an existing exploit, whereas our plan involved starting from an attack pattern.

Patcher: Patching Web application vulnerabilities via static source code analysis

We proposed symbolic string verification in Yu, Alkhalaf, Bultan, and Ibarra (2014), in which we developed several techniques for identifying vulnerabilities related to string manipulation in Web applications and generated characterization of user inputs that might exploit a discovered vulnerability. We also implemented our new string analysis tool, called Patcher, by incorporating patch synthesis techniques into our previous string analysis tool Stranger (the first public automata-based string analysis tool for PHP Web applications) (Yu, Alkhalaf, and Bultan, 2010). Stranger can automatically detect XSS, SQL injection, and MFE vulnerabilities in PHP Web applications, whereas Patcher can automatically generate patches to effectively prevent all possible malicious inputs from exploiting the detected vulnerabilities. These techniques form a solid, sound, formal security mechanism with which we can detect potential vulnerabilities and prevent malicious exploits. When new ICT-enabled services are introduced, it is essential to build confidence in their security mechanisms. The techniques we have developed represent the first step in building such confidence by using formal verification techniques to secure the server side of the NPM's applications.

We conducted static source code analysis (Yu, Alkhalaf, Bultan, and Ibarra, 2014) according to the stages shown in Figure 10.3. The analysis had two inputs, the source code of the Web applications and attack patterns that characterize

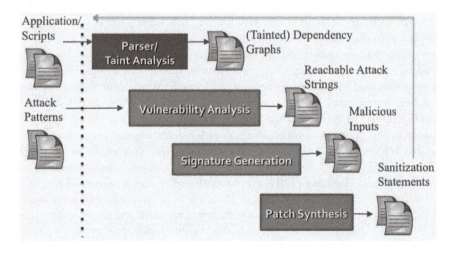

Figure 10.3 Static source code analysis stages

malicious strings for specific vulnerabilities. We first needed to incorporate other sub-projects to collect the source code of their Web applications. We then performed taint analysis (Huang et al., 2004) to identify sensitive functions in the (PHP) programs that may take user input values. These sensitive functions (sink nodes) are potential vulnerability points and required further inspection. We then constructed dependency graphs based on data flow analysis. These graphs specified how the user input values flowed to the sink nodes. We then conducted symbolic string analysis (Yu, Alkhalaf, and Bultan, 2009; Yu, Bultan, Cova, and Ibarra, 2008) of the dependency graphs. This vulnerability analysis combined forward and backward symbolic reachability analyses. In the forward analysis, we first assumed that the user input could be any string, then propagated this information accordingly on the dependency graph. When a fixed point was reached (we had explored all of the possible states for each node), we intersected the sink node values with the attack patterns. The result of this intersection identified all reachable attack strings. The next stage involved characterizing user inputs that could exploit vulnerabilities, called vulnerability signatures. Depending on the number of input nodes, we conducted backward reachability analysis on single-track automata to generate atomic signatures or forward reachability analysis on multi-track automata (Yu, Bultan, and Ibarra, 2011) to generate relational signatures. The second of these processes specifies the relationships between multiple inputs and presents a more precise characterization of malicious values from multiple user inputs. The final stage was to synthesize effective patches (Yu, Alkhalaf, and Bultan, 2011) that could be inserted into the programs in such a way that user inputs matching vulnerability signatures (the characterized malicious inputs) could be identified and modified to avoid exploits during the execution of programs. We implemented the tool Patcher to realize the static source code analysis described above. Patcher (Yu and Tung, 2014) can automatically analyze PHP4 programs end-to-end without user intervention. We also provided the Web version of Patcher so that users can directly upload their code and view the results as webpages. Patcher analyzes the script, points out potential vulnerabilities in the program, and generates sanitization statements with the appropriate positions at which to insert them. Developers can also upload the full application as a package. Patcher will automatically check all execution entries of PHP scripts in the application and report and synthesize all vulnerabilities and sanitization statements.

Although Patcher has been tested against several open-source applications, analyzing real web applications like those of the NPM is challenging. The contributions described in this part arise from enhancing Patcher to address the issues outlined below.

1   Input languages: The current version of Patcher uses Pixy (Jovanovic, Kruegel, and Kirda, 2006) as the front end to parse PHP scripts and to build the dependency graphs. To analyze Web applications developed in other languages, much painstaking work is required to develop or identify suitable parsers to replace the front end. One alternative for Java applications is Java String Analyzer (Christensen, Møller, and Schwartzbach, 2003).

2	Built-in functions: Another challenge arising in the analysis of real applications is the handling of the many built-in functions in these applications. For static analysis, we needed to implement additional routines for each of these functions, using basic operations such as concatenation and replacement functions on the automata. We implemented several routines for such built-in functions, but expect the NPM applications to contain others. In addition, some built-in functions cannot be handled precisely using basic operations; we plan to use (tight) approximations in this case.

3	Path-(in)sensitive analysis: The current analysis carried out using Patcher is path-insensitive. Overlooking branch conditions may result in high false-positive rates for applications that use branch conditions frequently. One way of addressing this issue is to develop path-sensitive string analysis. We plan to investigate how to carry branch conditions through to dependency graphs so that we can extend Patcher to cover path-sensitive analysis.

4	Performance and scalability issues: The static analysis presented may require extensive computational resources to analyze the complex behaviors of the programs. It is likely that Patcher will run out of memory during the analysis of NPM Web applications. One approach is to build Patcher on a scalable platform, for example, via private/public clouds, to enhance its scalability and reduce performance problems. Another way to improve Patcher's scalability is to apply abstraction techniques (Yu, Bultan, and Hardekopf, 2011) to adjust the performance and precision of the analysis. We proposed two abstraction techniques, alphabet abstraction and relational abstraction, to form abstraction classes as a complete abstraction lattice, and a heuristic for identifying a suitable abstraction class for the target program and property. By using this technique in Patcher, we will be able to improve the scalability further.

5	Program and vulnerability visualization: After our taint analysis and string analysis have been carried out, the results need to be carefully reviewed by the developers of the target applications. We plan to develop user-friendly visualization interfaces to display the results of analysis. This part of the research will involve both program and vulnerability comprehension. We plan to use Utility to develop a 3D interface and to develop mobile applications to provide a brief summary report and facilitate remote control of the viewing process. This will require us to work closely with developers to identify real vulnerabilities, fix potential software defects, and improve the security of the applications. Hence, it is essential that this project is integrated with future NPM proposals.

The extension described above is not a trivial one and clearly has major requirements in terms of labor and time. In addition to the development of a sound tool, however, it will potentially provide research contributions on path-sensitive analysis and vulnerability visualization, and empirical contributions on the analysis of real government Web applications.

Application-level protection on the client side: Revealing the behavior of mobile applications

With the dramatic growth in mobile users and smart devices over the past decade, mobile applications have become the most popular and dominant software applications. Most of these applications only have an executable available. To identify a sound mobile application, it is essential to be able to reveal its real behavior in the executable. AppBeach (Yu, Lee, Tai, and Tang, 2013) provides a systematic approach to reveal the behavior of a mobile application directly from its executable. Unlike analysis based on the description or appearance of a mobile application, this analysis reveals the behavior of the executable based on embedded system call sequences. The main element involves syntactically counting call sequences that are directly resolved statically from the executable. This is done on the scale of the Hadoop framework by distributing routines to mappers with an assembly tool that resolves explicit and implicit system method calls directly from iOS executables. The reducer then collects the counts from the mappers to characterize the behavior of apps. Patterns of malicious behavior are identified from the differences between pairs of normal and malicious apps and the probability of potential behavior of commercial apps is reported by matching these patterns to their call sequence counts.

We extend AppBeach to characterize mobile application behavior by call sequences embedded in app executables in the work (Yu, Tai, Tang, and Wang, 2015). To effectively analyze a large number of apps, we performed our analysis using a distributed algorithm on the Hadoop framework. We sliced the app assembly file into pieces using routines and fed these slices to the mapper that we had set up separately on the Hadoop environment. Briefly speaking, the mapper reads and tokenizes every single line of an assembly file slice, then locates every call invocation within every previously resolved assembly command. Next, the mapper combines these calls in sequence according to the number set by us, for example, in pairs or in triples, and sends these to the reducer that we defined while processing the whole slice. The reducer generates the total call sequences of every app by collecting the contributions of each slice. After obtaining the call sequences of a mobile app, we were able to characterize its behavior by analyzing the content of the call sequences.

After generating method call collections for mobile apps, we examined these collections and determined the existence of malicious behavior. We defined categories of sensitive functions and generated malicious patterns by building the pairs of a malicious app and a benign app in such a way that the only difference between them was a single, specific inserted malicious behavior composed of the sensitive functions of interest. After analyzing these self-developed pairs of apps using the proposed syntax analysis, we used differences in the key-value pairs of system calls/sequences to identify malicious patterns. We collected a large number of these to create a pattern library for detecting the behavior of apps.

There are many types of malicious behavior. After investigating the functions that produce malicious behaviors, we classified these into the following major categories based on purpose: first, the retrieval of sensitive information, including user information (e.g., address book, calendar) and device information (e.g., GPS location); second, the conveying of information outward from mobile devices (e.g., transmitting data via HTTP or TCP). For each purpose there were specific functions to fulfill. We used the functions from built-in frameworks or well-known public packages as the basis of our sampling. Our malicious (suspicious) pattern was composed of these specific functions (this will be covered in the following sections).

To characterize malicious behavior, we used the approach proposed in App-Beach (Yu, Lee, Tai, and Tang, 2013) to build malicious applications that are developed in pairs comprising one normal app and its abnormal counterpart. Both apps have identical behavior except for an inserted malicious behavior that is to be characterized. Figure 10.4 shows the steps required to characterize a malicious behavior. Instead of simply counting methods, we counted call sequences.

We inserted the malicious behavior targeted for characterization in the source code to produce the abnormal app and left the original code alone in the normal one. The two apps were therefore identical apart from the malicious behavior embedded in the abnormal version. After compiling the source codes of the pair of apps, we applied our binary analysis to their executables and characterized the differences in their behavior as the malicious signature for the embedded behavior.

As we used call sequence analysis, we expected to generate patterns of sensitive behavior under different given sampling conditions. Different patterns were

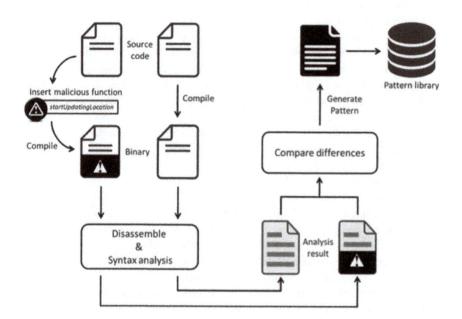

Figure 10.4 The processes of building up a malicious pattern library

generated for the same behavior. For example, the call sequences for class invocations and method invocations generated different patterns and the length of the sampling sequence also revealed different patterns.

We built a pattern library from the collections of these malicious signatures and used them later to detect whether the target app included the malicious signature. If so, the target app might be able to execute the malicious behavior; if not, it cannot execute the malicious behavior. The soundness of this approach arises from counting with respect to a malicious signature. It should be noted that the learned malware signature depends only on the embedded malicious behavior and not the application itself.

Finally, we have developed the website of AppBeach (Yu, Lee, Tai, and Tang, 2013), as well as providing a chain of tools that allow users to evaluate and investigate applications developed on the Apple iOS operating system. The AppBeach website also reports updated analysis results for modern iOS mobile applications to public users. We analyzed more than 7,000+ online apps against patterns that we collected. Figures 10.5 and 10.6 are screenshots of the AppBeach website showing analyzed apps with their (potential) behavior. Figure 10.7 shows sample patterns for sensitive behavior.

To sum up, we introduced a novel static sequence analysis to reveal the behavior of mobile applications directly from their executables. The main concept involved resolving the method calls embedded in apps and counting their appearances in a syntactic order. Through using these call sequences, we were able to build up

Figure 10.5 The AppBeach website

Figure 10.6 Behavior of apps on the AppBeach website

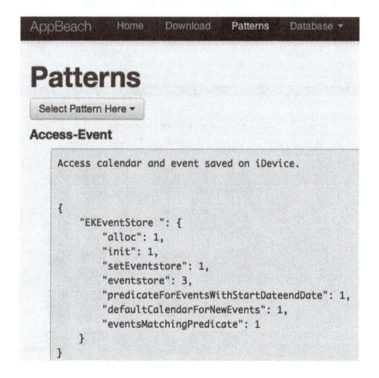

Figure 10.7 Patterns in system method calls

patterns of sensitive/malicious behavior and use these patterns to reveal behavior in modern apps. The evaluation of thousands of online apps demonstrated some promise for the approach presented.

Content-level protection: From passive authentication to active execution

Digital Rights Management (DRM) is one of the most important issues for the NPM in terms of deploying its ICT-enabled services. After addressing system-level and application-level protection, the final part of this project shifted focus to data hiding in digital content, with the aim of providing protection for the content itself. Data hiding has been used in various applications, such as copyright protection, authentication, fingerprinting, error concealment, broadcast monitoring, and covert communications. We can embed watermarks that contain non-perceptible digital data such as ownership information, contact details, usage rights, and even programs, thus using the content itself as a covert communication channel between owners and users. Watermarks can involve text, images, or computer programs. As they are invisible and hard to detect, they are difficult to remove. They can also be very robust and remain almost intact when the content they are watermarking is altered. Properly embedded, watermarks will not affect a host video's quality and such watermarked videos can be played without requiring any special software.

The objectives of this part of the project are to investigate potential watermarking techniques to support the authorization of digital content, and to embed programs (rather than signatures) into digital content to achieve active execution (in addition to passive authorization). By using such techniques, we can prevent copyright from being infringed, trace the users and uses of the content, and actively check or authorize legal uses.

To hide data in videos via watermarking techniques, we adopt the framework proposed by Yu, Lin, Tang, and Wang (2014) for video watermarking protected by asymmetric keys. The encoding process embeds watermarks in selected frames of the target video. The process involves first remixing the video into a series of frames, selecting appropriate frames and inserting watermarks based on private keys into these, then replacing the original frames with the watermarked ones and mixing the series of frames back into the video. Note that a watermark can be divided into parts, copied, and embedded into videos separately. To extract the watermark from the video, additional information is required to compose the parts back into the original watermark. The main concept underlying this framework is the use of a PGP key pair to provide the additional information and protect integrity. The decoding process requires a public key for identifying which frames are watermarked and where the messages are embedded in the frames. In this way, we can ensure that messages are embedded using the corresponding private key and maintain integrity.

Note that a message can be a signature or a program, as long as it can be represented as a bit stream. Our focus is on how to use videos as a medium for carrying information (programs) and how to execute programs on the client side when watermarked videos are played.

Instead of developing a new watermarking scheme, we will use an existing one that fulfills our needs. The following watermark properties are required: robustness (the watermark should be impossible to remove from the video without sufficient knowledge of the process used to embed it); imperceptibility (the watermark embedded in the digital video sequence should be invisible); unambiguity (the extracted watermark should uniquely identify the original owner of the video); and loyalty (the watermark should have a high level of reliability, i.e., any degradation it causes should be very difficult for the viewer to perceive). Robustness is a primary requirement for ownership protection, for example, in schemes such as spectrum watermarking (Cox, Kilian, Leighton, and Shamoon, 1997) and cocktail watermarking (Lu, Huang, Sze, and Liao, 2000). However, for content authentication, for example, Zhu, Swanson, and Tewfik (1996), the embedded watermark should be fragile so that changes or modifications to an image will be reflected in the hidden watermark. Lu and Liao (2001) proposed a multipurpose watermarking scheme for images that satisfied both of these needs. This part of the project includes investigating modern watermarking techniques to find a suitable and feasible watermarking algorithm for our purposes.

Although image watermarking techniques can be extended to the watermarking of videos, applying watermarks to original videos will entail additional mechanisms for maintaining the embedded watermarks so that they and the necessary properties remain intact during video compression and decompression processes. In particular, we need to ensure that information is not lost from embedded watermarks due to video compression. The most common standard for video compression is H.264/MPEG-4 Part 10 AVC (Advanced Video Coding), which is used widely as the standard format for the recording, compression, and distribution of high-definition video. Watermarking techniques based on transform domains, such as discrete cosine transformation (Chen and Li, 2008; Naik and Holambe, 2010), discrete Hadamard transformation (Ramanjaneyulu and Rajarajeswari, 2010), and discrete wavelet transformation (Sun, Shao, and Wang, 2008), may provide better resistance than techniques based on spatial domains; however, these usually involve more complex computation to take video compression into account during the encoding and decoding processes. To provide an elastic computation platform, we are interested in developing distributed algorithms for these techniques within the Hadoop framework presented. Watermarks may also be directly embedded into and extracted from compressed videos rather than original videos, but this may involve additional online processing and delay, and may reduce display quality.

In addition, for active program executions, a special decoder for extracting and executing the embedded programs needs to be designed. This decoder will ideally be a plug-in from the standard library of common media players. Our research will focus on media players available in mobile devices.

Finally, various attacks on watermarks, such as frequency-based compression, addition of noise, cropping, correction, zooming, rotation, and pixel permutation, removal or insertion, pose significant challenges. During this study, we will investigate techniques for handling these issues so that the encoding can maintain the watermark properties in the face of attacks. We summarize our proposed research steps below.

1 Investigate watermarking techniques for images and apply them to frames.
2 Develop PGP key-based selection algorithms and mechanisms.
3 Investigate techniques to maintain the integrity of watermarks before and after media compression, and develop a prototype tool to encode and decode video watermarks.
4 Develop routines and programs for enhancing intellectual rights and properties as the payload (watermark).
5 Develop a decoder (or plug-in functions for common media players) on mobile devices, to extract and check watermarks and trigger program execution.

Yu, Tang, Lin, and Wang (2014) described the prototype system, which uses a cryptography and steganography technique to design a mechanism for claiming digital ownership, focusing solely on H.264 video files due to the popularity of this format on the Web. We investigated the properties of the H.264/MPEG-4 AVC standard and the concept of PGP software and public-key encryption/decryption, and applied it to our prototype. We also bound a scripting language run-time to the player, enabling developers to design their own variants according to their requirements.

However, the technique used to embed messages in videos is fragile and therefore not resistant to attack. Following the generic embedding framework, it is envisaged that it will be replaced by modules.

Conclusion

Cloud services and mobile and Web applications will surely become the dominant software platforms of the future. Security and dependability are the major roadblocks to the increasing reliance of society on services provided by cloud, mobile, and Web applications. This project focused on the research in this area, aimed at finding a sound and practical security mechanism for cloud services and mobile/Web applications. We realized our concepts as several tools and Web services that may provide security assurance for the ICT-enabled services of the NPM. Due to its focus on facilitating the dependability of clouds and ubiquitous Web applications that influence every aspect of society, including commerce, entertainment, communication, healthcare, and security, this research is potentially of far-reaching significance. Any improvement in the dependability of such systems and applications will translate to the improved dependability of IT in every aspect of society.

This chapter summarized the three directions of our work on this integrated project: the cloud platform and the VIS system, the extension of the string analysis tool Patcher, and data-hiding techniques for digital content. We have worked on these three directions in parallel. In the first year, we focused on building a KVM-based private cloud and developing a prototype of the VIS system on this platform. We refined our string analysis tool Patcher to support vulnerability visualization and path-sensitive analysis, and also investigated watermarking and media compression techniques. At the end of this year, we were ready to conduct advance analyses for system-level and application-level protection. In the second year we shifted our attention to the analysis of modern security threats and prevention mechanisms for enhancing the VIS system, and the deployment of the iPalace Video Channel and other ICT-enabled services on the cloud platform. In the final year, we tested Patcher against real-world Web and other applications, and continuously refined the tools in the chain, collected malicious signatures, and reported useful results to the public. After a thorough study of watermarking and media compression techniques, we were able to apply image watermarking techniques to videos and to develop a prototype tool for hiding data in digital content.

In future work, we plan to develop security routines for mobile applications that address intellectual property issues and embed these as watermarks in digital content. We will investigate the development of a media decoder (or a plug-in function for common media devices) that is able to extract watermarks and execute the corresponding programs on mobile devices. We also hope to launch the VIS system (Lee and Yu, 2014) and Patcher (Yu and Tung, 2014) to the public and thus provide protection in other cloud and web service contexts.

As final remarks, connections exist between the techniques we have developed in this project. The string analysis and automata construction techniques investigated in (Yu, Alkhalaf, and Bultan, 2011) and (Yu, Alkhalaf, Bultan, and Ibarra, 2014) can be used to identify malicious patterns in the system calls of VMs in the VIS system. The back end of Patcher can be deployed on the cloud platform that we developed for the VIS system (Lee and Yu, 2014). The concept of using distributed syntax analysis with the Hadoop framework (App-Beach [Yu, Lee, Tai, and Tang, 2013]) can also be used to develop distributed algorithms for media encoding and decoding, deploying the process to parallel computations in the cloud. The identified patterns of malicious behavior aimed at gaining private information may be used to develop routines for collecting user information to enforce the protection of digital content. Last but not least, the visualization skills developed to improve the interface of Patcher can also be used for the VIS, providing intuitive reasoning regarding system status and application behavior.

References

Beck, J., Han, S. H., and Park, J. (2006). Presenting a submenu window for menu search on a cellular phone. *International Journal of Human-Computer Interaction*, 20(3), 233–245.

Bouajjani, A., Habermehl, P., and Vojnar, T. (2004, January). Abstract regular model checking. In R. Alur and D. A. Peled (Eds.), *Computer aided verification* (pp. 372–386). Berlin, Heidelberg: Springer.

Bouajjani, A., Jonsson, B., Nilsson, M., and Touili, T. (2000, January). Regular model checking. In E. A. Emerson and A. P. Sistla (Eds.), *Computer aided verification* (pp. 403–418). Berlin Heidelberg: Springer.

Chen, L., and Li, M. (2008, June). *An effective blind watermark algorithm based on DCT*. In Intelligent Control and Automation, WCICA 2008. 7th World Congress, 6822–6825. IEEE.

Christensen, A. S., Møller, A., and Schwartzbach, M. I. (2003). *Precise analysis of string expressions* (pp. 1–18). Berlin, Heidelberg: Springer.

Common Vulnerabilities and Exposures (CVE). Retrieved from http://cve.mitre.org/

Costa, M., Castro, M., Zhou, L., Zhang, L., and Peinado, M. (2007, October). Bouncer: Securing software by blocking bad input. *ACM SIGOPS operating systems review*, *41*(6), 117–130.

Cox, I. J., Kilian, J., Leighton, F. T., and Shamoon, T. (1997). Secure spread spectrum watermarking for multimedia. *Image Processing, IEEE Transactions*, *6*(12), 1673–1687.

Elhage, N. (2011). *Virtualization under attack: Breaking out of KVM*, DEF CON, 19.

Gould, C., Su, Z., and Devanbu, P. (2004, May). Static checking of dynamically generated queries in database applications. In *Software engineering, 2004. ICSE 2004. Proceedings. 26th International Conference* (pp. 645–654). IEEE.

Huang, Y. W., Yu, F., Hang, C., Tsai, C. H., Lee, D. T., and Kuo, S. Y. (2004, May). Securing Web application code by static analysis and runtime protection. In *Proceedings of the 13th international conference on World Wide Web* (pp. 40–52). New York, NY: ACM.

Jovanovic, N., Kruegel, C., and Kirda, E. (2006, May). Pixy: A static analysis tool for detecting Web application vulnerabilities. In *Security and privacy, 2006 IEEE Symposium*. Washington, DC: IEEE.

Kiezun, A., Ganesh, V., Guo, P. J., Hooimeijer, P., and Ernst, M. D. (2009, July). HAMPI: A solver for string constraints. In *Proceedings of the eighteenth international symposium on software testing and analysis* (pp. 105–116). New York: ACM.

KVM (2010). Kernal-based virtual machine. Retrieved from http://www.linux-kvm.org.

Lee, S. W., and Yu, F. (2014, January). Securing KVM-based cloud systems via virtualization introspection. In *System sciences (HICSS), 2014 47th Hawaii International Conference* (pp. 5028–5037). Waikoloa, HI: IEEE.

Lu, C. S., Huang, S. K., Sze, C. J., and Liao, H. Y. M. (2000). Cocktail watermarking for digital image protection, *Multimedia, IEEE Transactions*, *2*(4), 209–224.

Lu, C. S., and Liao, H. Y. (2001). Multipurpose watermarking for image authentication and protection, *Image Processing, IEEE Transactions*, *10*(10), 1579–1592.

Minamide, Y. (2005, May). Static approximation of dynamically generated Web pages. In *Proceedings of the 14th international conference on World Wide Web* (pp. 432–441). New York, NY: ACM.

Naik, A. K., and Holambe, R. S. (2010). A blind DCT domain digital watermarking for biometric authentication, *International Journal of Computer Applications*, *1*(16), 11–15.

National Palace Museum annual report. (2010). National Palace Museum, Taipei.

OpenStack. (2013). *Open source software for building private and public clouds*. Retrieved from http://www.openstack.org

Padmanabhan, N., and Edwin E. B. (2011). An architecture for providing security to cloud resources, *IJCA Proceedings on International Conference on Emerging Technology Trends*, *2*, 34–37.

Payne, B. D., Carbone, M., Sharif, M., and Lee, W. (2008, May). Lares: An architecture for secure active monitoring using virtualization. In *Security and privacy, 2008. SP 2008. IEEE Symposium* (pp. 233–247). Oakland, CA: IEEE.

Ramanjaneyulu, K., and Rajarajeswari, K. (2010). An oblivious and robust multiple image watermarking scheme using genetic algorithm, *International Journal of Multimedia and Its Application (IJMA)*, *2*(3), 19–38.

Seshadri, A., Luk, M., Qu, N., and Perrig, A. (2007). SecVisor: A tiny hypervisor to provide lifetime kernel code integrity for commodity OSes, *ACM SIGOPS Operating Systems Review*, *41*(6), 335–350.

Shannon, D., Hajra, S., Lee, A., Zhan, D., and Khurshid, S. (2007, September). Abstracting symbolic execution with string analysis. In *Testing: Academic and industrial conference practice and research techniques-MUTATION, 2007. TAICPART-MUTATION 2007* (pp. 13–22). Windsor: IEEE.

Sun, T., Shao, X., and Wang, X. (2008, November). A novel binary image digital watermarking algorithm based on DWT and chaotic encryption. In *Young computer scientists, 2008. ICYCS 2008. The 9th International Conference* (pp. 2797–2802). Hunan: IEEE.

Tang, W. S., and Yu, F. (2014). *Hiding code in digital contents: From passive authentication to active executions*, The MOST Undergraduate Student Research Project Report.

Tsaih, R. H., Lin, J., Han, T. S., Chao, Y. T, and Chan, H. C. (2012). *New ICT-enabled services of National Palace Museum and their designs*, Presented at the 17th International Conference on Cultural Economics, Kyoto, Japan.

Wassermann, G., and Su, Z. (June 2007). Sound and precise analysis of Web applications for injection vulnerabilities. *ACM Sigplan Notices*, *42*(6), 32–41.

Yu, F., Alkhalaf, M., and Bultan, T. (2009, November). Generating vulnerability signatures for string manipulating programs using automata-based forward and backward symbolic analyses. In *Proceedings of the 2009 IEEE/ACM International Conference on automated software engineering* (pp. 605–609). Auckland: IEEE Computer Society.

Yu, F., Alkhalaf, M., and Bultan, T. (2010). Stranger: An automata-based string analysis tool for PHP. In *Tools and algorithms for the construction and analysis of systems* (pp. 154–157). Berlin, Heidelberg: Springer.

Yu, F., Alkhalaf, M., and Bultan, T. (2011, May). Patching vulnerabilities with sanitization synthesis. In *Proceedings of the 33rd International Conference on software engineering* (pp. 251–260). Honolulu, HI: ACM.

Yu, F., Alkhalaf, M., Bultan, T., and Ibarra, O. H. (2014). Automata-based symbolic string analysis for vulnerability detection, *Formal Methods in System Design*, *44*(1), 44–70.

Yu, F., Bultan, T., Cova, M., and Ibarra, O. H. (2008). Symbolic string verification: An automata-based approach. In *Model checking software* (pp. 306–324). Berlin, Heidelberg: Springer.

Yu, F., Bultan, T., and Hardekopf, B. (2011). String abstractions for string verification. In A. Groce and M. Musuvathi (Eds.), *Model checking software* (pp. 20–37). Berlin, Heidelberg: Springer.

Yu, F., Bultan, T., and Ibarra, O. H. (2009). Symbolic string verification: Combining string analysis and size analysis. In S. Kowalewski and A. Philippou (Eds.), *Tools and algorithms for the construction and analysis of systems* (pp. 322–336). Berlin, Heidelberg: Springer.

Yu, F., Bultan, T., and Ibarra, O. H. (2011). Relational string verification using multi-track automata, *International Journal of Foundations of Computer Science*, 22(8), 1909–1924.

Yu, F., Lee, Y. C., Tai, R., and Tang, W. S. (2013, June). AppBeach: Characterizing app behaviors via static binary analysis. In *Proceedings of the 2013 IEEE Second International conference on mobile services* (p. 86). Washington, DC: IEEE Computer Society.

Yu, F., Tang, W. S., Lin, Y. and Wang, W. (2014). *Active authentication via hiding programs in digital contents*, Proceedings of the 14th International Conference on Electronic Business, Taipei, 2014.

Yu, F., Tai, R., Tang, W. S., and Wang, W. (2015, April). AppBeach: A static behavior checker for iOS mobile applications, *Communications of the CCISA, 21*(2), 2015.

Yu, F., and Tung, Y. Y. (2014, January). Patcher: An online service for detecting, viewing and patching Web application vulnerabilities. In *Proceedings of the 47th Hawaii International Conference on system sciences* (pp. 4878–4886). Waikoloa, HI: IEEE Computer Society.

Yu, F., Wan, Y. W., and Tsaih, R. H. (2013, June). Quantitative analysis of cloud-based streaming services. In *Services Computing (SCC), 2013 IEEE International Conference* (pp. 216–223). Santa Clara, CA: IEEE.

Zhu, B., Swanson, M. D., and Tewfik, A. H. (1996, September). Transparent robust authentication and distortion measurement technique for images. In *Digital signal processing workshop proceedings, 1996* (pp. 45–48). Loen: IEEE.

Index